Flight from Wonder

Flight from Wonder

AN INVESTIGATION OF SCIENTIFIC CREATIVITY

Albert Rothenberg MD

OXFORD
UNIVERSITY PRESS

OXFORD
UNIVERSITY PRESS

Oxford University Press is a department of the University of Oxford.
It furthers the University's objective of excellence in research,
scholarship, and education by publishing worldwide.

Oxford   New York
Auckland   Cape Town   Dar es Salaam   Hong Kong   Karachi
Kuala Lumpur   Madrid   Melbourne   Mexico City   Nairobi
New Delhi   Shanghai   Taipei   Toronto

With offices in
Argentina   Austria   Brazil   Chile   Czech Republic   France   Greece
Guatemala   Hungary   Italy   Japan   Poland   Portugal   Singapore
South Korea   Switzerland   Thailand   Turkey   Ukraine   Vietnam

Oxford is a registered trademark of Oxford University Press
in the UK and certain other countries.

Published in the United States of America by
Oxford University Press
198 Madison Avenue, New York, NY 10016

© Oxford University Press 2015

Library of Congress Cataloging-in-Publication Data
Rothenberg, Albert, 1930–
Flight from wonder : an investigation of scientific creativity / Albert Rothenberg, MD
pages cm
Includes bibliographical references and index.
ISBN 978–0–19–998879–2
1. Creative ability in science.   2. Discoveries in science.   3. Creative ability.
4. Critical thinking.   I. Title.
Q172.5.C74R68 2015
501'.9—dc23
2014014267

1 3 5 7 9 8 6 4 2
Printed in the United States of America
on acid-free paper

TO JULIA, *golden sunlight*

The process of scientific discovery is, in effect, a continual flight from wonder.

ALBERT EINSTEIN

Science is not a heartless pursuit of objective information; it is a creative human activity.

STEPHEN JAY GOULD

{ CONTENTS }

{ PREFACE }

When I set out to investigate creativity, I knew that it was a very grand and challenging task. I had long been a lover of all arts—literature, music, visual arts, theatre, and dance—and as I learned the sciences in the course of becoming a physician, I also admired and was dazzled by outstanding scientific achievements. All of these fields, I knew, manifested what was designated deservedly as creative processes and creativity. At that time, I had not thought very much about the factors involved in such a distinction, either from a popular or a scientific standpoint. But soon I came to make out that with regard to matters of designation or definition and, even more, the attribution of *deservedly* or *deserving*, I right away entered the widely adopted but spiraling complexity of the positive valuation of creativity—the idea, the realizations, and the applications. For it is hard to utter seriously the words *creative* and *creativity* in an uncomplimentary way or, indeed, without intending to signal something worthwhile or, beyond that, something even great and awe inspiring. To be sure, part of that positive valuation derives from the idea of original creation, both of the world and of humankind, by a divine or other hallowed source. Leaving deity aside, however, there is a special luster to human creation or creative activities: having creative ideas is good; creative art, whether poor or astounding, is worth doing; and creative achievements are better than ordinary ones.

The positive valuation of creativity poses special problems for scientific investigation. I have confessed that I have always prized and admired creative work. I shall not try to list all the fields but I do esteem them all, including workday creativity or so-called everyday creativity, and such an orientation could introduce known and unknown biases into a necessarily objective research pursuit. But then again, why does anyone passionately pursue any type of investigation unless there is love for the field and the nature of the problem? One of my known biases, then, is that I do find myself impatiently out of hand—even now, so far along the investigative path—with formulations attributing creativity to negative sources. This positive bias, I believe, may actually have some benefits for interpretation similar to the positive biases and orientations in other fields, such as the study of health practices, beneficial social developments, and the like. Nevertheless, positive valuation of creativity is strong and pervasive, and problems for objectivity do arise. How, for example, does one decide which artists and works of art are good, better than others, or specifically worthy of being designated "creative"? Is creativity in science primarily a matter of the degree of influence rather than the uniqueness of a particular discovery? These and many other questions of valuation with respect to creativity have been issues for my research all along the way. I hope, therefore, in the material to follow in this investigative report, to clarify how I have attempted to deal with the difficulties presented and, I hope, solved them.

In addition to matters of good, better, and best pertaining to creativity and creations, another challenge is the accepted definitional feature that creative acts come about in different and irregular ways (not pertinent are any such common linguistic usages as "creating a scene" or "creating an Internet connection"). They do not result directly from ordinary ways of thinking. Creative actions come neither from what we generally think of as common sense, nor from logical thinking—no matter how rigorously applied—nor simply from finding different types of connections or from strong desire. Creative ideas often have been reported as coming spontaneously or all at once but they frequently develop from long deliberations. Moreover, and sometimes with a sense of appreciation and adulation, creativity is pronounced to be mysterious. This idea sometimes has been offered in different ways by creative people themselves, both sincerely as well as primarily in the service of self-promotion.[1] Consequently, the results of any type of concrete investigation, whether psychological or philosophical, are at times viewed with disappointment and even disdain.

In addition to positive value, creations and creativity are widely considered to possess newness, novelty, and uniqueness. The most meaningful investigative criterion for these phenomena therefore is the production of both valuable and new entities. Early in my investigations, I believed that ordinary psychological tests and experimental devices would not capture the nature of new and valuable productions, the unusual and sometimes breakthrough thinking involved in creativity. A way of identifying the appearance of the new rather than using standardized formats based on static preexisting categories or measures was necessary. Although studying personality features, backgrounds, and other qualities of proven creative people (e.g., openness, spontaneity, affective involvement with work) could provide some valuable correlational information, that method also would not reveal the specific attributes or processes directly producing creative results. Spontaneity alone, for instance, could not be shown to produce creative scientific achievement or even a well-designed work of art. Broadening the field, even effective political sloganeering could not be reliably connected with combinations of the features of affective involvement, openness, and spontaneity. It is necessary to trace the specific course and connections, the actual processes of creation, from qualities to outcomes. If creative people were found largely to have personality attributes such as introversion or, as several have tried recently to suggest, severe or moderate mental illness, how might impairments produce meaningful literature, art, or scientific discoveries?[2]

An investigation of physical processes such as brain activities and functions, on the other hand, might well be a productive approach to creativity. The current state of knowledge, however, about the relation between psychological processes and the brain—about all types of mind–body relationships, for that matter—is still very meager and unstable. The matter is also made more challenging by the functional complexity of human creating and creativity. A primary consideration, therefore, must be to understand the psychological processes in creativity as thoroughly as possible. This will be useful in its own right and its own level of scientific understanding, and someday may lead to understanding of accompanying physical factors.

With these considerations, I decided early to attempt to study the psychological creative process as it unfolded. If I could delineate the factors within a series of thoughts, feelings, and activities that led directly to a creative result, then I and others would know that indeed I had a creative factor or factors in tow. To study the process, it would from the first be necessary to determine the nature and composition of the outcome, the created product. As I knew that there was little question in general consensus about the presence of creativity in literature and literary products, I began there and attempted to develop procedures for getting as close as possible to observing or investigating the literary creative process. I chose to study outstanding writers first, not out of an elitist perspective but because, with respect to the matter of creative value, objective criteria could to some extent be applied by consensus to clearly high level creation. In other words, the factors operating for outstanding writers should also be found in some degree or related way with unrecognized or to-be-recognized creators. So, I focused on Pulitzer Prize winners, Nobel laureates in Literature, National Book and National Book Circle Awardees, and winners of the Bowdoin Poetry Prize.

To study the ongoing creative processes of these outstanding writers, I devised a method of intensive psychiatric research interviews to be carried out as frequently as possible during a time period when the writers were actively engaged in creating a literary work. This meant meeting with the research subjects as early as possible in the creative endeavor, and in most cases I succeeded in meeting with them regularly from the time of the first idea for a poem, short story, play, or novel until the time of publication of the work. In practice, these research periods lasted from a few weeks for individual poetic works to up to two years for a series of poems, short stories, or complete novels. The semistructured interview protocol was focused on the ongoing work in progress. It was a confidential, candid, and specialized investigation. Exploration was carried out as a mutual endeavor enlisting the interest and cooperation of the subject; it was based on associations to and analysis of the following: written literary revisions, initial ideas, characters, metaphors, and proposed and completed aspects of plot or poetic statement. Confidentiality and pre-approval of publication of any interview-derived material was guaranteed. For me, it was a heady experience. I was exposed to some of the best writing in the English language and, I believe, I learned a great deal about the circumstances and substance of literary creativity. One of the writers I worked with won the Pulitzer Prize for the novel we were exploring, and another writer, a previous Pulitzer Prize winner, wrote one of his worst novels during our research time.

Less rigorously, I carried out a series of comparison interviews with young creative writers at Yale University, where I was a professor at the time. Here the idea was to see whether I could predict future established creativity on the basis of similarities with the outstanding writer subjects. Many of the young subjects had good writing skills, but my final assessment was that only one applied the same type of creative psychological processes I had observed with the outstanding-writer group. On that basis, I predicted that this particular person would become a successful creative writer, a prediction that has proved to be correct. A few years later, my former subject, Leslie Epstein, has become a creative and well-established novelist; he is also director of the Boston University Creative Writing Program.

I also carried out several experimental studies with different writers and other creators, specifically visual artist groups. After many years of performing both experiments and interview studies regarding literary and artistic creativity, I turned to science. At first, the possibility of interview-tracking the scientific creative process—the complex work that often took place with copious interchanges from other persons in the same and different locales—did not seem possible. So, I constructed experiments using psychological tests in new ways to assess the creative thinking of individual scientists. With these, I measured aspects of the type of processes I had up to then identified in writers and artists and looked for other possible factors. I turned again to investigating outstanding consensually defined creators, in this case Nobel laureates in the designated scientific fields of physics, physiology or medicine, and chemistry.

Testing results were encouraging and important, as I shall describe in chapter 9. In addition, shortly after the session began, I found that in each case these very creative scientists spoke in detail, because of my explicit interest and focus on creativity, about the factors involved in their creative scientific formulations and discoveries. As they clarified their individual ideas, thoughts, and feelings, I realized that I could right away apply the same type of research interview protocol to these scientific discussions as I had used to investigate the literary creators. The difference was that descriptions of the mental processes involved were largely retrospective rather than from current work in progress as with the literary group. Therefore, there were more possibilities of memory lapses and inaccuracies. As it turned out, however, this was only clearly true for one of the Nobel-winning scientist subjects, who was in his eighties at the time. With the others, including the larger number added later to the group, the breakthrough and arduously achieved discovery experiences were both important and life changing at the time they occurred and in subsequent application; they were therefore remembered in great and vivid detail. To me, a psychiatrist trained to assess authenticity of memory, the descriptions seemed reliable and accurate, although a minimal degree of hindsight distortion could not possibly be ruled out. All scientists accompanied their reports with very positive emotion.

On the basis of these investigations, I stopped administering the psychological test and continued interviewing other scientific Nobel laureates with a systematic focus on reconstructing and defining the processes leading to their prize-winning discoveries as well as on their current work in progress. In addition to meeting with US Nobel laureates, I arranged, while I was spending a fellowship year in the Netherlands, to extend and culturally diversify the investigation to Nobel scientists from European countries. These subjects were from France, Germany, and Switzerland (all spoke English fluently) as well as England.

The use of interviews as an empirical approach provided rich and complex data that denoted factors leading to creative scientific production, as will be seen in the chapters on creative discovery (chapters 9–13). Earlier, I noted general biases and preconceptions in creativity research; an interview methodology, it should be recognized, might introduce specific preconceptions and biases of its own. Primarily, there is the risk of what is called "confirmation bias" or "self-fulfilling hypotheses," the investigator's choosing to recognize only data and factors that fit his or her preconceived theories and formulations. This risk was present with my interviews of outstanding literary creators, so to deal with it I constructed a semistructured interview research protocol that allowed for consideration of alternate theories and data, permitted cross-checking, and provided means for refuting or altering preconceptions. With the Nobel laureate interview group, I designed and applied an even more rigorous semistructured interview protocol, presented in detail in chapter 8, because I was aware of the broad complexity of the scientific data discussed and the risk of overinterpretation. The protocol spells out procedures for minimizing or altering experimental and theoretical biases.

In addition, a major means of dealing with bias and preconceptions was the development of an interviewer-"blind" (i.e., with the criterial distinction hidden) comparison control group for an experimental design of the investigation. I had intended from the first to develop an appropriate control group for the Nobel laureates, but the circumstance of composing a rigorously framed comparison control group presented itself to me in an unexpected way. During the same period when I was interviewing the science Nobel laureates, I had been consulting with a number of research and development organizations in California and New York to learn whether I could extend the study of creativity to other types of related scientific groups. Engineers on the faculties of universities, the organization managers suggested, were often highly competent technologists and could therefore be models of a different type of creativity. As successful applied scientists, versus research and pure scientists, they might serve to supplement my findings with the Nobel laureates, all of whom were also on university faculties.[3] I took up the suggestion and applied at the Mechanical Engineering Department of a prominent eastern US technological university, and subsequently gained permission to interview members of the faculty. When I explained my research project on creativity, the department chairman became very enthusiastic and introduced me to department members whom he and other faculty members considered to be creative engineers. All of these faculty engineers agreed to be interviewed and I used the same semistructured interview research protocol with them that I used with the Nobel laureates, searching for creative processes. The engineers told me about a number of technological projects and theories as well as some patents they had achieved. They were intelligent, with a seemingly good memory for their accomplishments. Overall, they were good problem solvers and clearly competent teachers, but except for one case, none had made any creative (i.e., both new and valuable) achievements. Several had produced various useful devices and products that were not identifiably new. The patents they had obtained, as is often the case with US patents, were for individually different but not new commercial item changes or processes. Many of these were never used (possibly, of course, I may have missed some minimally creative products). Therefore, as I had studied a group believing them to be creative and using exactly the same creativity research protocol as with the Nobel laureates, I was ideally blind throughout regarding any preconceived findings. As this group was comparable in many ways—scientific, intelligent, university status, diversity—I realized that their interview results would serve as a meaningful control comparison for the Nobel group.

After all interviews were over, therefore, to be sure that my blindness and comparison judgments were reliable, I engaged a group of science and technology experts for consensual assessment. This group went carefully over the achievements of all the members of the interviewed Nobel group and all the interviewed professional engineers. As I shall describe in more detail later, they concluded that, according to the criteria of both newness and value (social, scientific, instrumental), the Nobel laureates were highly creative, whereas only one engineer was comparatively creative to any degree. Overall, the engineer group was noncreative or very low in creativity. Therefore, as this group was interviewed in the same manner as the Nobel group, they were a suitable consensually determined minimal or noncreative comparison control group for the consensually determined creative experimental group.

Did I perceive overall group differences? Both within the Nobel and engineer groups there was a large range of personality variation; and variation between the two groups was the case in many other aspects. The most specific difference between groups was an overall lack of aesthetic interests among the engineers. As with the Nobel laureates, however, these technical experts were often highly motivated and all were diligent. I shall report, on the basis of the intensive and detailed analysis of the scientific creative process in the pages to follow, a number of significant types of cognitive differences and some strong and distinct emotional dispositions between the laureate and engineer groups.

Overall, all of the investigations, including several other psychological experiments associates and I have carried out with groups of different types and degrees of creativity,[4] and also involving independent controlled testing of psychological factors found in the research interviews, have been enjoyable as well as deeply moving. One of these factors, the effect of developmental components on creative motivation, was also subsequently tested in a controlled assessment of family background structure of Nobel science laureates. In addition to specific findings regarding creativity, the source of human adaptation, as profound gratifications, I have had the privilege of close contact with extraordinary and diverse types of persons. I hope some or all of them found the experience worthwhile and that my readers particularly will benefit from my findings.

The overall experimental investigation of scientific creativity presented here is in two parts. The first part lays out the conceptual background, a review of creativity research literature, and the specific hypotheses regarding both cognitive and accompanying or separate emotional factors in creativity. The second part, beginning with chapter 8, on empirical design, describes the application of the hypotheses to the experimental methodology and findings: the semistructured interviews with Nobel laureates in science and the verbatim recorded descriptions (either on tape or as MP3s for all interviews in the study) of their creative conceptualizing and work, as well as the verbatim recorded interview results with the comparison control group of university engineers. I constructed the scientific creativity hypotheses in the first part both from discoveries in my previous empirical studies on literary and artistic creativity and from primary documents consisting of detailed autobiographical or scientific reports that presented the creative thinking of eminent scientists of the past. I describe three hypothetical cognitive creative processes operative in science: janusian, homospatial, and sep-con articulation. Involved in all three processes are disruptions from the past and of the customary leading up to creative results: The janusian process involves logical and temporal disruption; the homospatial process entails spatial disruption; and part and whole disruption occurs together with the sep-con articulation process. Emotions accompanying these processes include motivation to create, passion, intention to deviate, problem finding, aggressive feelings, courage and risk-taking, and others.

Next, I detail the methodology of my empirical study of living Nobel laureates in Medicine or Physiology, Physics, and Chemistry from throughout the 20th century, and I delineate the contents of the semistructured research interview protocol. Following that, I present the scientists' verbatim recorded interview descriptions of their thought sequences and the experimental procedures leading to their individual creative discoveries. The findings are that the cognitive creative processes—janusian, homospatial, and sep-con articulation, as well as the postulated emotional factors—have played key roles in creative scientific discovery. I also present the work of interviewed Nobel scientists who primarily reported collaboration with others rather than individual contributions. Throughout the work of all the Nobel laureates interviewed, primary or varying degrees of successful collaboration resulted in part from a special devotion to learning and teaching.

I also carried out an empirical study of the family background of 435 scientific Nobel laureates from 1901 to 2003. Findings from this study indicated a statistically significant number of same-gendered parents of Nobel laureate offspring in an applied or performance-equivalent occupation, suggesting early environmental effects on creative motivation.

Comparisons of the results of the blind interview study with the engineer control group in chapter 15 show, in distinction to the experimental group's use of cognitive creative processes and emotional accompaniments, tendencies to conceptualize with the use of schemas, visualization, analogy, reversal, connections, and connecting alone, in their problem solving and technological work.

{ ACKNOWLEDGMENTS }

I would like to thank Dr. Charles Radding, Dr. Robert Wallerstein, Professor Fred Balderston, and Dr. Lawrence Crowley for their early aid in helping me to recruit several of the science Nobel laureates in this study. I am grateful also to the Netherlands Institute for Advanced Study in the Humanities and Social Studies, Wassenaar, where I spent the year beginning the outline for this book and from where I made direct contact with and traveled to interview the Nobel laureate subjects in France, Germany, and Switzerland. I appreciate the work of the anonymous members of the creativity rating group and the help and participation of the Mechanical Engineering Department chairman and faculty at the eastern US technological university. I, together with all persons in modern times who have benefited from the work of the science Nobel laureates studied here, thank them for their achievements. For all subjects interviewed, I feel great gratitude for their hours of time, confidence, and efforts at complete clarity and openness. Both Margarethe Bohr and Claudia Köhler graciously provided me with information through correspondence regarding details of the achievements of their husbands Niels Bohr and Georges Köhler, respectively. With regard to the book itself, I thank Joan Bossert, who saw the worth of this project and made many contributions. To my wife, Dr. Julia J. Rothenberg, I here record my deep appreciation for her wisdom, her insatiable passion for learning, her own creativity and helpful contributions, and her patient support regarding my collection of data and writing, especially in the darkest and most head-spinning hours.

Flight from Wonder

Introduction

I begin with what may seem a dizzying leap: an application of one of the cognitive creative processes I have found, sep-con articulation, to workday creativity. The process of sep-con articulation consists of conceiving and using concomitant separation (SEP) and connection (CON). The term derives both from common usage and the root meaning of articulation. These are incorporated in the often used phrase, "an articulate speaker." The expression connotes that the person referred to speaks in a smooth, flowing, and totally connected manner, and also that he or she clearly discriminates and separates the words and ideas within the flow of speech and thought. An articulate speaker both connects and separates at once. Another application of this feature of articulation is in the sense of "carving out" or "bringing into realization."

The root meaning of the term *articulation* is "a joint or joining," an element or elements that both connects and keeps things separate concurrently. In an organic structure such as the human body, the articulations that construct an overall integration, that at once keep things together and separate, range from the anatomically structured joints between bones to the functionally and operationally jointed osmotic membranes between all cells and the very important functional synapses, the bringing-together gaps between neurons. These are all aspects of a creation that was and continues to be produced by nature.

Although sep-con articulation specifically involves the carving out of disruptions of parts and wholes, joints and joining, both mental and physical, the other two cognitive creative processes to be described, janusian and homospatial processes, also possess an aspect of this operation. These processes all lead to creations and creative results. In science, they function as mental processes used to produce discoveries. I would speculate that a possible reason for the effectiveness of these cognitive creative processes in scientific creativity particularly may be based on the nature of physical reality. The well-known and widely touted figurative scientific investigative goal of "cutting [or carving] nature at its joints,"[1]—learning all there is to know about nature—may contain an intrinsic truth that such a goal is meaningful and worthwhile, because all natural phenomena are jointed rather than smooth and seamless. Joints or joinings differ from continuous connection, bridging, combination, simple bringing together, merging, and fusion. The joint or joining structure provides for the interaction of functionally independent and separate entities. Whereas separation of components is vital for joint functioning, as evident from ordinary experience with elbows and knees, a functioning joint does not comprise separation alone. Rather, concomitant connection of bones, cartilage, muscles, tendons, and ligaments is necessary for walking and lifting. Interaction among these separate components creates the style and means of action. The entire human body is composed of parts that are joined and interact, from the simplest molecule to the largest organs—the heart, lungs, liver, and others—leading to an integration in which the whole is greater than its parts. The interactions and integration at conception and birth each time produce a new and intrinsically valuable human being. The newness achieved is the result of emergent novelty, novelty that is not reducible to any of the previous stages.[2]

The dizzying leap I spoke of goes from the investigative focus on a high level, or outstanding creative achievement and the organization of nature, to applications to what is usually termed "everyday" or workday creativity. By this, I do not mean such loose and commonly used applications as simply doing something differently or changing an habitual approach. Neither do I refer to such practices, applauded by a limited few, as "creative makeup," nor to such clever production of artifice as "creative accounting." I mean more valuable and lasting, distinctly new productions of creative cooking, business practice, sports performance, education, theatre, design, advertising, and politics. I believe I can show here an application of the sep-con articulation process to such workday creativity with an example from sports. To do this, I shall illustrate the operation of the process in the creative baseball activity of the New York Yankee ballplayer Joe DiMaggio.

This is the Joe DiMaggio who is the fabled hero of song and story and who, for me as a boy, was the very epitome of baseball—the king who could do no wrong at bat or in that special area of center field he seemed both to inhabit and possess during a particularly prolonged and legendary period of New York Yankee ascendancy in baseball.

I shall not focus on his famous and unmatched record of having hit in 56 consecutive games, a feat that seemed to inspire the entire Yankee team and raise them out of a year of doldrums up to that point to a level where they were able to go on and win both the pennant and the World Series. This was indeed a great and as-yet-unmatched accomplishment, and accomplishment surely has something to do with creativity. It is not, however, the whole story. Accomplishment is not synonymous with creativity, although as with other general usages, the two are sometimes confused. Every accomplishment is not a creative one, but a creative effect or result does typically involve tacit or explicit accomplishment. In Western culture, creative accomplishment is usually a tangible matter, but, according to Eastern religions and philosophies, creativity can lead to intangible but nevertheless valuable results.

The creative aspect of Joe DiMaggio's way of playing baseball that I am focusing on was what appeared when he performed in the outfield, specifically when he fielded balls, be they fly balls, line drives, or grounders. What he did, unlike every other outfielder of his time (many have copied him since) was make his highly effective catches look easy and beautiful.

Whenever a ball approached him, regardless of whether it looked like it was going over his head, driving on a line with tremendous momentum, or low and grazing the ground, DiMaggio moved toward it with a long-legged loping gait and, manifesting amazing speed, got himself into a position either directly in front of or underneath the ball. This much would serve to demonstrate the high-level skill of almost any major league ballplayer. Then, in an absolutely characteristic way, he reached up or out just as the ball came within the scope of his arm length, smoothly plucked the ball out of the air, and with the same unbroken motion, brought it cupped within mitt and bare hand down or backwards into the region in front of his abdomen, roughly at the level of his belt buckle. There, if you watched, it seemed to rest for a split second before he threw it toward the infield. We saw him make the catch in this manner whether the ball looked too far out of the way and impossible to catch or was a clearly easy blooper. It was a truly aesthetic experience.

In Joe's characteristic movement of bringing the caught ball down or backward into the central region of his body, he smoothly continued the impelled trajectory of the moving sphere. At the same time, the ball and his body were brought into mobile juxtaposition with each other. There were the coordinated initial clutching movements of his arms, the angling of his shoulders and hips, and the long flexing arm movements together with the firm, slightly bent planting of his long legs.

Someone attempting to describe the aesthetic factor in the performed activity might call it a kind of artistic dance. To do so appropriately points up the beauty of the movement and the way in which the smooth, lengthened trajectory of the ball within Joltin' Joe's arms and hands coordinated with and emphasized the rhythmic moving image of his slender, long legs, arms, and body—this despite a curious biographical report we have that, as a young man, Joe disliked dancing.[3] Nonetheless, calling it an artistic dance points to the kind of positive intrinsic value the action contains. Focusing on the aesthetic factor alone would, however, overlook another type of positive value in creativity, both Joe's and other types: instrumental value or usefulness, the fact that catching the ball the way DiMaggio did was an extremely effective way to play baseball. He was one of the most proficient center fielders in the history of the game. At baseball's 1969 Centennial Center, Joe was named the game's greatest player.

As I have said, the other factor in addition to value—either intrinsic or instrumental—that is required for creative accomplishment is newness or novelty. This criterion was also met in DiMaggio's outfield catching because it constituted an aspect of his own unique and novel style. Although it may have been copied since, it was new when he began it. Beautiful to watch, effective in helping to win ball games, and DiMaggio's own invention, the catching was *both* new and valuable, a defined creation.

Now, in saying that Joe was creative, I would also say that he made catching the ball organic. The term is constantly used in art criticism and theory as an indicator of aesthetic value—that is to say, an artwork is judged to be good, meaningful, and also beautiful when it is considered to be organic or when its parts are seen or experienced as being in organic relation with each other—and it applies to DiMaggio. Why is this term so all-around meritorious? Because, among a number of reasons pertaining to taste, form, and meaning, *organic* means that the artwork is composed, constructed, and organized like an organism, a living, breathing entity. It is beautiful because its parts work together like an integrated organism. The artwork is integrated because the parts interact dynamically as separates within a whole, and the whole therefore is greater than its parts. Artistic integration may apply to all features: character or characters, the story, colors and shapes, musical elements and themes, and movements or works of dance. Joe's catching also is organic because it is integrated. His catching is integrated with his body, his movements, and with his whole manner of playing baseball, a factor called style.

As the model for all organic integration is a living organism, we usually focus on the human organism out of anthropomorphism. The integration and function derive from having parts that are both functionally separate and connected at the same time. These parts—skin, stomach, liver, and arteries on down to molecules—all operate individually and separately and in connection with one another and with the body as a whole. Such integration, when applied in creative activities, is derived from the sep-con articulation process through which functional separates are concomitantly connected.

DiMaggio's use of the sep-con articulation process, his articulation of the catching of a baseball into a creation, consisted of seeming to join the ball to himself and to his body. Composing the catching event overall, both ball and body flowed in a smooth, continuous trajectory motion but each was also clearly identifiable, distinct, and separate from the other. He did nothing to conceal the ball in some act of athletic legerdemain, and instead of stopping the ball at the place where it came in contact with his body, the place where separation between ball and body was most clear, then emphasizing in usual fielder fashion the break in the line of motion by winding up and throwing to home or to second base, he continued the smooth dual aspect trajectory in a process of ball-body separation-connection.

Joe's creative catching in the Yankee center field exemplifies features of creativity in everyday life. Joe's process of sep-con articulation is, as I shall show with specific instances from my research, similar to the more complex and prolonged processes that are responsible for artistic and scientific creations. In art, for example, Michelangelo very likely used a similar process when, as several documents suggest, he saw the form of a sculpture in an unworked block of marble. Starting in this manner, Michelangelo realized the image in the work of art[4]; the work grew through the process of sep-con articulation into a creation. Although my purpose in this investigation is to determine and delineate the nature and structure of creativity, especially scientific creativity, the results should, as I shall outline in greater detail in Chapter 16, apply to everyday creativity as well.

The Search for Creativity

Creativity is beautiful and highly elusive. It is justly hallowed as a quintessentially human capacity often responsible for our progress in the physical and social world and our deepest gratifications in art, literature, and music. The lexical definition of the word *create* is, however, simply "to bring forth or make," and these functions literally can apply to any type of production or change including the most infinitesimal and inconsequential. Of course, even a small switch may lead to something beneficial or valuable, and creating, even in the most limited sense of making, is usually considered worthwhile. In addition, one of the everyday beneficial features are applications of the term to tasks such as problem solving. The special value and usefulness of what is recognized as truly creative problem solving begins to raise it to the levels of creativity with wide social significance in special fields of endeavor such as the arts, science, and government. For these fields, the feature of *creating-as-worthwhile* has been elevated far beyond that involved in simple making, and therefore may sometimes seem quite different from other types of creating, including the type done in everyday life.

The other feature of creativity not strictly included in a lexical definition is the production of *newness*. Although the designations "being creative" or "creative thinking" are often applied, both popularly and in a large amount of creativity research and inquiry, to somewhat unusual, spontaneous, or just very intelligent thinking, a challenge for the appreciation and understanding of creative achievement is the bringing forth of something original and new. Unlike the matter of degree of usefulness or value, newness may be a more absolute attribute.

Determination of newness is a key issue for the essential understanding of creativity; value alone is not a satisfactory criterion for creative events. For persons of Western culture, the use by some Eastern cultures of value alone as a designation of creativity is a shortcoming. In China, Japan, Korea, and India, creations are often considered to occur internally within individuals and to be positive, valuable, and unseen.

The newness aspect, however, even applies to the malevolent creativity of the likes of Adolf Hitler, where manifest products are still valuable to someone or to some group. Not only is value alone difficult to assess—in Hitler's case, of course, it would overwhelmingly be considered a negative value—but in the Eastern culture variations it is also especially difficult to tease out an aspect of newness. Moreover, brashly labeled constructions such as *nouvelle cuisine* or *new politics,* despite the emphasis on the new in the term, may not be creative but essentially a matter of different wine in old bottles. Another consideration regarding newness is that it must have some degree of endurance to become allied with the value aspect of creativity. It must stand the "test of time." Constantly produced extremes in art, literary, and music styles may be clearly new at the time they appear but may seldom endure as meaningfully creative; sometimes, although they are not creative in themselves, they may inspire other creations. A further factor is that historians or others broadly knowledgeable about developments in fields such as the natural and behavioral sciences often describe complex and surprising backgrounds for seemingly new events. They propose, implicitly and explicitly, that there is essentially nothing new under the sun. Accordingly, nothing is unprecedented and causation is intrinsically ubiquitous. Other specialists, however, have argued that creations consist of exemplars of a type, and in that sense are truly unprecedented rather than simply different.[1]

Human beings in general have respected and sought newness, and although sometimes discomfited by and repudiating newness and change, they frequently also have been awed by the appearance of newness together with clear-cut value. Does that awe and respect derive from a sense that, rather than completely predetermined and derived from past factors, newness intrinsic to creativity may actually in some way be truly unprecedented and without forebears? Such is implied in notions of creativity exercised by a deity or other mysterious or supernatural forces. Perhaps the degree of value in high-level creativity itself instills awe and great appreciation. Nevertheless, to say today that creativity involves the unprecedented does not require reference to supernatural or mystical notions of the cause of newness. Widely accepted current philosophical and scientific formulations, such as those applied in quantum mechanics, indicate acausal or so-called emergent processes, defined as the product of multiple interactions determining the rise of new and coherent properties of self-organization in complex systems.[2] Such newness involves a break or discontinuity with the past in both temporal and spatial spheres.

Integration is an example of a phenomenon that has always been recognized as having acausal aspects in the sense that the integrated whole is always greater than the sum of its parts. Unification, in distinction to integration, requires that all components lose their individual identities to become a single entity. The components of integration retain separate identities while they interact within an organized whole. Integration is an important characteristic of the human body; of high aesthetic accomplishment; of scientific, social, and philosophical theories and constructions; and of effectively functioning groups. It is intrinsic to creative results, and as will be manifest in the investigation to be described here, integration may be considered the *sine qua non* of creativity.

Again, like the use of "to create," the term *integration* is often applied non-specifically to a range of operations and phenomena. As with the distinction from unification, moreover, integration is not synonymous with other conflated terms in creativity theories such as *blending,*[3] *connecting, fusing, combining,* and *merging.* Nor are integration and synthesis the same. All these terms involve a bringing together with change of component elements. With integration, multiple separate elements retain their discreteness and identity while connected and operating together in a whole. By specifying *multiple,* I mean to include the minimum of two but to allow also for numerous additional elements operating within that whole. I am not simply proposing here a lexical or linguistic analysis but a clarification of a sometimes loosely used concept. Also, I am specifying the nature of concrete created entities. In other words, it is important to understand a created product as an integrated entity in order to determine how it is produced. As I am searching to clarify the nature of creativity, I cannot stop at a general outlining of the creative process, but I need to go on to attempt to account for how the process leads to an integrated created product.

To say a created product is integrated indicates reasons for the newness together with value. The outcomes of unifications and the other types of bringing together I have listed may well be valuable, even very valuable, but they will lack newness without integration. The merger of a large corporation with another one, for example, may often require designating an entity with a different name, and the merger and the name together may even be called a creation, in both financial and popular circles. This larger corporation may only consist, however, of a unification that is different from its components in composition and name, and it therefore lacks both newness and value until it becomes integrated. There may be valuable aspects to the merger itself such as potentially less overhead, overall increased capacity, or better financial solvency, but none of these features will make the organization new unless the two corporations function as an integrated entity, the separate elements interacting and contributing to the whole. Otherwise, they could be a collection of individuals from each of the corporations occupying the same building and following practices appropriate only to their previous jobs or pursuing lesser combined and dysfunctional pursuits. To use another example from the business world, a worker or the head of a corporation may get a really new idea such as using rain clouds to develop alternate sources of industrial energy, but he or she cannot define any known structure, either within the corporation or anywhere else, in which that idea can be put into practice or become functional. It cannot be integrated and cannot be valuable.

Similarly, within the artistic enterprise, integration is required to imbue a work of art with both newness and positive value. A writer, for example, may combine or merge two or more words or blend multiple stories to produce a new-sounding word or subject matter. Until these elements are integrated into a poem, play, novel, or other literary structure, however, they do not become creations with positive value. Many of the critics and judges of aesthetic taste who use the term *organic* to indicate an important attribute of subsequently successful works of art are using, as I pointed out earlier, a complex concept based on analogy with integrated living things.

Notable examples of the differences between creative integration and the blending of stories come both from James Joyce and Shakespeare. Joyce, the master of 65 languages, combined words and sounds from many of these languages to produce several new-sounding words or "neologisms" in his literary works. Consider the English-language-derived phrase "Willingdone Museyroom" in *Finnegan's Wake*.[4] The phrase is a merger of the words *willing, done, muse,* and *room,* with the *musey* portion a neologism of its own merging *muse* with a *y* adjective ending. Similar types of combining or merging neologisms are also characteristically produced by persons suffering from schizophrenia. I have elsewhere documented word examples actually produced by such patients as *rambrewfully* and *warons* in the phrases squared *rambrewfully* and *warons ticking.* These too seem like combinations of other words—possibly *ramble, brew,* and *fully* as well as *war* and *on* for *warons.*[5] However, they are different from the Joyce neologism in that they have only personal resonance and meaning to the person suffering from schizophrenia who uttered them. Careful listeners do not hear any contextual indication that the utterer integrated them within an intelligible communication, much less a literary outcome. "Willingdone Museyroom" is, on the other hand, richly integrated by Joyce to contribute to a literary creation. In *Finnegan's Wake,* the Museyroom allows a guided tour through a museum in the Wellington Monument in Phoenix Park, which commemorates the fatal fall of the hero Finnegan. The fall has occurred at the battle of "Willingdone" at Waterloo, a word connected to the sound of *Wellington* and suggesting "willing-to-be-done." This represents the book's tragic and archetypal family drama in military-historical terms.[6] Joyce, rather than using a combined word with meaning only to its maker as produced by the severely mentally ill, has given this neologism or new word a positive value and produced a literary creation by integrating it as a discrete entity within the whole work of art. For those who might deny the literary value of the writing in *Finnegan's Wake* because it seems so abstruse, there are similar examples, widely extolled aesthetically, of integrated neologisms in the more accessible poem by Lewis Carroll, *Jabberwocky,* as well as

Joyce's clearer and groundbreaking novel *Ulysses*, and more recently in the literary works of John Barth and Thomas Pynchon.[7]

With respect to Shakespeare, several versions of the story of King Lear were available when he wrote the play. According to most scholars, he brought together at least two sources, one of which was the 1587 histories of Holinshed, which he consulted for a number of his plays, and the other a popular, anonymously written play, produced 12 years earlier, titled *The True Chronicle History of King Leir and His Three Daughters, Gonorill, Ragan, and Cordella*.[8] Here, too, the actions of simply bringing together, blending, or combining the two sources do not account for the creation of Shakespeare's drama, *King Lear*. Elements of Lear's blindness, his belief in Cordelia's betrayal, the poetic descriptions of the tragedy of aging, and of course the character and language constructions themselves are all individually distinct as well as connected entities within the overall integration. These qualities and many others produce the integrated literary work, *King Lear*, with attributes of both newness and value.

In artistic creativity, the example of the work of the Post-Impressionist painter Paul Cézanne also demonstrates the difference between combination or merger and the development of integration. Cézanne is often considered the artist whose work launched the artistic era widely designated as "Modern Art," comprising the styles and artworks of Picasso, Braque, Matisse and many others. He brought the earlier Impressionist style of painting, in which form was dissolved into light and color, together with form as constructed or structural. This French painter, at the end of the 19th and the beginning of the 20th centuries, produced a new artistic mode within a movement known as Post-Impressionism. His work was functionally separate from and at the same time connected with the Impressionists. He painted their favorite types of bright land, seascapes, and ordinary household scenes and emphasized strong geometric underpinnings and shapes. He considered these shapes to display ideal forms in natural things. In his new mode, in paintings such as *The Bathers*, colors, hues and lighting, geometric shapes, and textures were integrated into a whole. These artistic creations inspired the work of the Modernists and many generations of artists after him.

In all three of these examples, integration characterized individual works. Just as integration is a crucial factor for positive value in the arts,[9] according to artistic experts, practitioners, and critics, it is, as shall be evident from the results to be reported here, a significant factor in scientific creative discovery. Breakthroughs are integrated into theories and pragmatic or instrumental uses. Although it might be argued that factors in nature are preexisting and discovery of them therefore does not actually produce anything new, integrations provide both emergent and relative newness. Relative newness in science consists of the appearance of something radically different with an unknown or hidden causal history. The social and environmental effects of influential and valuable discoveries certainly appear as new. Also, the thinking processes leading to influential discoveries in science almost invariably involve creative structures and operations.

Integration, as indicated by Cézanne's artistic impact, is also manifest in the relation between new styles as well as entire bodies of work and their predecessors. Newness in isolation or for its own sake does not necessarily advance knowledge, aesthetic apprehension or appreciation, or usefulness. New and separate elements, forms, or mechanisms must be connected with essential aspects of previously existing elements, forms, or mechanisms to become creations. New and creative postmodern sculptural or painting styles are in some part connected with Realism, Op and Pop Art, action painting, and many other previous approaches; Joyce's and Shakespeare's literary creations are connected both in subject matter and form with their own and others' previous works of literature and life events. New factors, clearly distinct and separate, are at the same time connected in some measure with the past. Creations are concomitantly separate and connected with aspects, sometimes totalities, of the past. This is especially true in scientific creativity. Creative achievements involve new experiments, new theories, and new structures that always are connected to some degree with existing scientific knowledge.

Creativity, therefore, consists prototypically of the production of both newness and value, properties that are difficult to determine objectively. Consequently, a scientific investigation of the creative process in science requiring objectivity must depend on independent consensual agreement regarding presence of these factors. In the empirical investigation to follow, I have used the award of the Nobel Prize for individual achievements in physics, chemistry, and physiology or medicine together with a judgment panel of experts as this independent consensual measure. Findings, therefore, apply specifically to creativity and the creative process. Specific creative processes identified involve breaks with the past in both the temporal and spatial spheres. All lead to creative integration.

In speaking of creativity and discovery in science, Albert Einstein once said, "The process of scientific discovery is, in effect, a continual flight from wonder." I hope in the pages to follow to show both how and, in some way, why that flight from wonder occurs.

Research on Creativity: Scientific and General

Although determination of the new and valuable components of creativity together is difficult, recognition of the new, whether relative or absolute, is usually more feasible. Moreover, persons recognized as creative producers of valuable entities have sometimes been unapproachable, unapproached, or otherwise nonparticipant in scientific explorations. Perhaps this is the reason why, despite the voluminous literature, scientific and other, on creativity,[1] empirical scientific studies of living persons consensually defined as creative are rare. Meaningful objective criteria for the value aspect of creativity are widely absent. Tests, theories, manuals for achieving creativity, and other approaches, therefore, have attained reliability and repeatability in some sense, but in the absence of meaningful applicability to creativity they lack validity. Although many introspective or anecdotal accounts of creativity are interesting and even ingenious, often commendably attempting to explain the complicated matter of creativity in everyone, the authors seldom base their speculations on similar work done before them, and many set out as though starting at the beginning.

Although assessment of the value aspect of creative products and endeavors is often in particular cases controversial, there is usually general agreement about the social and intellectual usefulness or intrinsic worth of products from the fields of art, literature, music, scientific discovery, and particular approaches in business and politics. Consensually defined creators, therefore, are those persons who have shown potential or made achievements in these fields. Notably, empirical studies of such defined creators have been done at the Institute of Personality Research (now called the Institute of Personality and Social Research) in California, by Mihaly Csikszentmihalyi and his associates in Illinois; by Bernice Eiduson, Anne Roe, Nancy Andreasen, and Kay Jamison; and within our own investigations. In the cases of Andreasen and Jamison, the foci of the studies were specifically on associations between creativity and mental illness rather than on any directly operative creative factors.

Howard Gruber, who did not study Charles Darwin personally, used an empirical approach of meticulously investigating Darwin's diaries, in which that scientist documented his thinking and the work involved in the development of the principles of evolution and natural selection. Dean Keith Simonton also did not investigate living creators directly, but he used empirical data extensively in his comprehensive statistical studies using a method known as historiometrics. This consisted of retrospective assessments of the personal, social, cultural, developmental, and cognitive factors correlated with the lives and work of great artists, musicians, writers, scientists, and social leaders. Other presumptive but nonempirical explorations of factors related to creativity by Arnold Ludwig and Howard Gardner were based on the secondary sources of written biographies of creative persons both recent and historical. Ludwig's study, like Andreasen and Jamison's, was focused on creativity and psychopathology.

Creativity in Science

Bernice Eiduson[2] and Anne Roe[3] each carried out empirical investigations of scientific creativity involving direct explorations with living scientists. Eiduson interviewed and applied projective psychological tests to 40 US West Coast research scientists working in diverse areas; no subjects were defined as controls. Her husband, a scientist, was the sole identifier of competent investigator subjects and helped make them available for the study. Two of the subjects identified were Nobel laureates and 16 had received scientific honors. Her findings, all of which pertained to the scientists' personality features, consisted primarily of the following: intellectual competence involving a lukewarm emotional temperament, sensitivity to stimuli, reliance on mentors, and cognitive interest in the new and different. Also, their personalities and lifestyles mirrored their early childhood environment. She was most impressed by a general sense of rebelliousness, also found in the investigation reported here (chapter 12), among members of the group as follows: "Subjects look for the novel, the new, the interesting in their thinking; they are oriented toward rejecting the obvious, the hackneyed; they quickly tire of the usual in everyday ways of seeing reality."[4] In some cases, this was accompanied by manifest personal aggressiveness; in others, it appeared to be expressed through the overall orientation of the group in which the scientist worked.

Anne Roe also interviewed and tested research scientists chosen as eminent in their field in this case by an independent panel of scientist judges. In addition, she interviewed and tested distinguished social scientists selected by other panels. She too primarily used projective tests as well as an intelligence test. The research group consisted of 20 biologists, 22 physicists and chemists, and 22 social scientists. Among a number of broadly defined personality features she identified in this group, her most distinct finding was a tendency of biologists and experimental physicists to use visual imagery in their work, as compared with both theoretical physicists and social scientists. Theoretical physicists used verbal, symbolic, and imageless thought, and the social scientists primarily used verbal imagery. She also found that, with regard to familial factors, a subject who tended to use primarily verbal imagery often had a father who had been in a "verbal" profession such as law, ministry, teaching, and editing (see chapter 14 for findings regarding literary prizewinners with fathers in verbal professions).

Gregory Feist has recently carried out a meta-analysis of studies of personality of scientists (including social scientists) as well as artists. Out of a total of 83 studies, 26 contained comparisons of creative and less creative scientists as well as nonscientists. Criteria for the differentiation of creative and noncreative were not described. Using factor analysis and multiple regression, Feist identified the following personality characteristics of the designated creative scientists: "more aesthetically oriented, ambitious, confident, deviant, dominant, expressive, flexible, intelligent and open to new experiences than their less creative peers."[5] Including his analysis of studies of nonartist and artist subjects, who were art students and persons making a living from art, he derived an overall composite of the creative personality as autonomous, introverted, open to new experiences, norm doubting, self-confident, self-accepting, driven, ambitious, dominant, hostile, and impulsive.[6]

Recognizing that a good deal of modern science is carried out by collaborative groups, Kevin Dunbar conducted a direct observational investigation of four working biological-laboratory blocs. Using judges' assessments of coded categories of thought, he determined that the groups' productive scientific thinking was based on analogies, attention to unexpected findings, and "distributed reasoning" (group correction of individual errors and introduction of new elements). Although this study was a rare instance of observations of scientists at work, it essentially described factors in scientific problem solving with no direct connections to creative results.[7]

Dean Keith Simonton's extensive statistical assessments focused on the distributions of achievements and lifestyles of outstanding persons in a number of types of activities and occupations. With respect to scientists, he assessed research productivity as measured by the number of publications and citations by others. He also measured the incidence of multiple discoveries. Showing especially that multiple discovery in science was quite frequent and occurred according to a Poisson or random distribution, he concluded that scientific creativity was what he called a "constrained stochastic process."[8] Stochastic or chance occurrence of ideas and events were subjected to the constraints of the particular scientific field or discipline. Personality attributes and what he called "domain skills" are, according to this formulation, the factors producing the constrained aspect of the process.

Using the numerous diaries in which Charles Darwin wrote on close to a daily basis, Howard Gruber systematically analyzed that scientist's creative thinking.[9] He especially traced Darwin's conception of the metaphor of the tree of life, which guided the course of his formulations and conclusions. Emphasizing that this analysis had delineated conscious problem solving, "the growth of thinking in a real, thinking, feeling, dreaming person,"[10] Gruber developed the point later in a more general theory of creative problem solving as utilizing "ensemble of metaphor"—figures of thought defined as images, symbols, allegories, and analogies. These, he believed, also produce paradigms and metaphors tending to cluster within various disciplines.[11]

Other writers on scientific creativity have formulated theories based on their own frameworks of ideas and conceptions derived from their familiarity with scientific products and achievements. Using excerpted published comments by creative scientists as evidence and support, physicist and philosopher of science Arthur I. Miller at first attempted an analysis based on Gestalt psychology and Jean Piaget's genetic epistemology in which he emphasized that visual imagery was a key ingredient in scientific thought.[12] More recently, he has continued his emphasis on imagery and has proposed that aesthetics, consisting of invariance and symmetry factors, is used as a means for discovery and decisions among differing theories. Metaphors, analogies, and what he now calls "network thinking" are significantly involved. His description of network thinking is "concepts from apparently disparate disciplines are combined by proper choice of mental image or metaphor to catalyze the nascent moment of creativity."[13] He also proposes that the interplay among unconscious parallel lines of thought as well as parallel processing of information (as described by Margaret Boden[14]) eventually emerges into conscious thought as the problem's solution.

Physiologist Robert Root-Bernstein, singly and together with his wife, Michele, also emphasized the importance of aesthetic factors in creative scientific thinking.[15] Robert Root-Bernstein singly presented a noncontrolled listing of outstanding scientists who had been cited anecdotally in various sources as having artistic, musical, and literary interests and skills,[16] and the Root-Bernsteins together proposed the theory that polymathy (having great or varied learning) was a key factor in successful scientific discovery. They have applied this theory to the field of education with advocacy of early teaching of artistic skills, including word capacity, analogy, and graphic thinking, to children of special ability. While acknowledging the hypothetical nature of his conclusions, Robert Root-Bernstein has spelled out specific ways in which he believes these tools are applied in scientific thought: analogizing, pattern recognition, visual thinking in several dimensions, modeling, play-acting, kinesthesis, and manual manipulation. Two particular modes of cognition were, he thought, especially important. The first is transformational thinking, "the ability to translate a problem expressed in one form [such as numbers] into another more amenable to problem solving [words, perhaps, or mental images]; to mentally manipulate these words, images, or models, to solve the problem, and then to translate this solution into yet another form [such as an equation or diagram or experimental protocol] that can be communicated to other scientists."[17] The second is synscientia, "the knowing in several different ways at once."[18]

Some working physical scientists have, on the basis of their own experience and what they have considered to be the logic of scientific creativity, also proposed an importance of aesthetic factors. Touched on by the great mathematician Henri Poincaré,[19] his colleague Jacques Hadamard,[20] and Nobel Prize–winning formulator of the existence of antimatter, Paul Maurice Dirac,[21] the applications were developed more extensively by the investigator of the structure and evolution of the stars, particularly white dwarfs, Nobel laureate Subrahmanyan Chandrasekhar. On the basis of his own experience, the literary works of both E. A. Milne and Arthur Stanley Eddington in astrophysics, and the account of Albert Einstein's development of general relativity, Chandrasekhar theorized that aesthetic factors were crucial for the motivation for, and achievement of, truth in science. Particularly, he described both the aesthetic result and scientific goal as "strangeness in the proportion and conformity of the parts to one another and the whole," as well as "harmoniously organizing a domain of science with order, pattern, and coherence."[22]

Historian of science Gerald Holton has studied motivation for scientific discovery through extensive analysis of the thematic origins of scientific thought, starting historically from the works of Johannes Kepler up through those of Albert Einstein. Holton has attempted to show that the scientist himself or herself, both in personality and cognitive orientation, embodies the themes he or she works on. For Albert Einstein, it was the factor of paradox, which operated throughout his life and work. Holton also showed that one of Einstein's contemporaries, Niels Bohr, was similarly focused on, if not actually enamored with, paradox.[23] This factor was a theme in both great scientists' pursuits. Holton documented as well the thematic uses of specific metaphors such as the "Big Bang" and "black holes in space" for experiment and theory in the history of scientific discovery.[24] Philosopher of science Nancy Nersessian postulated that scientific creativity was based on cultural factors and model-based reasoning,[25] a type of cognition emphasized by her philosopher predecessors such as Max Black.[26]

Creativity in General

Beyond explorations in science, there has been some recent controversy among investigators and commentators regarding the domains of creativity. Some allege that there is no commonality of creativity across fields, and others assume that the factors they identify apply to creative achievement in all fields as well as to everyday creativity. Advocates of noncommonality declare the existence of "domain creativity," but those commentators, with the exception of the ones who postulate different types of intelligence in different fields, have neither produced meaningful theory nor empirical data to support the claim.

With regard to the long-standing conception of creativity as manifest in all types of fields and domains including artistic, scientific, and others, there have been a number of approaches. Although there is some overlap among these, the primary characteristics of each have tended to fall into particular categories as follows: motivation and goal relevance; associationism; cognitive mechanisms or processes and problem solving; deviant modes of thinking; personality characteristics; and biological mechanisms.

MOTIVATION AND GOAL RELEVANCE

On the most general and manifest level, a motivation to create, as emphasized in the following studies, is very strong among successful creators. Intense devotion to work, sacrifice, single-mindedness, and drive toward high achievement and gratification are constant features of scientific discovery, artistic production, and often of everyday creative solutions as well. An empirical study of the motivational factor of "flow" for creative people has been led by Mihaly Csikszentmihalyi.[27] Stipulated as a necessary factor in creative work as well as general happiness, flow is a motivational mode consisting of an automatic, effortless, yet highly focused state of consciousness. The characteristics of flow, as defined by Csikszentmihalyi, are the following:

1. clear goals at every step,
2. immediate feedback to one's activities,
3. a balance existing between challenges and skills,
4. merging of action and awareness,
5. distractions are excluded from consciousness,
6. no worry of failure,
7. disappearance of self-consciousness,
8. sense of time becomes distorted, and
9. activity becomes autotelic [that is, something that is an end in itself].[28]

Csikszentmihalyi and his graduate students interviewed 91 subjects considered on the basis of consultation with various professional colleagues to meet the criteria of having "made a difference to a major domain of culture." Following a semistructured protocol, they asked the subjects general questions about motivation, background, interests, relationships, and working habits. In addition to postulating the importance of flow as a motivating factor in their work, Csikszentmihalyi concluded there were general personality traits consisting of a number of opposing characteristics in temperament, emotionality, playfulness, energy, imagination, and knowledgeabilty. No control procedures with other types of subjects were used for these determinations.

In an earlier experimental study of 31 art students at the University of Chicago, Csikszentmihalyi, together with Jacob Getzels, had discovered the motivational factor of "concern for discovery," and of problem finding—the formulation of worthwhile artistic matters or questions to pursue and solve in their creative work.[29]

Teresa Amabile, on the basis of a well-designed controlled means-end experimental investigation with 95 female college students and 115 children in Grades 1 to 5 on intrinsic motivation versus external pressure in creative work, concluded that the "intrinsically motivated state is conducive to creativity whereas the extrinsically motivated state is detrimental."[30] Although Amabile carefully worked out a scheme for consensual validation of creativity for these and other experiments, neither her scheme nor findings were empirically applied to the achievements of socially proven creators.

Robert Sternberg and Todd Lubart have proposed a motivational theory based on the model of financial investment. According to the theory, creative people are like good investors; in the world of ideas, they buy low and sell high. Some ideas are unpopular or treated with disrespect but they nevertheless attempt to convince other people of their worth. Then they sell high, allowing other people to pursue the ideas.[31] As a researcher on intelligence, Sternberg has independently proposed that three aspects of intelligence are key for creativity: synthetic, analytic, and practical abilities.[32]

Motivational approaches are often derived from conceptions of the nature of the ends and goals of creativity.[33] Instances of these conceptions come from two psychoanalytic theorists whose work on creativity has been frequently adopted in a wide range of psychoanalytic and psychological writings. Ernst Kris's concept of creative achievement as the result of "regression in the service of the ego" focuses on the gratifying, ego-building (largely in a conscious, reality-oriented mode), and managing aspects of creating.[34] A key factor is the role of regression and therefore unconscious modes in the process indicating a deviation in creativity from usual adult and conceptual ways of (secondary process) thinking. This formulation, however, does not take into consideration that the contents of the unconscious and therefore of regressive production are essentially the same forbidden elements in everyone. These are difficult to connect with the distinct newness component of creativity. The other major psychoanalytic theorist, Lawrence Kubie, writing on the neurotic distortion of the creative process, attempted to denote a freer motivational and cognitive state than Kris by emphasizing the function of the preconscious rather than deeper unconscious roots of creative thought and action. Whereas the preconscious mode—thoughts, ideas, emotions, or memories not in immediate awareness are available to consciousness without intrapsychic resistance—allows for more flexibility than Kris's formulation, this mental conformation also involves the release and use of universal types of psychological content.[35] Notably, Kubie's emphasis on flexibility serves as a strong psychoanalytic argument against recent popular as well as semiscientific assertions of a connection, cited hereafter in the Deviant Thinking Modes section, between creativity and psychopathology based on rigid or regressive psychological functions.

ASSOCIATIONISM

Associationist approaches are characterized by explanations based on affiliations, combinations, blends, connections, mixtures, and other assemblages of related or unrelated entities. Two widely cited formulations regarding the creative process or "creative act" (Koestler) are the closely similar "bisociation" of Arthur Koestler and the remote association theory of Sarnoff Mednick. Koestler's bisociation consists of the association of two self-consistent but habitually incompatible frames of reference in the physical, psychological, or social world.[36] Mednick's conception, which is based on word association studies and has become the basis for one of the most broadly used tests or measures of creativity, the Remote Associates Test, consists of the bringing together of words and other entities that are remotely associated or connected with each other.[37] Although the test is frequently used as a measure in creativity studies, it is important to note that it has never been assessed or validated with consensually designated creative persons. Nor has Koestler's bisociation been validated with creative persons or achievements in his or others' related work, except anecdotally.

The major fault or limitation of theories of association such as these two and those to follow is the lack or exclusion of determinative or causative factors. Association based solely on passive contiguity of two or more elements does not result in a new or novel entity. When elements that are incompatible or remote simply become associated, another element, factor, or condition is still necessary for a new and valuable result—that is, a creation. Even if the associated elements were considered primarily as inspirations, foundations, or content for creative acts, processes, or events, it would still be necessary to account for the transformations, facilitations, or constructions present in the ultimate created product.

Other approaches, oriented toward cognitive formulations regarding the creative process, have also been based on associative mechanisms, and have so far not been able to indicate any factors producing newness, value, or both. Margaret Boden has proposed an artificial intelligence–derived concept of creative connections or connectionism based on parallel processing and analogical representation. A parallel processing system consists of many simple computational units linked, Boden suggests, "as brain cells are" by excitatory or inhibitory connections. Analogical representations, on the basis of the connectionist mechanism, involve associations with one structure transferred to another.[38] The connections are made unconsciously (not through the psychoanalytic unconscious) and their evaluation, according to Boden, requires an undefined "deliberative thinking."[39]

Another associationist approach also stipulating an unconscious mechanism for the outcome is the theory of cognitive "blending" by Mark Turner and Gilles Fauconnier. Unconscious blending, considered a general development of the evolution of thought processes in all human beings, is alleged to produce unified (inappropriately termed "integration"—see chapter 1 for definitions) meanings. The mechanisms producing such meanings are, in ordinary conceptualizing, a matter of "mapping" an input structure or frame upon another to produce a "single space blend."[40] Innovation and creativity, according to this theory, result primarily from an advanced type of "double scope blending," both a source and target input organized by structure taken from each input frame. Artistic activity is produced by compression of both disparate and similar elements in the blend.[41] The theory involves various types of unconscious mixing and coming together of elements on the basis of an unguided type of association. Although this and the other associationist approaches have not successfully elucidated creativity, they have emphasized bringing together and connecting. These are in some ways an aspect, as I shall attempt to show, of a creative process.

COGNITIVE MECHANISMS OR PROCESSES
AND PROBLEM SOLVING

Many of the studies so far outlined—those of Roe, Gruber, Robert and Michelle Root-Bernstein, Miller, and to some extent Csikszentmihalyi, Boden, and Turner and Fauconnier—have necessarily included or been focused to some degree on cognitive mechanisms or processes in creativity. Howard Gardner specifically names his explanations as "a cognitive approach to creativity."[42] As the theorist of multiple intelligences, delineations of which have been broadly applied and valued in the field of education, Gardner has construed these multiple intelligence modes to be thema in the lives and thinking of historically creative people such as Sigmund Freud, Albert Einstein, and Pablo Picasso. He analyzed the thema for each subject as extended capacities primarily in one of seven intelligence modes: interpersonal, logical-mathematical, visual-spatial, music, linguistic, bodily-kinesthetic, and intrapersonal.[43] More recently, he has described an eighth mode, naturalistic intelligence.[44] His conclusions, despite a very thorough analysis of biographies and other secondary sources, have not been based, as he acknowledges, on "sustained studies of the creative process as it unfolds in acknowledged masters."[45]

Studies of creativity as a form of high-level problem solving, although also not carried out directly with living, acknowledged creative masters, have consisted of carefully controlled experiments of problem features. Other types of imaginative and complex controlled experimental explorations of particular hypotheses also have been based on modeling of previously solved scientific and conceptual problems. Norman Maier et al. have found experimentally that good problem solving involves what they describe as "integrative or creative" solutions rather than compromise. The integrative solutions were those integrating the facts stressed in conflicting points of view.[46] Summarizing the findings in other such modeling studies, David Klahr and Herbert Simon differentiate between strong methods of problem solving supplied by each discipline and weak methods that supply commonalities. Creative problem solving may, they say, involve both. They state that, overall, creative problem solving has been considered to be based on "(a) heuristic search in a set of problem spaces, spaces of instances, of hypotheses, of representations, of strategies, of instruments... (b) the control structures for search are such general mechanisms as trial and error, 'hill climbing,' means-ends analysis and response to surprise... (c) recognition processes, evoked by familiar patterns recognized in phenomena, [which in turn] evoke knowledge and strong methods from memory, thereby linking the weak methods to the mechanisms that are domain specific."[47]

Pat Langley, who had previously worked extensively with Herbert Simon on artificial intelligence problem solving, has recently described an interactive method of computational problem solving involving collaboration between human investigators and computerized systems (named CLUSTER, AUTOCLASS, RETAX, NGLAUBER, DALTON, STAHLP, MECHEM, ASTRA, IDS, and KEKADA). He outlines the following steps in the scientific discovery process: formation of taxonomies, basic concepts, or categories; discovery of qualitative laws; discovery of quantitative laws that state mathematical relations among numeric variables; creation of structural models that incorporate unobserved entities; and development of process models that explain phenomena in terms of hypothesized mechanisms that involve change over time.[48]

DEVIANT THINKING MODES

Creative achievement is an often infrequent, out of the ordinary event. Many explicators have therefore focused on different, out of the ordinary, or deviating thinking operations or processes. On the basis of factor-analytic assessments of the nature of intellect, J. P. Guilford described "divergent thinking" as a primary method for achieving creative ideas.[49] Divergent thinking (also divergent production) is a form of thought that consists of generating ideas directed toward an undefined solution, whereas the obverse, "convergent thinking," is the following of a series of logical or known steps to a correct or previously known outcome or solution. The concept has been broadly and actively applied to creativity tests and measurements for experimentation, especially by Mark Runco[50] and Ellis P. Torrance,[51] and additionally by the latter to educational practices. Both have used the measure for identification of creative talent and for creative approaches in a number of productive fields.

Runco has recently proposed that "ideational creativity," the number of ideas produced, may be an even better measure than operations and productions of divergent thinking.[52] Frank Barron and George Welsh, on the basis of an assumption that preferences for complexity and design asymmetry were generally unusual and particularly correlated with creative capacity, designed a measure, the Barron-Welsh Preference Test, that until recent years was widely employed in empirical creativity studies.[53] A notable shortcoming is that, with respect to art, preference for design asymmetry has been a distinctly recent time popular orientation for both artists and viewers.

Another type of creative thinking differing from ordinary modes, "lateral thinking," has been proposed and widely disseminated in practical guides by Edward deBono.[54] As the term implies, lateral thinking consists of a sideways shifting from the usual and stepwise modes to achieve creative ideas. deBono advocates choosing random, provoking, outlandish, and challenging ideas and expanding the range and number of concepts.

A fuller type of deviance involving thought, emotions, and behavior is involved in the popular and sustained idea, given impetus during the Romantic period of the 19th century, that creativity and psychopathology are intrinsically tied together. Without going here into the many conceptual and methodological flaws of recent putatively empirical studies in this area, as I have documented those extensively in other places,[55] I shall only describe the approaches of the three most cited and well known. Nancy Andreasen interviewed 30 writers at the Iowa Writers' Workshop and a variety of types of local control subjects.[56] Kay Jamison interviewed a mixed group of 47 British writers and artists and found that several had sought mental-illness treatment for self-reported affective illness (no differential diagnosis assessed). She included no control subjects.[57] Each concluded that depressive illness was connected with literary creativity. Arnold Ludwig and his assistants did not use primary scientific sources or perform diagnostic interviews, but instead studied 1,004 persons whose biographies were reviewed in *The New York Times Book Review*. They concluded that a high degree of various types of psychopathology appeared in artistic types of creators but less so in the scientist portion of the group.[58]

PERSONALITY CHARACTERISTICS

As with cognitive approaches, many of the theories and explorations already cited, especially those of Roe, Eiduson, Csikszentmihalyi, Feist, and Holton, have included descriptions of personality factors thought to be related to general creativity. Simonton also cites such factors (capacities for using a combinatorial process with chance-produced events) but he does not spell out the particular natures of these capacities. The most extensive empirical investigation of creative personality factors was carried out under the direction of Donald MacKinnon at the California Institute of Personality Assessment and Research (IPAR; later renamed the Institute of Personality and Social Research). Persons consensually identified by experts as consistently or moderately creative in their fields typically spent a weekend or more at the Institute, where they were given a battery of psychological tests, observed in their interpersonal interactions, and individually interviewed. One hundred and four subjects were studied directly: 40 architects, 30 writers, and 34 mathematicians. Forty-five promising space-scientist students also were included. Subjects were all found to be intuitive rather than sensing or sensation based. Male subjects all showed high scores on measures of femininity and openness to feelings and emotions. The majority of the subjects, both male and female, possessed the following qualities: perceptive rather than judgmental, introverted rather than extraverted, concern for meanings and implications, cognitive flexibility, interest and accuracy in communication, intellectual curiosity, high theoretical and aesthetic valuation, psychological-mindedness, and achievement through independence. Consistent with most creative personality studies, little relation was found between creativity and intelligence.[59] The male mathematicians in the group, who had been studied separately by Ravenna Helson and Robert Crutchfield, especially showed a high degree of adaptive autonomy—a mixture of complexity, autonomy, and effectiveness—but were low on assertive self-assurance.[60] Frank Barron, who also separately studied the writers in the group, found that they had more extreme experiences of emotion and fantasy life than the other subjects.[61] Helson also studied creative female mathematicians later and found that they were flexible, introverted, and had rebellious independence and symbolic interests.[62]

BIOLOGICAL MECHANISMS

In a famous and still-cited 19th-century study, English scientist Francis Galton attempted to show that genius and eminence and, by extension, creativity, was an inherited capacity from fathers to sons.[63] In his sample, he found that 48% of eminent sons had eminent fathers, and 51% of the eminent sons had their own eminent offspring. He also found other eminent family connections. Although the study was an outstanding instance of the application of the statistical methodology of the time, the results were strongly affected by the English social and legal tradition of primogeniture, which dictated that property as well as social position and occupation passed from father to son. A number of different types of investigations regarding inheritance of creative genius have been carried out since Galton's time. These, cited in the references in chapter 14, show mixed results. Also described in that chapter are the results of my controlled investigations of the family backgrounds of Nobel laureates, winners of the Pulitzer Prize and Booker Prize literature, and Nobel laureates in science, which tend to indicate that environment as well as inheritance, to a lesser degree, plays a critical role in the development of creativity and genius.[64]

Joseph and Glenda Bogen, on the basis of observations of humans who have had split-brain operations for epilepsy, have proposed that interhemispheric transfer in the brain mediated by the central structure, the corpus callosum, was responsible for creative thought. This hemispheric transfer occurs between independently functioning brain hemispheres, the right "appositional" brain hemisphere—capacity for apposing or comparing perceptions and schemas—and the left "propositional" brain—responsible for speaking, reading, and writing. Stages of creative thought, they propose, may be due to variations, such as partial and transiently reversible hemispheric independence. The stages defined by the Bogans (previously proposed by Graham Wallas[65]) are: preparation or gathering of information, incubation where information is unconsciously rearranged, then illumination and reorganization and refinement.[66]

The availability of brain imaging techniques such as positron emission tomography (PET) and magnetic resonance imaging (MRI), as well as improved knowledge of brain chemistry and genetic factors, has led to a number of studies attempting to localize creative brain functioning. By and large, these studies have been limited by the use of minimally defined and nonconsensually validated creative persons as laboratory subjects. A recent example of a study of brain thalamus function and creativity used correlation with a divergent thinking measure.[67] High divergent thinking scores among 14 subjects were negatively correlated with the density of the D_2 type of receptors of the chemical dopamine in the thalamus, a finding suggesting lowered thalamic "gating" and increased information flow between the thalamus and the brain cortex. This dopaminergic function, the authors suggest, could increase excitation of cortical neurons and allow switches between representations and multiple stimuli across a wide association range. Andreasen recently has located creativity in the association cortex, areas of the brain cortex that have neither motor nor sensory functions but are thought to be involved in higher processing of information.[68]

{ 3 }

Empirical Background and the Bases
for the Investigation

I begin this empirical exploration of scientific creativity with the prototype scientific achievement of Albert Einstein. The term *genius*, nowadays too commonly draped thoughtlessly around the shoulders of a wide variety of types of persons, aptly applies to him. Such genius, or exceptional capacity of intellect, may not be required for creative work in many fields, but in the case of science his genius provides important insights.

Born in Ülm, Germany, in 1879, Einstein is generally described as having been withdrawn and slow to respond in his early years. Often he quietly sat by himself putting together shapes cut out with a jigsaw, making complicated constructions with toy building parts. His spoken language developed late, and although he did well overall later in school, he failed foreign languages at the secondary school or *Gymnasium* level and at his entrance examination for the Swiss Federal Institute of Technology at Zurich. Reportedly quite rebellious to his teachers throughout his secondary school years, he nevertheless managed later to be admitted to the Institute and graduate from it in 1900. After that, he was unable for two years to obtain a teaching post, but a family member helped him get a job as a technical assistant at the Swiss patent office in Berne. He continued to study while there and received his doctoral degree in 1905.

That year in his life is widely described by biographers and scientists as his *annus mirabilis*, his miracle year, because he published five papers then that incorporated his special theory of relativity. This theory holds that because the speed of light is constant for all frames of reference, perceptions of time and motion depend on the relative position of the observer. The type of productivity leading to this theory is very important, and deserves particular examination, but we lack any direct evidence from Einstein himself about his creative thinking during that time. It is only later, regarding a further development and another great theoretical breakthrough, the application of

gravitational function within the general theory of relativity, that he documented the exact sequence and substance of his thoughts. In an archived and
unpublished but authenticated manuscript entry titled "The Fundamental
Idea of General Relativity in Its Original Form," he wrote that in 1907, during the course of working on a summary essay on special relativity for the
Jahrbuch für Radioactivität und Elektronik he had generated what he called
the "happiest thought of my life." This thought was the following: *"For an
observer in free fall, e.g. from the roof of a house, there exists for him during his
fall, no gravitational field"* [italics original]. Applying what he has called his
characteristic method of using "thought experiments," he went on to state
that if the observer released any objects, they would remain "in a state of
uniform motion and the observer was 'justified' in considering himself in a
state of rest."

Next, he wrote the explanation of the physical basis of this thought that
made the conclusion so gratifying:

> The extraordinarily curious empirical law that all bodies in the same
> gravitational field fall with the same acceleration immediately took on,
> through this consideration, a deep physical meaning. For if there is even
> one thing which falls differently in a gravitational field than do the oth-
> ers, the observer will discern by means of it that he is falling in it. But
> if such a thing does not exist—as experience has confirmed with great
> precision—the observer lacks any objective ground to consider himself
> as falling in a gravitational field. Rather, he has the right to consider his
> state as that of rest, and his surroundings (with respect to gravitation) as
> field-free.[1]

Two aspects of this account must be immediately striking: first, Einstein's
passionate search and emotional involvement in his finding; second, the contradictory and oppositional nature of the elements in his conclusion, that is,
*a man falling from the roof of a house is both in motion and at rest at the same
time.* This conception is an aspect of the form of creative cognition I have
termed the *janusian process.* The term is based on the Roman god Janus, who
was the god of beginnings and doorways and whose multiple faces (two, four,
or six, on the basis of the number of opposing doorways in the usual Roman
stone dwelling) faced in diametrically opposite directions at the same time.
The janusian process consists of actively conceiving and using multiple opposites or antitheses simultaneously. The process usually occurs early in creative endeavors, and although out of the ordinary and sometimes sudden, it
is conceived and used in a clear and logical frame of mind. It was a crucial
aspect of Einstein's breakthrough to the general theory of relativity, and there
is evidence for its operation in many other important scientific creative processes as well. Einstein elaborated his breakthrough into a theory reconcil-
ing Newton's laws of gravitation and his own special theory of relativity. He

proposed the complete physical equivalence[2] and simultaneity of the opposite effects of a uniform gravitational field in a nonaccelerating or inertial frame and the effects of a uniformly accelerating or noninertial reference frame. This led to his later theory of the universe being curved as a geometric system of space-time.

Charles Darwin, like Einstein, meets extensive consensual criteria for creative genius. Although belief in the evolution of living entities was held by numerous scientists before Darwin began his work, his observational data together with his discovery of randomness and natural selection made him the progenitor of the principle of evolution of species. The validity of this principle has been reliably and scientifically established.

Born in Shrewsbury, England, in 1809, Darwin briefly studied medicine in Edinburgh, then theology at Cambridge University. Under the influence of Reverend John Henslow, a botany professor there, he undertook an extended sea voyage after his graduation. He spent 5 years on the ship *HMS Beagle,* captained by Robert FitzRoy, and circumnavigated the world. Three of the years were spent exploring the coastal flora and fauna of South America, including a portion at the Galápagos Islands. In 1838, he recorded his full observations and theory but did not publish them until much later in 1859 in the book, *On The Origin of Species.* If it had not been for the instigating stimulus of Alfred Russel Wallace's writings to him in 1858 to report an independently conceived theory nearly identical to his own, Darwin might have delayed publication of his work even further.

Darwin documented that his conception of natural selection first came to him as a creative breakthrough in the year 1838.[3] After having gathered voluminous data on his sea journey regarding the diversity of plants and animals, including numerous observations indicating the interchangeability and replacement of closely allied animals, Darwin said he was "haunted" for a long time by the "supposition that species became greatly modified." Then, at a point in 1838, 15 months after having started his "systematic inquiry," he was reading a book by Thomas Malthus on population[4] that, he said, indicated the widespread struggle for existence. While riding in a carriage and thinking of Malthus, the following occurred:

> It at once struck me that under these circumstances favourable variations would tend to be preserved, and unfavourable ones to be destroyed. The result of this would be the formation of a new species. I had at last got a theory by which to work.

In this short remembrance, the two elements I highlighted in Einstein's report of his breakthrough are also manifest. There is the emotional involvement, passionate to some degree, as indicated by his earlier statement that the modification supposition had haunted him. Also, there is his simultaneous framing of opposite circumstances, the "favourable and unfavourable," in a single mental construct of the natural selection function. Up to that point, Darwin had been focused on a theory involving only the extinction of characteristics and species—extinction of the unfavorable.[5] Then, in his reported conception of natural selection in evolution, the creative breakthrough, he brought the opposites of unfavorable extinction and favorable preservation simultaneously together. After making this postulate, Darwin later developed the features of the components, outlining that favorable and unfavorable variation could occur in successive generations for both individuals and species.

Another creative scientific breakthrough, the development of the theory of complementarity by Niels Bohr, contained the same type of elements in a form even more closely resembling the structure of Einstein's insight regarding general relativity. A scientific contemporary of Einstein's, Bohr was, according to most physicists and scholars, virtually Einstein's equal in genius and creative capacity. Among other achievements, Bohr was responsible for constructing a picture of atomic structure that, with some later improvements, still fits as an elucidation of the chemical and physical properties of the elements. For this he won the Nobel Prize in Physics in 1922. Later in his life, he developed the theory of complementarity, which preceded and accommodated Heisenberg's theoretical uncertainty principle. These two theories became the joint bases of quantum physics and also advanced quantum mechanics. Complementarity in itself touched upon all domains of human knowledge.

Bohr was born in Copenhagen in 1885, the son of Christian Bohr, a professor of physiology at Copenhagen University. He received his doctoral degree there in 1911. While still a student, he carried out studies of surface tension for which he received a prize from the Danish Academy of Sciences. Then, soon after receiving the doctorate, he became professor of theoretical physics at the University. In 1920, he was appointed the head of the specially established Institute for Theoretical Physics, where he worked for the rest of his life, mentoring as well as collaborating with leading world scientists who came to work with him. The list includes Werner Heisenberg, Paul Dirac, Erwin Schrödinger, Charles Darwin (grandson of the evolutionist), Max Delbrück, Wolfgang Pauli, Hendrick Kramers, and his son, Hans Bohr (also a Nobel laureate in Physics).

He was long concerned, together with some of the just-named contemporary physicists and others, with the known contradictory properties of light, which sometimes acts in the form of waves and sometimes as particles (corpuscles). These poorly understood and confusing properties were serious impediments to scientific knowledge and to the important development of quantum physics in particular. Then in 1927, as described to me by his wife, Margarethe Bohr,[6] he came to feel great relief and happiness at arriving at a creative breakthrough regarding the nature of light. On a skiing trip to Norway, he conceived the following, documented in his first version of a report to the journal *Nature*:

> I...think...of optical properties which are accounted for so directly through the principle of superposition of waves but are quite foreign to a corpuscular theory. It seems that we here meet with an unavoidable dilemma, as there is no question of a choice between two different concepts but rather of the description of two complementary sides of the *same phenomenon* [italics mine].[7]

The breakthrough consisted of the idea of light as both wave and particle operating in the same phenomenon. He here indicated his first conception, within a janusian process, of the contradictory or antithetical properties of wave and particle as side-by-side composites operating simultaneously. Applying this creative insight to light, and by extension to electrons, he spelled out in his revolutionary and fully developed complementarity theory that the dual properties of wave and particle were both necessary, despite their mutual exclusiveness, for a complete explanation. Experimental results, he asserted, would sometimes yield data appropriate to one understanding of the properties and sometimes to the other in the larger, full description of natural phenomena. Both a traditional type of prediction based on spatio-temporal causation and a probabilistic prediction from the newly developed quantum theory were appropriate.

The two aspects of the episodes in Einstein and Darwin's reports were also present in Bohr's creative breakthrough. There was the adoption of opposites operating together—for Bohr, the two complementary sides of the same phenomenon. Also, there was a comparable passion and emotional involvement as reported by his wife. Bohr's second oldest son, Hans, later related, "One of the favorite maxims of my father was the distinction between two kinds of truths, profound truths recognized by the fact that the opposite is also a profound truth, in contrast to trivialities where opposites are obviously absurd."[8]

The janusian process also operated in James Watson's highly significant breakthrough conception of the double helix structure of deoxyribonucleic acid (DNA) and its application to the nature of genetic replication. Born in Chicago, Watson later became a young microbiologist member of the Luria-Delbrück phage group at Indiana University and Cold Spring Harbor. He then went to Copenhagen University, and after that to the Cavendish Laboratory at Cambridge University to collaborate with Francis Crick. Although some aspects of the account of the double helix discovery by Watson have been challenged, notably a lack of acknowledgement of the important contribution Rosalind Franklin made through her findings,[9] his description of the final step in the breakthrough clearly traces his own thought processes at the time. Regardless of considerations about the background and total circumstances of the discovery, the section of Watson's own documentation in his book *The Double Helix* is directly connected with the mental steps in the breakthrough itself. The account, personal, detailed, and certain, has been unchallenged as an authentic report.[10]

Watson says that, working in the morning in his "still empty office," he first continued to follow his "like with like" prejudices in order to conceive the structure of DNA. He believed that the composing chemical bases—adenine, cytosine, guanine, thymine—were each bonded together by the element hydrogen in similar pairs. Then, as he wrote:

> Suddenly I became aware that an adenine-thymine pair held together by two hydrogen bonds was identical in shape to a guanine-cytosine pair held together by at least two hydrogen bonds. All the hydrogen bonds seemed to form naturally; no fudging was required to make the two types of base pairs identical in shape....
>
> The hydrogen bonding requirement meant that adenine would always pair with thymine, while guanine could pair only with cytosine. Chargaff's rules [of base pairing] then stood out as a consequence of a double helical structure for DNA. *Even more exciting, this type of double helix suggested a replication scheme much more satisfactory than my briefly considered like-with-like pairing* [italics mine]. Always pairing adenine with thymine and guanine with cytosine meant that the base sequences of the two intertwined chains were complementary to each other. Given the base sequence of one chain, that of its partner was automatically determined. Conceptually, it was thus very easy to visualize how a single chain could be the template for the synthesis of a chain with the complementary sequence....
>
> Both pairs could be flipflopped over and still have their glycosidic bonds facing in the same direction. This had the important consequence that a given chain could contain both purines and pyrimidines at the same time, it strongly suggested that the backbones of the two chains must run in opposite directions.[11]

Watson shifted from conceiving the DNA strands having like-with-like pairing to the breakthrough formulation of strand chains operating simultaneously in opposite directions in the double helix, a janusian process formulation. Noting that he then told Crick of this determination, he says the two of them went to a local restaurant soon after and declared that they had discovered "the secret of life." The emotional excitement he describes is similar to the type felt by Einstein, Darwin, and Bohr.

So far I have described crucial solutions, creative breakthroughs, solely by Western scientists. Is there likely to be a cultural factor involved in the creative experience or might this type of gratification and thought structure be more widespread? At least one recorded incidence coming from a cultural setting quite removed from Europe and the West is that of the first Japanese Nobel laureate in science, Hideki Yukawa.

This scientist helped explain the nature of atomic nuclear forces through his prediction of the existence and description of the characteristics of previously unknown particles called *mesons*. The prediction was later confirmed in part and Yukawa developed a meson theory that served as the basis for the designation of a large class of subatomic particles and the subsequent wide development of elementary-particles knowledge. Others have extended his theory and discovery further.

Yukawa, born in Tokyo in 1907, was brought up in the venerable city of Kyoto. He attended primary and secondary school there. As described in his autobiography, he was both short and dark-skinned and consequently felt lonely and remote from other students.[12] Mathematics he loved and he later majored in physics at Kyoto University. He became a research associate, then a lecturer both there and at Osaka University. Receiving his doctorate at Osaka at the age of 31, a year later he became a full professor at Kyoto. He received the Nobel Prize in Physics in 1949, and he was widely designated by his colleagues as "a genius type." In his autobiography, he described his critical 1934 meson discovery at age 27 as follows:

> The problem that I focused on was...the nature of the forces that act upon the neutrons and protons making up the nucleus—that is, the nature of the nuclear forces. By confronting this difficult problem, I committed myself to long days of suffering....[13]
>
> The crucial point came to me one night in October. The nuclear force is effective at extremely small distances, on the order of 0.02 trillionth of a centimeter. That much I knew already. My new insight was the realization that this distance and the mass of the new particle I was seeking are inversely related to each other. Why had I not noticed that before? The next morning, I tackled the problem of the mass of the new particle and found it to be two hundred times that of the electron. It also had to have the charge of plus or minus that of the electron. Such a particle had not, of course, been found, so I asked myself, 'Why not?' The answer was simple: an energy of 100 million electron volts would be needed to create such a particle, and there was no accelerator, at that time, with that much energy available.
>
> I became increasingly confident. I spoke to everyone about the new theory during the meeting of the Kikuchi research group. [Seishi] Kikuchi said, "If there is such a charged particle, it should become visible in the Wilson cloud chamber, should it not?" I answered, "Yes, the particle can be found in the cosmic rays."...
>
> I felt like a traveler who rests himself at a small tea shop at the top of mountain slope. At that time I was not thinking about whether there were any more mountains ahead.[14]

In these passages, Yukawa indicated similar emotional involvement or, more particularly, emotional strain and happy release, with his reference to a commitment to days of suffering leading ultimately to relief. He describes the relief poetically with the Japanese simile of attaining rest at a mountaintop tea shop. As with the previously documented breakthroughs in this chapter, Yukawa's conception involved simultaneous opposition and a janusian process with his consolidated formulation of an inverse co-existing relationship between the distance of force effectiveness and the particle mass.

In understanding and assessing the psychological structure of these breakthroughs, these scientists' great store of specialized knowledge, skill,[15] and very high intelligence must not be ignored. I am, however, indicating the specific nature of creative thinking and creative processes. Although I have characterized all but one of these men as creative geniuses, in part because of their enormous intellect, there is, in fact, some evidence that in other fields than science the intellect of genius is not actually necessary for creative achievement. Special superior capacities and types of intelligence may be applicable in art, literature, and creativity in everyday activities but, with the possible exception of music, comparably high degrees of technical understanding are not crucial and might even restrict or hinder motivation and work habits.

The described breakthroughs by these scientists in diverse fields and cultures all indicate the operation of the janusian process in creative scientific cognition. As the descriptions all derive from autobiographical documents and scientific notes, they are potentially subject to the distortions attendant on faulty memory or public disclosure, even with such ordinarily reliable and objective informants. Therefore, I shall present the creative functions of the janusian and other specific cognitive processes as hypotheses and report pertinent primary investigative data and empirically derived conclusions later.

{ 4 }

Janusian Process

Oppositions and antitheses were important factors in the breakthrough conceptions of Albert Einstein, Charles Darwin, Niels Bohr, James Watson, and Hideki Yukawa. With respect to creativity, the significant creative feature regarding these oppositions and antitheses was that they were formulated and applied as simultaneously operative and valid.

In literature, I have presented evidence based on the content analysis of manuscript revisions together with pertinent life history information from Eugene O'Neill's last wife, Carlotta Monterey, that the playwright's initial conception for the drama *The Iceman Cometh* consisted of a simultaneous opposition. He conceived the lead character, Hickey, as a man who wanted his wife to be both faithful and not faithful at the same time. This formulation determined much of the plot of the play, an allegorical story of both faith and nondeliverance. It also underlay the dramatic unfolding and character development in the play, a work that many consider to be O'Neill's best.[1] Through intensive and extensive interviewing of literary prizewinners—winners of the Pulitzer Prize, the National Book Award, and the Bollingen Prize for Poetry—I also found evidence for critical formulations and use of simultaneous opposition within the janusian process in early and late conceptions of their major literary works. These ongoing interviews focused on the continuing creative process, usually from the first inception of the literary work until its final publication. Authors interviewed have included Arthur Miller, John Cheever, William Meredith, James Merrill, William Styron, John Hersey, Muriel Rukeyser, Maxine Kumin, John Updike, Richard Wilbur, and Robert Penn Warren. I found that Arthur Miller, for example, came up with the conception of the play *Incident at Vichy* while traveling through Germany: "Driving on the autobahn," he said, "I suddenly felt amazed and overwhelmed at how beautiful Germany had become." He conceived of writing a play that would simultaneously express the opposites of Germany's beauty and Hitler's destructiveness. "And then I remembered a story I'd been told about a sacrifice made by an Austrian nobleman for a Jew in a Nazi official's waiting room." He developed the story of the simultaneously anti-thetical components of the political sacrifice in his play. John Cheever, when first conceiving his most successful novel, *Falconer*, thought of expressing the central symbolic idea of a falcon as both aggressively predatory and victim-ized at once, a janusian process formulation.

Although the arts and science are markedly different endeavors, operative creative processes have appeared to be structurally the same. In literature, the working out of an initial conception of the simultaneous opposition or antithesis of the janusian process produces, among other effects, a central dramatic and formal conflict (tragedy or comedy) as well as irony, symbol, deep psychological meaning, humor, effective ambiguity, aesthetic truths, and intriguing paradox. In art and music, in addition, there are contrast-ing themes, syncopation, inversions, counterpoint, chiaroscuro, and color compositions of interacting complementaries and contrasts. Although such oppositional end products are critically well known and appreciated in liter-ature and other arts, it is not always manifestly apparent that similar struc-tural properties, particularly paradox, occur and are universal in scientific endeavor. In his Nobel laureate lecture, entitled "Asymptotic Freedom: From Paradox to Paradigm,"[2] physicist Frank Wilczek personally emphasized the importance of such paradox within science. "Paradoxes are good," he said. "When David Gross and I began the work that led to this Nobel Prize [con-tributions to the theory of the strong force] . . . we were driven by paradoxes." Historian of science Gerald Holton has extended this observation fur-ther: "Science has always been propelled and buffeted by . . . contrary or anti-thetical forces. Like vessels with draught deep enough to catch more than merely the surface current, scientists of genius are those who are doomed, or privileged, to experience these deeper currents in their complexity. It is precisely their special sensitivity to contraries that has made it possible for them to do so, and it is an inner necessity that has made them demand noth-ing less for themselves."[3]

Opposition together with antithesis, contraries, and contradiction is intrinsic to paradox. When a theory or fact of nature is considered true, the presence of an opposing actuality is paradoxical. Focused on the paradoxical and the resolution of paradox is the classical formulation of a dialectic, or dialectical argument and thinking, attributed to the philosopher Hegel. This dialectic consists first of an assertion of truth, a thesis, with the next step as the consideration of the opposite or antithesis, and last a resolution of the conflicting assertions or truths by synthesis.[4]

Although it involves opposites, the janusian process, I must emphasize, is not a dialectic or a dialectical structure because the opposites are formulated as simultaneously valid and not in sequence; they are not reconciled or solved with synthesis. Integration and metaphor are most commonly the outcomes. Because of the oppositional or antithetical content of the janusian process, it is relevant to the truthful factors underlying paradox and the pervasiveness of paradox throughout nature, thought, and human endeavor. It is not, however, a way of thinking obversely or even in a dialectical fashion because it consists of the active conception and the use of both multiple—not necessarily just two—and *simultaneous* opposites or antitheses. Concepts are posited as simultaneously true and not-true, contradictions are not resolved but are conceived as operating together or side by side, and multiple opposing events and facts of life and nature occur or in some way function at exactly the same time. These concepts are formulated actively and consciously in rational states of mind. Indeed, the positing of such conflicting and complex formulations about nature requires so much intellectual capacity and scientific knowledge, that the state of mind could be considered superrational and farseeing.[5] This was certainly the case when Albert Einstein, using the janusian process, had what he called "the happiest thought of my life," consisting of a man falling being at the same time in a state of rest. His conception of the simultaneous opposition of both motion and rest at once provided him with a physical example that led to a new conception of gravity in the general theory of relativity and later to what was called the principle of equivalence. His janusian conception, the creative breakthrough, needed to be extensively elaborated in the developed theory through various modifications as well as logical and analogical extensions involving mathematical and scientific skills.

Darwin's breakthrough conception of natural selection as the basis of evolution—"I had," he said, "at last got a theory by which to work"—was also formulated as a janusian conception of simultaneously operating opposites. Rather than unfavorable extinction alone as the cause of evolution, he brought together both favorable and unfavorable variations at once. Both were results of the same natural selection operation, survival, which brought about individuals or species. Darwin required both ordering and, as with Einstein, modification, logical, and analogical processes and skills to develop the full theory of evolution.

In developing the theory of complementarity, Niels Bohr's first formulation consisted of wave and particle as simultaneous opposites. "No question of a choice between two different concepts," he wrote, "but rather the description of two complementary sides of the same phenomenon." This concept, modified to state that the data pertaining to wave functions of light and electrons were in some situations valid and the data pertaining to light and electrons as particles were in other circumstances also valid, was elaborated into an extensive physical theory. He later applied this theory of complementarity to a broad range of fields, scientific and social.

James Watson stated dramatically that, working by himself, his formulation of the structure of the DNA molecule shifted from the idea of a like-with-like composition to a simultaneously opposing one of a double helix. He conceived multiple opposite perspectives of the backbones of the two helical chains running in converse directions at once and of the base pairs simultaneously being flipped over.

Hideki Yukawa thought of the meson particle as inverse in size to the infinitesimally small force field in the atom. This involved the simultaneous conception—a janusian formulation—of an extraordinarily large particle operating with its opposite-sized, infinitesimally small nuclear force field.

The janusian process illustrated in these creative discoveries characteristically proceeds through four identifiable phases: motivation to create; deviation or separation from the usual, the accepted canons and procedures; simultaneous opposition or antithesis; and construction of the theory, discovery, or experiment. Each of these phases bears on the development of the next one. In some cases, these phases, especially the deviation and simultaneous opposite ones, may occur in quick, almost instantaneous succession.

In chapter 3 I cited some of the passion and intense emotional investment of the foregoing scientists regarding their problems and breakthrough solutions. Later (chapter 7) I shall further describe some of the emotional factors together with the intellectual ones involved in the passionate motivation to create. It includes problem finding, passion for learning, aggressiveness and destructive feelings, courage, and self-confidence or ego strength. This motivation, which initiates every type of creative process, constitutes the first phase of the janusian process. I want to stress that motivation to create is a conscious factor. Although the scientist may not always have the term *create* in mind or use it while working or in public pronouncements, the goal is to look for or produce something new—a solution, an invention or innovation, theoretical point, or complete theory—not simply to extend material and knowledge or produce an alternative or a difference. There is little question that the scientist also intends to produce something valuable, and this ambition ranges from small scientific contributions to the achievement recognized in most if not all cases by the Nobel Prize.

Nothing is ever created without the intention to create. This means that so-called unconscious creating and the popularly alleged wide role of serendipity in scientific advance is overstated and incorrect. Even in vigorously touted cases of supposed serendipity or accidental discovery, to be detailed later (chapter 7), such as those of Alexander Fleming with penicillin and Wilhelm Roentgen with X-rays, both scientists were already actively working in the designated problem areas, Fleming on antiseptics and Roentgen on cathodes, and both had the understanding and goal to produce the creations. This understanding is what Louis Pasteur characterized as "chance favors the prepared mind," a preparation he declared was absolutely necessary for scientific discovery.[6]

The second phase of the janusian process, separation or deviation from the usual, occurs in every type of creative operation. Specific opposites or antitheses derived from ongoing and meaningful scientific issues and problems are separated and focused on. Deviation, whether occurring early or late, is then a necessary factor for the production of something new. In the janusian process it tends to occur early. This is because the creative thinker, focused on particular contraries, antitheses, and oppositions within and outside of paradoxes, often begins at that point to veer away from accepted formulations and knowledge. The interest in deviations comes in many cases partly from deep and wide-ranging scientific knowledge, but it is strongly fueled by the existing motivation to create, to find something new and even more valuable. As a necessary factor in the creative process, deviation is often included in and also inseparable from the choice to create.

The deviations and demarcations from the usual canons of procedure or knowledge set the stage directly for the newness and novelty of the third phase. The chosen opposites and antitheses, applied and elaborated simultaneously, substantially disrupt preexisting contexts and conceptions. Highly surprising—sometimes to creative thinkers themselves—even incredible and inconceivable, are propositions stating that contradictions or opposites of well-grounded facts, theories, or actualities are simultaneously valid. This is especially true when the simultaneous oppositions or antitheses are considered or described in isolation and before being elaborated into a final production. Previously held ideas and systems of ideas are split apart and broken, essentially destroyed. Because of the obversity, creative events are sometimes experienced as astonishing.

With respect to the newness of a created product, janusian formulations are out of time. The oppositions and antitheses are simultaneous and therefore without the factor of sequence that constitutes temporality and time. Because of this, janusian formulations can produce seeming or truly new properties without connections to antecedents. The properties arise in a direct line of causation, but are also products of emergent novelty as described earlier (chapter 1). As scientific investigation involves discovery of factors in nature that previously existed, both types of newness apply to a body of existing knowledge. Also, the creative process involves cognition leading to a previously unknown and ultimately valuable goal.

In the fourth phase, the new entity is developed. The valuable aspect of the creative effect in this phase, including construction of theory, discovery, or critical experiment, is produced through interaction among the simultaneously opposite components. These components are altered and often may not appear in the final product. Conflicting aspects of the opposites and antitheses induce production of creations in which they are integrated and transcended. The detailed factors of motion and rest, for example, were joined and mutually continuously modified and elaborated by Einstein in his general theory of relativity. The fully developed theory includes the effect of gravitation on the shape of space and the flow of time. Creative interaction effects lead, as in this theory, to the overall integration, and this type of interaction, as I shall describe, is characteristic of all three of the identified creative processes. The janusian process operates on logical and temporal effects; the homospatial process operates on spatial effects; and the sep-con articulation process operates on part and whole effects.

{ 5 }

Homospatial Process

Space and spatial locations are readily represented in the mind. This is so even for persons who are blind, both congenital and acquired, because living requires development of mental representation of spaces, particularly local ones, in order to move around and function. The mental representation does not, for everyone, usually include such extensions as veridical descriptions of locations in the universe or outer space unless one is a astronomer or other scientist using or exploring these realms. Capacity and uses of mental representation of space and spatial location through projection may nevertheless be more far reaching, extreme, and diverse than any physical actuality. The cognitive homospatial process responsible for many types of creative results, both in the arts and in science, entails a diverse type of mental presentation, one that defies or changes actual physical space. The homospatial process consists of actively conceiving two or more discrete entities occupying the same space or spatial location, a conception leading to the articulation of new identities. Shapes, patterns, written words, dimensions, distances, and other concrete entities are superimposed and interposed in conscious mental spatial representations. Subjectively, eyes closed or open, the resulting mental image totally fills the conceptualized perceptual area. Such an imaginary image location can be referred to as commonly occurring in the "mind's eye" but, because any sensory modality may be involved, terms such as "mind's ear," "mind's taste," "mind's touch," and so on, may also be applied. The discrete entities in the homospatial conception may be spatially superimposed or interposed within any of the sensory spheres: visual, auditory, tactile, kinesthetic, olfactory, and gustatory.

Although elements in the homospatial process are consciously and intentionally brought together, the mental construct may often be rapid and fleeting. The unstable and often perceptually conflicting components interact and both quickly and more gradually produce new identities, including new ideas. In the arts, these may often consist of effective metaphors and metaphorical phrases—literary, visual or artistic, auditory or musical. Broad metaphorical constructions in these areas may also be produced. Examples are Shakespeare's *Hamlet* as idealistic man and Rembrandt's self-portraits, which, as I have shown elsewhere, represent a genre of metaphors of self.[1] In music, an example of another type of use of the homospatial process is vividly documented in composer Paul Hindemith's general account of musical creation: "Within a second's time we see a broad landscape, not only in its general outlines but with every detail. . . .We feel that not even the smallest leaf of grass escapes our attention. We examine a view, immensely comprehensive and at the same time immensely detailed. . . . Compositions must be conceived the same way. If we cannot in the flash of a single moment, see a composition in its absolute entirety, with every pertinent detail in its proper place, we are not genuine creators."[2]

In my previous investigations in literary and artistic creativity, a writer subject described the course of creating a poem about the outdoors while sitting at his desk. A central metaphor of that poem was the phrase, "the branches were handles of stars." To create that metaphor he had first become attracted to the shared sound qualities—the assonance or shared "an" in the center of *handle* and *branch*—and the somewhat similar shapes of the outdoor types of these objects. Then, in his mind's eye, he actively superimposed both these words and their concrete images, bringing them together because he felt they ought to be together. In the next rapidly ensuing moments, he thought of how in reality they could be the same, and also fleetingly experienced a vivid impression of the letter *a* overlapping in the two words. At that point, the middle *a* and accompanying radiant word *stars* was generated, not before. Associational or analogical ideas of the country (or park) at night did not generate the metaphor "the branches were handles of stars." It was derived directly from the homospatial process that provided both the real scene and sound qualities that integrated the words and their meanings.

In the creation of another type of metaphor, "the tarantula rays of the lamp spread across the conference room," the same author was thinking of writing a poem about a symbolic vacation in the tropics. Among the various thoughts and words that came to mind, he became interested in the sound similarity between the words *tarantula* and *lamp*. Feeling that these words ought to be together, he then actively superimposed images of the spider and a light source as well as letters in the written words. A spidery light radiated out in his mind from a central source in the superimposed images, and he thought of the metaphor, "tarantula rays of the lamp." Deciding next to elaborate that fragment with a suggestive context, he conceived the phrase, "conference room." Once this entire metaphor was created, he thought of overtones such as wars in the tropics and the idea of the slow crawl of a tarantula in contrast with the dazzling speed of light; experiencing an awe-inspiring type of beauty, he was pleased. With both poetic creations, this author visualized a vague scene and found the answer in words. The created metaphors then induced more fully developed and vivid mental scenes similar to the ones experienced by a reader or audience, and he articulated the metaphors as well as descriptions of the scenes into fully developed poems. He was sure that those subsequently visualized scenes did not produce the metaphors, but rather added mainly to his feeling of the aptness of his creation.

In the realm of visual art, sculptor Henry Moore documented the crucial use of the same homospatial process in the creation of his sculptural works as follows: "This is what the sculptor must do. He must strive continually to think of, and use, form in its full spatial completeness. He gets the solid shape, as it were, inside his head—he thinks of it, whatever its size, as if he were holding it completely enclosed in the hollow of his hand. He mentally visualizes a complex form from all round itself; he knows while he looks at one side what the other side is like."[3]

Use of visual and spatial factors is often considered an important component of creative thinking of all types. Capacity and use of spatial imagery, spatial and topological calculations, and three-dimensional conceptualizations, are often attributed to creative persons and considered critical in their achievements. It has been alleged, for example, that Einstein had poor verbal skills and consistently used spatial cognition, although he himself never described his thinking in that way.[4] The vivid images involved in his thought experiments—imagining a train riding next to a beam of light, a gravitation example of falling in an elevator, as well as his key reference to a man falling from the roof of a house that I cited in chapter 3—do point to some use of spatial conceptions.[5] Claims for the importance in science of visual and spatial imagery have ranged from Galton's famous claim of minimal,[6] to very large by Roe,[7] and to Miller's assertion of the critical presence of visual and spatial imagery in all scientific creative work.[8]

Considering the visual nature of many creative results in both science and the arts, it seems likely that various aspects of the work have involved some degree of visual and spatial skills and conceptualizing. Despite Miller's far-reaching suppositions, however, spatial thinking in itself is not directly or adequately creative in science; used alone, it has not been shown to produce creative outcomes. Although the homospatial process does utilize both visual and other types of imagery, these do not alone lead to such outcomes; the cognitive operations of superimposition or interposition of spatial entities are required to produce the radical changes in the creative sequence. There is mutual occupation of the same space and violation of the veridical properties of concrete space. These radical conditions begin a break with the past necessary for the newness in creations and creativity. The apposition and mingling of discrete components produces mental interaction with mutual modification and change. Identities resulting from this process are integrated and intrinsically or pragmatically valuable.

Imagination involves not-yet-seen or realized actions, experiences, persons, and events. It is always based in part on some aspect of memory of the past that is combined with wishes, knowledge, fantasy, and freedom of thought. Patterns and elements of remembered persons and events are modified, extended, and mixed with anticipations, fears, and hopes; these are often projected into the future. Imagining the characteristics of an unknown person, for example, is based on anticipated similarities and differences from past acquaintances. Imagination is an adaptive human capacity; it originates adaptively as a spontaneous reflex in the face of danger, alerting one usually in images to the possibility of accidents or evildoing. Imagination may also signal immediate or delayed pleasure or work. These reflexes and experiences are extended throughout life to more complicated emotional circumstances. Frequent intentional imagining may often be fruitful in creative activities to provide images for paintings, procedures, and outcomes both in science and story. Sherlock Holmes author Arthur Conan Doyle, for example, said, "Imagination is the breeding ground of horror." Although such imagining may be quite extensive and even out of the ordinary, it is not a creative factor in itself; it does not directly produce newness and value. Consisting primarily of sensory images, as designated in the lexical basis of the word *imagination* in *images* or *imaging*, it is creatively molded primarily by the homospatial process, which utilizes all types of sensory images, visual, auditory, and other. Rich imagining is generally useful when applied in art, literature, music, and dance, and also for planning procedures and working out theories in science. For all productive fields, imagination also applies to the potentially facilitative expectation of personal and social gratifications. Nevertheless, in all creative activities, both images and imagination operate primarily as content used and molded by creative cognition. Extensive imagination content may provide increased opportunities for creative transformations. So-called imaginative people may also be creative; nevertheless, creative people may use little or no imagination in their work. As an instance of imaginative use in literature, writer Robert Penn Warren told me, "I see a movie in my head throughout the writing of a novel." This "movie," he attested, was used to develop character, metaphor, emotional scenes, suspense, ethical dilemma, and integration. Verbal, emotional, and conceptual aspects of imagination are creatively applied by the homospatial process; characterization particularly is developed by another cognitive creative process, sep-con articulation, as will be detailed in chapter 6. "Creative imagination" or "creative imagining" consists of imagination structured by the cognitive creative processes.

The homospatial process contributes in science to creation of a theory, models and metaphors, an experimental design and procedure, or a previously unconceived discovery. In art and literature, many other types of creative identities and integrities such as designs, themes, and formal structure also are produced. In all fields, the homospatial process works generally in conjunction with other creative processes described here for development and elaboration of creative results.

With respect to the arts and literature, I, together with co-investigator Robert Sobel, have carried out a series of controlled experiments with prize-winning artists and talented writers using superimposed visual images to assess the creative effects of the homospatial process. Forty-three writers were randomly assigned to view 10 different slide compositions presented either superimposed or as separated images. A frontal grouping of nuns, for example, was seen by half of the subjects as superimposed on a frontal grouping of racing jockeys, and the other half in a different room saw the nuns and jockeys in separated side-by-side presentations. All subjects were asked to create literary metaphors in response to the images seen. In another experiment with 46 writer subjects, the same procedures were followed with the modification of turning the slide projectors off and encouraging the subjects to shut their eyes and mentally visualize the images they had seen before creating the literary metaphors.

In the experiments with artists designed to assess the homospatial process, 46 of them were exposed in the same fashion to images presented either superimposed or side by side. In response to these, the artists were asked to create pastel drawings. Another artist experiment I later performed was designed to assess whether image superimposition rather than a change to Gestalt foreground–background perception had creative effects. In this procedure, the photo images were cut up to present the same scenes in a foreground and background display as the superimposed ones. Nuns, for example, were seen in the foreground of the picture with blocked-off shapes of the jockeys behind them. Thirty-nine prizewinning artists were randomly assigned to each of these viewing groups and also asked to create pastel drawings. In all four experiments, expert professional writers or artists were contracted to rate, blind to the experimental conditions, the creativity manifested by the literary metaphors or pastel drawings produced. Results for all four experiments were that the works produced in response to the superimposed-image condition, metaphors, or drawings, were rated by these experts as higher in creativity at a statistically significant difference level than those produced in any of the separated or foreground–background control conditions.[9] As the experimental superimposed presentation could be considered a representation of the mental homospatial process, especially in the eyes-shut delayed writing condition, the results support the proposition of the effective operation of the homospatial process in creative achievement.

Testimonial evidence from creative scientists indicates that the homospatial process has also facilitated direct solutions to scientific problems. One account comes from the French mathematician and physicist Henri Poincaré, whom some have credited as a codiscoverer of the special theory of relativity along with Einstein, and who made many discoveries in fields such as topology, thermodynamics, electricity, and cosmology. He detailed his formulation of the famous Fuchsian (automorphic) mathematical functions as follows: "One evening, contrary to my custom, I drank black coffee and could not sleep. [I began thinking of my mathematical work and] ideas rose in crowds; I felt them collide until pairs interlocked, so to speak, making a stable... [structure]. By the next morning, I had established the existence of a class of Fuchsian functions, those which come from the hypergeometric series; I had only to write out the results, which took but a few hours."[10] His description of interlocking ideas indicates interposition or superimposition of entities within the same mental space in a homospatial process leading to a group of functions that served to integrate and clarify results in several different areas of mathematics.

Another French mathematician scientist, Jacques Hadamard, made many contributions broadly to modern mathematics including number theory, differential geometry, and partial differential equations. He discovered the "valuation of a determinant," a formulation that started with inequalities of some mathematical determinants and led to the development of "Hadamard matrices" in which determinant equality holds. He wrote that his initial conception of the valuation was a schematic diagram consisting of "a square whose sides only the verticals are drawn and, inside of it, four points being the vertices of a rectangle and joined by (hardly apparent) diagonals."[11] His visualized concept consisted of a rectangle occupying the inside of a square, two discrete entities within the same spatial location.

Throughout history, many guiding conceptual metaphors and models for theory building and discovery have been used in scientific discovery.[12] Although there is no direct evidence, it seems likely that these resulted from the application of the homospatial process to the production of creative and evocative metaphors. Isaac Newton, for instance, applied the metaphorical concept that the moon is a ball thrown around the earth to his theory of gravitation. A metaphorical state of "suspended animation" was described by Dr. Henry Hill Hickman as his goal for developing an early form of inhalant anesthesia for painless surgery. Louis Pasteur brought together in a burst of inspiration the observation of the survival of previously infected chickens with Edward Jenner's injection of cowpox to prevent smallpox in his creation of the metaphor "vaccination" as the guiding formulation for what became preventive medicine. August Kekulé discovered the circular chemical structure of the benzene molecule from a probable homospatial process image consisting of a snake with its tail in its mouth.[13] Astronomer and priest Abbé Georges Lemaître conceived the metaphors of "Big Bang" and "cosmic egg" as bases for his theory of the origin of the universe. J. F. A. P. Miller's metaphors of "killer cells" and "the thymus is a school" helped to determine the functions of the thymus gland and set the stage for the birth of cellular immunology.[14] The metaphor "black holes in space," coined by physicist John Wheeler,[15] has led to findings providing for extension of Albert Einstein's general theory of relativity and other theories of energy, time, and astronomical events.

The homospatial process tends to have a primarily unidirectional effect. In the production of both conceptual scientific and literary metaphors, one of the elements in the metaphor is more in focus, more changed, or in terms of technical literary analysis, the "target,"[16] rather than its modifier. For the metaphor "tarantula rays" described earlier, the impact is greater on the sun's rays than on the tarantula; the rays are more definitively spider shaped than the tarantula is illuminated. Likewise, in scientific creation, one factor in a conception is more affected or changed than others, as, for instance, the square more than the rectangle in the previous Hadamard valuation.

The homospatial process proceeds through several phases. Like the janusian process, there is in the first phase an initial motivation to create, a phase similarly with specific and general emotional underpinnings. The second phase, concerning ordinary spatial problems and formulations, involves a deviation of a different type. Two or more discrete entities, usually in the form of sensory images of concrete space and spatial locations, are wrested from their ordinary contexts. They may be meaningful in some way to the overall sphere of investigation or production, but diverse other factors may also be included. The discrete entities chosen are individually, emotionally, and cognitively appealing, and even when out of context, in all cases have some relationship with one another.[17] For the poet, as with the handles and branches example, the components may often have sound as well as physical relationships. Sound and motion elements involving rhythm and theme are chosen by the musician along with representative visual images.[18] For the visual artist, there are both similar and related complementary or contrary connections in shape and color, and, for the scientist, some degree of component conceptual or physical relationships within the problem being worked on. In this phase of the homospatial process, elements chosen may also be previously formulated simultaneous antitheses or opposites from the janusian process. The two processes, in this way, then operate together. In the third phase, deviation from the usual continues together with the development of newness and novelty. The homospatial process continues to be conscious and intentional, and the related entities are interposed or superimposed in the mind because the creative thinker conceives that they *ought* to be together. Spatial continuities are broken. There are several reasons for this act of volition, pragmatic and intellectual as well as emotional in all generative fields. In the extensive last phase, the superimposed or interposed elements of the homospatial conception interact and are articulated into an integrated new identity, partial or complete, as a new and valuable final product.

Sep-Con Articulation Process

The sep-con articulation process consists of actively conceiving and using concomitant functional separation and connection. The term derives from the root meaning of *articulation* as joining, joint, or to join, used, as I pointed out in the Introduction, by the articulate speaker who joins words and ideas together while keeping them clearly separate. In the creative process, the creator articulates such concomitant separation (SEP) and connection (CON), a sep-con articulation, in many different spheres—conceptual, perceptual, affective, and physical. This type of bringing together differs from blending, fusion, combining, connectivity, and connecting alone. Component elements are brought together that are functionally separate and continue to retain their individual identities. Articulation in common parlance denotes "realizing" or "forming," and using the sep-con articulation process produces these results with a conscious sense or feeling of creating.

The concomitance of the separations with connection produces fluency or continuity together with distinctness, flowing elements shaped with internal form. In every creative outcome the separate entities retain their functional distinctness and identity as they interact through the joint connection. Interaction is a key factor in the creative process. Degree of strength of the connection determines the amount of interaction. When separate elements are weakly joined, or when they remain remote from each other, frequent interactions occur. Connected weak or remote separations induce cognitive strain, and interactions serve to reduce, modify, or resolve the strain, often resulting in a creative idea that bursts into consciousness. The functionally separate elements themselves are chosen early in the process. When these elements are strongly joined, as is sometimes the case with scientific creativity, there is less opportunity for interaction, mutual modification, and change. Interaction is produced in both instances, however, both because of the essential structure of the thought and the continuing creative and problem-solving motivations of the thinker.

Separation consists of being distinct and apart, whether regarding objects, factors, or actions. Sep-con articulation, which is a cognitive creative process, involves functional separation, apartness, and distinctness in any or all of these spheres. Effective separating alone, even when done meticulously, as in analyses or formal logical procedures, may have much usefulness but it is not sufficient to produce a creation. In the sep-con articulation process, joined and connected functional separations lead to creative integrations.

Integration, as I proposed earlier, characterizes created works and is a crucial factor in their newness and positive value. The creative thinker uses interactions within sep-con articulation structures to produce an integrated whole with concomitant functionally separated and connected parts. This integrated whole product or result has qualities not present in any individual component or factor and is therefore greater than any sum of its parts.

As a physical homolog or parallel function of the sep-con psychological process I have described, the brain synapse, especially the presynaptic and postsynaptic components, may also have features of concomitant separation and connection of chemical factors producing interactions, both macroscopically and microscopically. The joinings of the presynapse and postsynapse between neurons separate the adjacent neurons and concomitantly connect them by means of the chemical transport across the anatomically visible gap. This may account to some extent for integrated features of the neuronal system. It should be noted, however, that conceptions of underlying, genuinely integrated physical operations are currently incomplete, as synaptic chemicals also merge, blend, and combine.

The other creative forms of cognition, the janusian and homospatial processes, also manifest concomitant separations and connections of parts: functional parts connecting in the same space in the case of the homospatial process, and often widely separate opposites simultaneously present and therefore connected in time in the janusian process. Although these processes may both act alongside and contribute to aspects of the integrated product, the creator primarily uses sep-con articulation for the overall creative integration. In the creative process, new ideas and concepts; procedures; experiments; metaphors; word and sentence structures; plot themes; and artistic, dance, or musical patterns are integrated within the product through the cognitive and accompanying emotional effects of sep-con articulation.

In literature, development of characters results from the process of ongoing sep-con articulation of the author's self and self-conception with the developing characterization. Routine and formulaic literary characters are in distinction not created but are copies in whole or part of personalities depicted in other writings or media. Created characters, also, are not produced by direct autobiographic representation and simulation of the writer's own personality and life history, nor from blending, fusing, or combining of such factors with other persons, real or imaginary. The creative author uses the sep-con articulation process to mold images, emotions, and circumstances taken largely from memory and anticipations into new and vivid characters in the literary work. Throughout the course of writing a novel, play, or poem, the author functionally separates and concomitantly connects his or her images and conceptions—the content of imagination—as well as aspects of his or her own emotions, personality characteristics, and experiences, with the fictional characters being created. Continual interaction of features of the author's self and self-conception with the developing portrayal is mentally experienced.

As with other applications of the sep-con articulation process to be described, this interaction may be consciously felt and may also occur outside of awareness. Although critics and scholars often believe they have found evidence of parts or even large portions of an author's personal life in literary works, there is no direct or actual representation in a truly created story, play, or novel. Created stories and characters are integrations, distinct and unique. So-called autobiographical novelists such as Proust, Joyce, Hemingway, and Fitzgerald have stated, with conviction and sincerity, that none of their characters or stories actually represent them. The validity of these assertions is based on the results of the alterations and creative effects of the sep-con articulation process; functionally separate aspects of the author interact with developing conceptions of emerging characters and stories.[1] This is experienced in the course of writing as realizing, forming, and creating.

The sep-con articulation process and its accompanying interacting emotions also operate in the production of poetic structure or form, producing creative integrations within an entire work. Poetic metaphors produced by the homospatial process are often integrated into a poem by the sep-con articulation process. In 1970, the Weather Underground protest organization inadvertently blew up a Manhattan brownstone where they had been making bombs. This house, 18 West 11th Street, was the childhood home of the poet James Merrill who, soon after hearing the news, embarked on writing a poem. Merrill, who was born in New York City in 1926, was the son of the stockbroker Charles Merrill and his second wife, Hellen Ingram. His books of poems have won the Bollingen Prize for Poetry, the Pulitzer Prize for Poetry, and the National Book Award. Though primarily a poet, he also wrote a play and several novels, one of which, *The (Diblos) Notebook,* was a 1965 finalist for the National Book Award.

During his weeks of writing this new poem, I interviewed him regularly, and he and I systematically discussed (semistructured protocol) his drafts, thoughts, and revisions. Regarding the poem, his work shifted wistfully back and forth between memories of childhood and the later accidental devastation of the house by rebellious young terrorists (so-called Antiquarians in the poem—the Weather Underground).[2] At one point in the process, we focused specifically on his creation of a metaphor pertaining to a room in the house, the final form of which he described as an "inspiration." It was: "A mastermind/Kept track above the mantel," a metaphor vividly joining the bomb makers to a wall mirror in the home.

In his early manuscript, the first phrase he wrote eventually developing into this metaphor was about a "magic room" and a tilted decorative "lintel" (homospatial process). His next step was to bring together this phrase with the idea of an ideal room reflected in a mirror, and after a number of modifications he separated out the term "mantel." Several versions later, he conceived "a mental world." That, he changed to another separate and distinct word, "mastermind," and then articulated, both separating and connecting, the words "mastermind" and "mantel" into the mirror metaphor.

"I just thought it [mastermind] was better than 'a mental world,'" he said, "and it connected obviously with 'saboteurs.' I mean one imagines behind any plot there is a mind. And to make it the mirror!...I just turned my attention to that line...and then that came to me. I suppose from the word 'mental' it's not so far to get to mind. But it seemed to me *it was already there* [italics mine] in a way, an embryo in the original phrase."

Merrill's feeling that the mastermind idea was an embryo in the original phrase indicates how he used the sep-con articulation process to realize and produce an integration within the poem. Through several versions, he distilled out the functional separate parts "mastermind" and "mantel" and then connected them concomitantly in the created metaphor "mastermind kept track above the mantel." The metaphor itself was an integrated structure and it was also concomitantly separated and connected with the sad and sinister saboteur themes (e.g., in the final poem the mirror metaphor appears as a dramatic pun, "breakfast *mirror*," and explicitly near the end where it is connected with "debris," "airquake," and "flame"[3]). Note that "mastermind," "mantel," and "mirror" are both separated and connected and not blended into composite words such as "mirrormind" or "mantelmind" or the phrase "mastermind mirror," nor is there only connection consisting of fusion of a mirror into a science fiction–like object with flashing eyes on a reflecting plate.[4]

The sculptor Michelangelo, as I touched on earlier, described a similar process when he famously reported, "In every block of marble I see a statue as plain as though it stood before me, shaped and perfect in attitude and action. I have only to hew away the rough walls that imprison the lovely apparition to reveal it to the other eyes as mine see it."[5] He saw a figure in the stone. To realize the integrated human figure, it was very likely necessary to separate stone elements and concomitantly connect ("hew away the rough walls") their forms as he proceeded.

A more extended literary example concerning a pivotal creative structure comes from my research interviews with the novelist John Hersey. Winner of the Pulitzer Prize for the novel *A Bell for Adano*, Hersey was also known for the nonfiction work *Hiroshima*, a vivid documentary tale of victims of the atomic bombing of that city; *The Algiers Motel Incident*, a dramatic report of racist killings in Detroit; and several additional novels. Born of missionary parents in Tientsin, China, he came back with them at the age of 10 to live in the United States. His secondary schooling was at Hotchkiss in Connecticut, his undergraduate college was Yale, and he did graduate study at Cambridge University in England. He worked at a summer job as secretary for Nobel laureate novelist Sinclair Lewis and subsequently was a journalist at *Time* magazine for some years.

His novel *Too Far to Walk*, which we regularly explored throughout its creation, is about a mixed-up college student who loses interest in his classes and schoolwork and searches for gratification in sex, debasement, and drugs.[6] Much of the story involves a complex unfolding of the young man's relationship with his parents and his attempts toward meaningful freedom and independence. In a key scene in the novel, he rebelliously brings home a young prostitute to meet them. Developing the literary picture subsequently in the manuscript, Hersey wrote three versions of a sentence indicating different degrees or kinds of both functional separation or else connection between the father and the son. The first version was: "Excuse me, Pop (he said, going into his bedroom to dress, leaving the non-king staring at himself in the mirror)." He crossed this out and wrote: "Excuse me, Pop (he said, going into the bedroom to dress, leaving his friend staring at himself in the mirror)." Finally, he changed it to: "Excuse me, Pop (he said, going into his bedroom to dress, leaving the old man staring at himself in the mirror)." He first used the deprecating term "non-king" to indicate a separating rift, then introduced a connecting "his friend," and shifted back to the functionally distinct separations of "old man," and son.

This development of separations was the initial portion of the sep-con articulation process manifested in a later, defining version regarding the relationship between the young man and his father that produced new dramatic and aesthetic power. Hersey introduced one of the young man's later LSD-produced fantasy visions consisting of the two of them, son and father, fighting in Vietnam. In the fantasy, they move together through heavy embattled woods, and the son believes he sees a sniper's head in the crotch of a tree. Then, as they continue forward through some slender saplings, the son feels he somehow is maneuvering his father's path; he steps aside little by little and constantly keeps up a murmured conversation so that his father needs to inch sidewise to catch the words. Then, as they move toward the tree crotch, his father's body, back exposed to the menace, shields him. He defensively assures himself in the fantasy that the shape in the tree is only "a queer growth, a burl, perhaps a paper-wasp nest," and Hersey describes the next moment as follows: "But then a whine came ridden hard by a snap. As his father fell, with the faintest sign of reproach on his otherwise empty face, John felt such an exquisite pain in his chest that he thought the bullet must have passed through both generations."[7] Hersey had, in the fantasy, constructed the sep-con articulation of a bullet passing through and thereby tragically connecting the functionally separate and distinct generations of father and son. After his earlier work on separations and connections between father and son, Hersey derived a moving concomitant separation and connection between the generations to produce a specific literary creation.[8]

In science, the sep-con articulation process leads similarly to creative results. The theory of immunization of the German Nobel laureate in Physiology or Medicine Paul Ehrlich—also the discoverer of the anti-syphilis drug Salvarsan—provides one example. Born in Strehen, Germany, Ehrlich was educated at the Universities of Breslau, Strasburg, Freiburg-im-Breisgau, and Leipzig. For his doctorate of medicine, he wrote a dissertation on the theory and practice of staining animal tissues, and he retained an interest in dyes, especially aniline dyes, throughout his career. Working on tissue staining at the Berlin Medical Clinic, he became ill with tuberculosis for a short time, but then went on to become a professor at the Faculty of Medicine in the University of Berlin. There, he first was assistant to one of the founders of the science of bacteriology, Robert Koch, and then he successively became director of the Berlin Institute for the Control of Therapeutic Sera, the Royal Institute for Experimental Therapy, and the Georg-Speyer-Haus Institute for Biomedical Research. Although his discovery of medications for the treatment of syphilis was clearly important, as the disease was a widespread scourge in his time, his contributions to the science of immunology, especially his creative "side-chain theory," earned him the Nobel Prize.

With the side-chain theory, Ehrlich attempted to explain the immune response in living cells with a focus on the functionally separate and distinct toxins and antitoxins. He conceived that, in response to toxins, cells in the body would produce a variety of cell-bound receptors that he called "side-chain receptors." The subsequent interaction between a toxin or infectious agent and a cell-bound receptor would induce the cell to produce and release antibodies. As he wrote, "If it is assumed that such a side chain carries a group of atoms with the specific linkage,...the living protoplasm (so long as the linkage lasts) is brought under the continuing physiological influence of the...toxin, which causes gradual and long-lasting functional disturbances. If it is assumed—and the long duration of sickness[es] suggests it to be true—that the reciprocal linkage of side chain and toxin is a durable one, we arrive at the view offering a fitting explanation for the creation of antibodies."[9]

In the process of sep-con articulation, Ehrlich conceived the concomitant connection of the functionally separate toxins and side chain receptors. The separate components retained their identities and characteristics while joined and interacting over a period of time to modify each other and produce antibodies. Ultimately, Ehrlich's theory would all be proven correct except for one aspect—the receptor exists both as a soluble antibody molecule and a cell-bound receptor. The soluble form is secreted rather than the bound form being released.

In the science of physics, Max Planck's core formulation of the theory of blackbody radiation was a creative breakthrough leading to the quantum of action concept and the construct known as Planck's constant. In conjunction with Einstein's special theory of relativity, this constant became the basis of modern quantum physics.

Born in 1858 in Kiel, Holstein, a territory that later became part of Germany, Planck was educated at the University of Munich and there first learned to do experimental work in physics. Later, he taught at the University of Kiel until he joined the faculty of Berlin University. There, he rose to Professor of Physics and was their first theoretical physicist. Electrical problems of radiation became his primary interest, specifically blackbody or cavity radiation in oscillators. The blackbody, an opaque or nonreflective body or surface that absorbs all radiation falling on it and reflects none, was at that time used as the standard for measurement and theoretical investigation of radiation. Wilhelm Wein had proposed a widely accepted energy distribution law regarding this radiation called normal spectral energy distribution. His law, which took account of high energies but not low ones, brought out the dependence of the radiation intensity on temperature.

In his scientific autobiography, Planck first described both his creative motivation and a deviation from the mainstream as follows:

It was an odd jest of fate that a circumstance which on former occasions I had found unpleasant, namely, the lack of interest of my colleagues in the direction taken by my investigations, now turned out to be an outright boon. While a host of outstanding physicists worked on the problem of spectral energy distribution... every one of them directed his efforts solely toward exhibiting the dependence of the intensity of radiation on the temperature. I suspected that the fundamental connection lies in the dependence of entropy [system disorder] upon energy. As the significance of the concept of energy had not yet come to be fully appreciated, nobody paid any attention to the method adopted by me, and I could work out my calculations completely at my leisure, with absolute thoroughness, without fear of interference or competition.

Since for the irreversibility of the exchange of energy between an oscillator and the radiation activating it, the second differential quotient [derivative] of its entropy with respect to its energy is of characteristic significance, I calculated the value of this function [mathematical operation performed on a variable that results in an output] on the assumption that Wien's Law of the Spectral Energy Distribution is valid—a law which was then in the focus of general interest; I got the remarkable result that on this assumption the reciprocal of that value, which I shall call here *R,* is proportional to the energy....

Planck determined two separate functions regarding entropy and energy in spectral energy distribution. Later measurements indicated that one function was proportional to small energies and another larger function was proportional to the square of the energy.

He then had the conception to construct a formula for *R* and for the law of the distribution of energy in which there was "a term proportional to the first power of the energy and another term proportional to the second power of the energy, so that the first term becomes decisive for small values of the energy and the second term for large values. In this way, *a new radiation formula* was obtained [italics mine], and I submitted it for examination to the Berlin Physical Society, at the meeting on October 19, 1900...."[10]

With this formulation, Planck had, in the first portion of the sep-con articulation process, focused on the factor entropy and connected that with the neglected factor of energy. Then, he turned to the measurement of functionally separate small energies and large energies in a formula for blackbody radiation. He concomitantly connected these functionally separate proportionalities in a single formula, a sep-con articulation structure. The separate values of the proportionalities varied together, the small going up when the large went down.[11]

He indicated that he knew he had made a creative breakthrough and he devoted himself to "the task of investing it [the formula for blackbody radiation] with true physical meaning." This key breakthrough led to his development of a constant number for energy steps in an oscillator that became known as Planck's constant or the quantum of action.[12] He was awarded the Nobel Prize in Physics for this achievement in 1918.

In another physics breakthrough, Paul A. M. Dirac predicted the existence of the positron (a particle opposite in nature to the electron) and thereby initiated the recognition of the existence of the world of antimatter particles. He was born in 1902 in Bristol, England, and remained there and eventually studied electrical engineering and mathematics at Bristol University. He also attended the Varenna Physics School in Italy for the study of history of science. Later, he became a professor of mathematics at Cambridge University. The Nobel Prize was awarded to him for his theory in 1933.

Although postulation of antimatter as an opposite state from matter might superficially suggest the operation of janusian processes entailing simultaneous opposites, that type of cognition was, for Dirac, only minimally involved.[13] That he primarily used a process of sep-con articulation with functionally separate components to determine the concept of the positron is indicated by his personal reference in his Nobel lecture that he conceived of and established a connection "between electrons in negative energy states and positrons."

In a talk he gave on a return to the Varenna Physics School titled "Recollections of an Exciting Era,"[14] he recounted how he had been working on the transformation theory of quantum mechanics and was concerned with how he could get a satisfactory relativistic theory of the electron. Seemingly empty spaces within and between atoms were not, he thought, really empty but were occupied by a sea of an infinite number of electrons existing at negative energy levels.

If one of the negative energy levels was given enough energy, he thought, it would at that time produce an electron-sized "hole" in the electric energy field. Next, he considered that this hole would be occupied by the positron having the same mass and the same properties as an electron except that it would be positively charged. According to this dramatic formulation in a sep-con articulation process, these functionally separate entities, electron fields, and positrons, were at once concomitantly connected by infused energy within the negative energy state. Four years after Dirac postulated the theory, the positron particle was found by experimenter Carl Anderson. The Dirac theory, with its conception of a "hole" filled up with a particle, reverberates ideationally with both the poet Merrill's feeling that the metaphor was "an embryo in the original phrase" and the artist Michelangelo's seeing a sculpture in the rock.

The sep-con articulation process may be either bidirectional or unidirectional, symmetrical or unsymmetrical. When it is unidirectional, dual or multiple functionally separate components are more in focus, more operant, or more changed than others, possible or real. With respect to the interaction produced by the sep-con articulation of father and son in Hersey's novel, the father who was killed was a more emotionally affecting and in some respects more important character than the son. In the Dirac conception, interactions between positive and negative states focused more on the negative states containing the positive positron result.

There are four specific phases in the sep-con articulation process structurally similar to the creative sequences of the janusian and homospatial phases: motivation to create; deviation from the customary and the choice or construction of separate functional entities or identities (these separate entities may have some degree of operational, structural, or other similarities with each other); connecting while maintaining the functional separations and identities; interactions leading to partial or complete integration.

Subsuming all four phases overall, the sep-con articulation process has a biphasic configuration. In the initial portion, the person motivated to create—scientist, artist, or other—takes in cognitively and emotionally laden stimuli, experiences, and concepts. Analogous with the literal meaning of the term *inspiration* in breathing or respiration, the contents taken in, like elements in inspired air, are modified and mentally interact both consciously and unconsciously. This does not lead to a phenomenon such as the classically postulated catharsis or release of unconscious contents or emotions in creativity. In a second, dyadic phase, the elements are neither simply expelled, nor expired, nor revealed, but are consciously articulated. Similar to the production of human speech, in which inspired air is articulated by the voice apparatus and the brain to produce words and language, sep-con articulation modifies conceptual and emotional inspirations that lead to a final construction.

Creative Emotions and Motivations

In the creation of art, literature, and music, which often overtly focus on emotions, various types of emotional elements are clearly important. In scientific creativity, when I earlier recounted the achievements of the scientists Einstein, Darwin, Bohr, Watson, and Yukawa, I pointed out their emotional states, particularly their excitement and passion—a powerful and compelling emotion—in discovery and creation. As with those creative scientists, Werner Heisenberg, the reputedly cold and unfeeling discoverer of the uncertainty principle and a founder of quantum mechanics, described the following in his autobiography: "It was about three o'clock at night when the final result of the [quantum mechanic] calculation lay before me.... At first I was deeply shaken.... I was so excited that I could not think of sleep. So I left the house... and awaited the sunrise at the top of a rock."[1]

There are likely many reasons for strong emotional involvement with a particular scientific exploration as well as—given the value of the solutions—very strong and positive emotion on reaching the goal. Emotion in artistic fields is also strong but the recognition of achievement is slower and more protracted. For Einstein and Darwin particularly, the passion was connected with the relevance of the problem to all of their scientific work up to that point. Why these and other scientists choose to work on a particular problem is surely in part a result of their knowledge and the conceptual understanding of that problem's importance in their fields. The goal of creative scientific achievement is usually more ambitious, however; it involves recognition of the need to produce an advance, something both new and significant, often widely so.

The passion of creating is formed at the outset. Work toward the goal begins with, and is sustained by, an intentional motivation to create. All cognition and cognitive processes, including those directed toward creation, have emotional aspects and components. As I said earlier, the sep-con articulation process particularly is accompanied by the feel of creating. Both the janusian and homospatial processes also have associated feelings of opening up, surprise, and radical change in the process of creating. The initiating emotional drive within all three creative cognitive processes is the motivation to create. That it is a necessary component of all creative endeavors is indicated by the ineffectiveness of chance, fantasy, intelligence, or unconscious operants alone. None of these factors have been shown to lead individually and reliably to the production of both new and valuable products. Motivation or emotional drive as well as knowledge are required, particularly for recognition and production of entities that are new. A new plot, character, or structure in a novel; new metaphors and conceits in a poem; new melodies and rhythms as well as structures in music; new compositions in visual art; and new theories and discoveries in science must be intentionally and knowingly constructed even if their initial elements arose unbidden or occurred accidentally. Although accidents and spontaneous or intuitive thoughts, ideas, and emotions may provide initiating content for a creation, all must be specially designed and applied for production of something new. All creditable accounts of the creative process, whether in artistic fields or in science, have given evidence of this constituent: the creator's drive and motivation to create.

Creativity must be regularly differentiated from simply making or doing something different. This is clearly apparent in art and literature, where lasting and meaningful production of both newness and value is universally recognized. Many writers, however, despite popular use of the word, do not *create*. They intentionally produce formulaic "stock" characters and plots, often with much general appeal. Many artists also aim at simply producing skilled reproductions, and many composers construct thematic and rhythmic but unoriginal music. These types of products may become prized and acclaimed, and therefore are to some degree valuable, even different, but are not in any sense new. Moreover, the literature on creativity is replete with personal accounts of spontaneous and so-called unconsciously derived inspirations that suggest unmotivated (and, some believe, magical) creative sources. These accounts, it should be recognized, are eventually and invariably revealed to be posturing and unreliable. Intended as aura and mystique, they are declarations by poets, authors, artists, and musicians who actually spend a great deal of time both before and afterward intentionally producing concrete creations. The most famous of such accounts is Samuel Taylor Coleridge's allegation that, in an opium dream, he received the entire text, word for word, of his poem "Kubla Khan." That creativity is more multiform than such an involuntary outpouring, even by a skilled creator, is indicated by the scholarly discovery of numerous revisions and insertions made by Coleridge himself within his first written manuscript of this poem.[2]

In both science and artistic fields, the initial conscious goal may be to solve a particular problem; in science, for example, the nature and function of an enzyme, the replication of genes, or the characteristics of dark matter; in art, music, and literature, the patterning of light, a resonating melody, or the behavior of terrorists. Many projects with problems of these types are adequately solvable in science through what Thomas Kuhn called "normal science,"[3] on some level in art through skilled design and painting, and in music through vibrant harmonics. In literature, crafted romantic and genre poems or novels might serve as examples. The creative thinker in any field, however, chooses projects and problems known in advance to require creative solutions, or else readily determines at some point in the course of working on a problem aspect that such a solution would be necessary. Differing from motivation to solve problems alone, including valuable ones, the sustained motivation to create is purposefully directed to producing something new and valuable together. Creative solutions may be individually new or new in kind or type. Scientific theorists especially initiate work on problems requiring new elements for solution, but all types of scientists may, later during the course of an investigation, begin a specific creative process and become actively motivated to create. As scientists are focused on nature and the complex details and stringencies of both problems and investigations of function and discovery, they, unlike persons in artistic fields, have not always spoken of, or been explicitly aware of, this specific motivation.

Serendipity, or inadvertency and chance, is often claimed to play a large role in scientific discoveries, even very important ones. The term was originally coined in 1754 by Horace Walpole to describe strange accidental discoveries reported by traveling princes in the land of Serendip, modern Sri Lanka. In science, it has been applied to many discoveries, most prominently to penicillin by Alexander Fleming, and X-rays by Wilhelm Roentgen, as well as the creation of the drug Valium by Leo Sternbach. In each case cited, as well as many others, an unexpected result was attributed to some factor external to the investigation or to an outright accident. On the basis of careful analysis of these presumably serendipitous discoveries as well as many others, however, it seems clear that all have involved what Louis Pasteur has characterized as chance favoring the prepared mind. Insisting that scientific accidents always favored a discoverer prepared by knowledge, intent, and the mental capacity to develop them, he firmly contended that these events would not have been perceived or appreciated in every case by a less knowledgeable scientist or one unable to put them into context and develop them. Clearly, he was indicating that such a scientist was "prepared" to formulate a creative achievement.[4]

Regardless of the circumstances in which a creative achievement occurred, the motivation to create is a constant factor. From the beginning, Fleming was searching for an effective antibacterial product. Prior to his discovery of penicillin, he discovered the antiseptic lysozyme when a tear falling on an agar culture plate obliterated a growing colony of bacteria. Later, after going on vacation, he returned to find an airborne-yeast contamination on an agar plate in his laboratory due to an open window. Similar to the action of lysozyme, Fleming right away recognized that this yeast also had antibacterial action. Because it was a biological organism, he and others designated it an "anti-biotic" agent even more effective than antiseptics, an idea that had never been previously conceived.[5]

Wilhelm Roentgen, the German physicist who was awarded the first Nobel Prize in Physics, also is thought to have accidentally discovered X-rays when an electrostatically sensitive barium platinocyanide plate he had placed on a bench became illuminated by cathode rays overnight. At the time, however, he had been investigating how a fluorescent effect was produced by invisible cathode rays from various types of vacuum tube equipment. He was fully motivated and prepared to make that creative discovery and he named the cathode rays "X-rays" because "x" stood for the unknown in mathematics.[6]

Leo Sternbach, an American organic chemist, discovered a number of drugs in his many years at Hoffman-La Roche. During the 1950s, he was put in charge of the company search for a better anti-anxiety agent to compete with the then popular but fairly unsafe drug Miltown. As he told me in an investigative interview several years later, he had come to a point after a long search when he was disappointed with the activity of all the chemical compounds he had made, so he decided to discard all those remaining in his laboratory. During this activity, however, an assistant helping came and notified him that there was one more untested compound in a previously used laboratory area. Still determined to find the new kind of drug he sought, he readily stopped discarding and decided to set up use of the untested compound in one more animal experiment. It turned out that this particular one had all the efficacy and improved safety features he was looking for. Sternbach carried out this unplanned but not chance procedure with a possibly lessened but still purposeful motivation to create the new tranquillizing agent. It became the first benzodiazepine anti-anxiety drug, named Librium. Of the several other drugs he later produced of this type, the most successful was Valium.[7]

In all three cases, the chance or spontaneous event, reported by the investigators themselves, was constructed into a creative discovery. Accidental or chance occurrences are very frequent in every area of life, and they may favor some devoted and potentially creative scientists over others. Nevertheless a successful outcome is invariably produced and proclaimed by a scientist who is already deeply steeped in a particular investigation and who both recognizes the potential value of the chance event and is motivated to mold it into a creation. A creative procedure involving the use of chancelike or deviating events, to be discussed in chapter 11, has been called by the scientist Max Delbrück "the principle of limited sloppiness," and in my own investigations "the articulation of error."[8,9]

In the conscious and intentional motivation to create, a first component step may be what Getzels and Csikszentmihalyi determined as the drive toward "problem finding" within creative scientific work.[10] Although such problem finding may in some respects apply broadly to various types of problem-solving work in general, it does seem to play a particular role for creative solutions and discoveries.[11]

Choosing or finding a seemingly worthwhile scientific problem may work to some extent as a lead to the ultimate value of a creative achievement. Knowledge of the field may guide a scientist who is so disposed to a problem that seems to have important and far-reaching consequences. The potential newness or novelty aspect of creation, however, may not yet be apparent.

Altruistic motives—beliefs that particular solutions would be beneficial to humanity or particular groups—often play a significant role. Emotional determinants at a problem-finding phase of the work help to produce the passion of the creative process. Specific personal factors together with cognitive considerations and opportunities help determine the choice of the problem. For example, after his admired teacher died of an infection contracted while performing an autopsy, the 19th-century physician Ignaz Semmelweis chose to study the problem of a mysterious infection among pregnant women in hospital wards. Working regularly at a hospital, he devoted himself to years of investigation and later discovered the cause of this infection: puerperal sepsis, the devastating infection of childbirth.[12]

When James Watson, codiscoverer of DNA, was a young child, he and his father spent a great deal of time bird-watching. This was an important sharing and emotional experience for him, and he later spent his first earnings on a pair of binoculars. When he began to pursue the important field of genetic microbiology, he heard a lecture by Maurice Wilkins about the use of X-ray crystallography for the study of DNA. Crystallography, as with Watson's valued bird watching with his father, involves a constant visualizing procedure; partly for this reason, he was influenced to study the problem of the structure of DNA.[13]

Such personal emotional factors very likely enter into all problem finding and motivations to create, just as with cognitive pursuits of all types including the rigorously logical and objective. Because they are singular and specific, however, any such factors do not necessarily apply to more than an individual case. Nevertheless, together with other types of emotional determinants of chosen problems and procedures, they may be strongly motivating, and may then play a role in the passion, ultimate exultation, and relief associated with creative discovery.

Along with or following the problem-finding phase, scientists making creative discoveries or theories have described the distinct motivation to create. French mathematician Henri Poincaré made the following comments regarding his creation (described in chapter 5) of the Fuchsian (non-Euclidean geometry) automorphic groups:[14] "There are Fuchsian groups other than those which are derived from the hypergeometric series, the only ones I knew up to that time. Naturally, I proposed to form all these functions. I laid siege to them systematically and captured all the outworks one after the other.... All this work was perfectly conscious."[15] Forming all the functions and capturing the "outworks," as he then describes, refers clearly to his motivations for creative work. He goes on to state generally later, "To know how to criticize is good but to know how to create is better.... Logic teaches us that on such and such a road we are sure of not meeting an obstacle, it does not tell us which is the road that leads to the desired end."[16]

Similarly, Hideki Yukawa declaimed shortly before he developed the meson theory, "I was unable to produce creative ideas during the day, getting lost in the various equations written on pieces of paper. On the other hand, when I lay down in bed at night, interesting ideas entered my head."[17]

In addition to humanitarian and personal emotional goals, the developed motivation to create may be primarily educational, utilitarian, or geared either to the acquisition of skill and knowledge or sometimes to gratifications resulting from aesthetic pleasure. They may focus on extrinsic rewards ranging from recognition or admiration of peers and associates to major forms of material success involving money and fame.

I have previously cited the intention to deviate in the early phases of all of the cognitive creative processes. Such deviation or choice of an individual path is sometimes colloquially described as "thinking outside the box" and often is driven by an emotional factor underlying or related to the motivation to create. Max Planck's statement, previously cited, that the disinterest of his colleagues allowed him to work out his calculations completely at his "leisure, with absolute thoroughness, without fear of interference or competition"[18] indicated his deviating motivation for individual creative discovery.

Connected with deviation as well as the breakthrough aspect of the creative cognitive processes are aggressive feelings and dispositions. Aggression undoubtedly has been overtly evident in the prevalent degree of high competition in scientific investigation, the wishes for priority and struggles to supersede in both small and large findings. In artistic pursuits, aggression is manifest, especially in the performance and aesthetic competition among artists, actors, playwrights, painters, novelists, and musicians.[19] As applied in scientific, artistic, and other creative processes, aggressiveness is in part annihilative and involves destructive feelings and the wish to taint, spoil, split, break, eliminate, displace, and supplant all or part of previously existing works and knowledge. These destructive feelings range from full-blown intentions to overthrow a theory, do away with a widely accepted fact or belief, bring down a government, or destroy an institution or personal/cultural activity, to a minute but essential severance and separation from the past. The destructive effect is not inadvertent or circumstantial in the creative process; it is not, for instance, only a side product or incidental result of producing something new. If a preexisting factor or connection is not intentionally eliminated, a relatively new or unprecedented effect cannot occur. A split from a past element, large or even infinitesimal, is required for appearance of the new. Even when the new element or phenomenon is embedded or else accompanies a vast body of preexisting substance, knowledge, or art, a creative discovery contains a necessary element of real or relative separation from the past.

The motivation to deviate eventually leads to interruption or obliteration of antecedent or preexisting formulations and factors and the production of new entities. Such obliterations or interruptions are begun through the disruptive structures of the cognitive creative processes: logical and temporal disruption of the janusian process; spatial disruption within the homospatial process; and part and whole disruption together within the sep-con articulation process. These disruptions all require aggressive and destructive feelings to some degree.

Aggressiveness and destructive feelings operate at varying levels and degrees when involved in creative achievement. Seldom do they entail full extinction of a preexisting mode, procedure, belief, theory, paradigm, or entire corpus of creative art, literature, music, or other types of valid creations. Even when the break with past causative factors is minimal, however, a destructive motivation is necessary to produce the manifestly new aspect of a creation. Attempts to supersede, negotiate, or otherwise continue all or part of previous theory side by side with the new still requires some elimination and disjunction. Seldom, however, do destructive feelings in themselves initiate a creative process; rather, they function at certain intervals, early and late.

With his complete formulation of the general theory of relativity, Einstein knowingly intended to eliminate aspects of Newton's theory of gravitation. Bohr, also knowingly, eliminated classical conceptions of causation (and discussed this effect actively with Einstein at the famous Solvay Conference) with his theory of complementarity. Watson was actively engaged in overthrowing Linus Pauling's alpha helix and triple helix models of DNA. When he arrived at Cambridge for the final leg of his investigations, his explicit goal was to "imitate Pauling and beat him at his own game."[20] Yukawa remembered the following when working on the problem of the nuclear force: "One day, among the newly arrived periodicals, I found Fermi's paper concerning beta decay [ejection of nuclear particles], I think I must have grown pale as I read it."[21] He felt beaten by Fermi and went on, with his conception of the meson, to eliminate elements of Fermi's beta decay.

The motivation to create and destructive emotions operate side by side, and the intensity fuels the passion associated with creating. However, although a creative person usually recognizes a need to do away with an existing or past element to produce a new entity, there may sometimes be reluctance, denial, and even fear of acknowledgement. Therefore, unlike the modal, even laudatory motivation to create, destructive feelings may often be experienced as unacceptable and be only dimly or partially conscious.

When Darwin described the circumstances of his conception of the theory of natural selection, his immediate written comment following was, "but

I was so anxious to avoid prejudice that I determined not for some time to write even the briefest sketch of it."[22] This statement suggests his concern or even fear of destructive wishes and effects at the time. One way to discover such aggression and destructive feelings that are partially conscious, or may be masked and denied, is through an appearance in dreams. This principle of representation of unconscious or partially conscious feelings in dreams was established by Sigmund Freud and has continued to be affirmed by modern dream investigators.[23] The following fragment, therefore, of a pertinent dream recorded by Charles Darwin in his working notebook does, I believe, indicate his incipient destructive feelings and a denial. The dream occurred on September 21, 1838, 7 days before he conceived the theory of natural selection while riding in a coach. On September 22, Darwin wrote the following: "Was witty in a dream in a confused manner. Thought that a person was hung and came to life, and then made many jokes about not having run away and having faced death like a hero, and then I had some confused idea of showing scar behind (instead of front) (having changed hanging to having his head cut off) as kind of wit showing he had honourable wounds...and because of the impossibility of a person recovering from hanging."[24] As a depiction of death and rebirth, including "honourable wounds," "scar," and "recovering from hanging," this dream from shortly prior to Darwin's breakthrough theory indicates destruction together with positive effects, regeneration, or creation. Despite the trifling and downplaying references to confused wittiness and jokes, he is concerned in the dream with death by hanging or beheading, heroism, and the return of life. This focus on destruction[25] was very likely a motivational factor in his shortly ensuing break with previous conceptions of evolution together with the intent to produce a creative idea.

As I described earlier, Darwin did not publish his natural selection theory of evolution for approximately 20 years after its formulation. Alleged reasons for this were a fear of the reaction of the Church and especially of offending or betraying his religious wife. Whatever the specific concerns, it seems likely that he struggled with having unacceptable destructive feelings and their realization in his creative accomplishment.

Another instance of reluctance to propose a creative discovery because of the destructive element was overtly indicated by Paul Dirac in connection with the conception of the positron:

> Well, when I first thought of this idea [the mass of the new particle], it occurred to me that the mass would have to be the same as that of the electron because of the symmetry.... At that time the only particles that were known were the negatively charged electron and the positively charged proton, and the other atomic nuclei which were believed to be composite things. So I put forward the idea that these "holes" [in negative states] correspond to positively charged protons, and I left it as an unsolved problem

why they should have such a widely different mass from the mass of the electron.

That, of course, was wrong of me; it was just a lack of boldness. I should have said in the first place that the "hole" would have to have the same mass as the original electrons [i.e., a positron].[26]

Dirac's "lack of boldness" must have derived from fear of disapproval of his expunging current beliefs regarding existing particles.

Outside of its application in the creative process, personal aggressiveness is not necessarily a general characteristic of creative achievers, although it may have been a component of Eiduson's finding of a tendency to rebelliousness emphasized in her study of accomplished scientists.[27] Aggressiveness and rebellion do seem readily apparent in creative literature, postmodern art, and some forms of song lyrics, where the attacks on culture and institutions are overt, consistent, and sometimes strongly influential. Because the motivation to create and aggressive destructive feelings occur side by side in creative work itself, many creators, rebellious or not, may experience a good deal of strain and emotional ambivalence in their work. Such ambivalence may actually be productive. It may, in literature and art, facilitate patterns of aesthetic ambiguity, features that experts have often considered to be highly effective and intriguing.[28]

Creative people are neither generally harsh, vicious, rageful, murderous, nor chronically angry. Many are, overall, temperate, unaggressive, and strongly altruistic. The aggressive impulses and actions are usually applied exclusively to the creative work itself.

Other emotional and passionate factors, more properly termed *emotional predispositions*, are courage and risk taking. These have the positive or productive aspect of making one willing to put oneself and one's work on the line, risking total failure, to achieve success. Such firm conviction and willingness to take chances for an important or idealistic goal requires the stable formulation of self-worth and the capacity termed *ego strength*. The strong sense of individuality and self associated with ego strength provides an ability to withstand deleterious internal and external demands. There are many historical examples of major risk taking by creative scientists, such as Galileo's insistence on such factors as planetary motion around the sun despite the Church's opposition; Darwin's decision, after long reluctance, to go ahead and publicly propound the theory of natural selection despite widespread social and religious hostility (continuing in some quarters to this day); Freud's revolutionary and initially widely rejected psychoanalytic precepts; and Bohr and Heisenberg's daring quantum mechanics propositions. Without frequent willingness to take risks, even in lesser ways, it is safe to say that science would not have produced the giant benefits and advances of today.

Emotional factors frequently operating in creative work that do not necessarily or directly cause creative achievement are the interest in and love for materials used, the gratification of constant learning, and (in artistic fields) aesthetic goals and satisfaction. For literary creators, love of materials consisting of words and discourse starts very early in their lives—for artists there is love of paints, brushes, and shape forming materials; for musicians there is love of tones, multivariate rhythms, and particular musical instruments. This love is not incidental or superficial but is continuously influential; immersion in the material helps generate both the idea and form of the final created product. A case in point is James Joyce, whose love of words and extensive multilinguism led him to produce thousands of literary neologisms (like the one described in chapter 1), a rich sense of inner thought and speech, and new literary constructions in his writings. In a similar way, many creative experimental scientists love the chemical equipment, properties of chemicals, optical and electronic instruments, spectrometers, calorimeters, gravimeters, DNA sequencers, growth media, as well as corollary clinical contacts that allow them to trace data and also inspire ideas. Theoretical scientist creators often love numbers and symbols as well as puzzles, problems, and pure thinking.

Gratification in learning infuses all aspects of the creative process. Choice of a problem or type of investigation requires and induces further learning in its own right. Constant learning from doing and applying or from trial and error is critical for carrying out the project. Acquiring learning may guide and dictate risk taking and venturing on new and uncharted paths. Large, gratifying bursts of learning may often accompany the achievement of the goal. Leading to that culmination is the need in the preceding creative process to collect all that is known in a particular realm and the enlightenment derived from going beyond that. More learning probably results from the process of going beyond the realm of what is known than in any other type of human activity. Motivation to achieve such extended learning is intrinsic to creating. It may be a factor in goal achievement or a sufficient intrinsic gratification whether or not the goal—and final enlightenment—is reached. Learning is a driving factor and an inevitable reward.

Intuition often is thought to play an important role in creativity, especially in science. Every year at the Nobel Prize ceremonies in Sweden, the science award recipients are invited afterward to participate in a local radio program regarding their achievements. Bengt Feldreich, the host of the program for many years, has invariably asked what role intuition played in the participants' discoveries. Many of the science Nobelists have then described rather sudden realizations, which they and the host assumed were successful intuitions. Although intuition, as they suggested, was certainly productive in some cases, its success was in fact likely to have been based on further unrecognized creative transformations. As a partly cognitive and partly emotional factor, intuition does not itself lead to a creative achievement; it may in many cases supply some of the content. Although sometimes sudden, and seeming to be inspirations, intuitions are not themselves creative ideas. The cognitive aspect of intuition is lack of direct reasoning with the retrieval of partially remembered knowledge or thought processes, often in an area of expertise. The emotional aspect is a vague sense of appropriate confirmation, aesthetic, instrumental, or other. Seldom is there passion or great relief. The partial knowledge or thought processes, which may or may not be conscious, may approximate aspects of a solution or the nature of a problem. Together with appropriate emotional predispositions, such partial knowledge may lead to tentative or sometimes effective problem solving and interpersonal judgments. Many times, in intellectual work, intuitions may arise from fully developed ideas and conclusions that at one time appeared briefly in consciousness and that reappear later. Gruber reports, on the basis of Darwin's work diaries, that such a phenomenon occurred frequently in Darwin's case,[29] and Yukawa explicitly reports in his autobiography similar mental reappearance events.[30]

When intuitions have roots in specially charged emotional experiences and events, a sense of suddenness and seeming validity are conveyed. Partial knowledge, together with previous thinking and consideration, combines with intense or important emotional matters. The following example of a very famous and important intuition described by Enrico Fermi serves to demonstrate a previously unrecognized emotional factor.

Fermi gave the following report to his colleague Chandrasekhar regarding Fermi's discovery of the induction of radioactivity, for which he was awarded the Nobel Prize. It was initially told to Segrè and is here reproduced verbatim.[31] It has long been considered an intuition by Fermi himself and others:

> I will tell you how I came to make the discovery which I suppose is the most important one I have made. We were working very hard on the neutron-induced radioactivity and the results we were obtaining made no sense. One day, as I came into the laboratory, it occurred to me that I should examine the effect of placing a piece of lead before the incident neutrons. Instead of my usual custom, I took great pains to have the piece of lead precisely machined. I was clearly dissatisfied with something: I tried every excuse to postpone putting the piece of lead in its place. When finally, with some reluctance, I was going to put it in its place, I said to myself: "No, I do not want this piece of lead here; what I want is a piece of paraffin." It was just like that with no advance warning, no conscious prior reasoning. I immediately took some odd piece of paraffin and placed it where the piece of lead was to have been. [This led to the induction of radioactivity.]

At first, neither Fermi nor his laboratory colleagues understood why the paraffin filter succeeded for induction of radioactivity, but by the late afternoon, Fermi had worked out that the neutrons were slowed down by elastic collision and in that way became more effective. As for the idea itself, he dramatically stated to Chandrasekhar (as well as his working colleagues and his wife[32]) that he had no realization at all where his idea to use paraffin had came from. Although the circumstances of the use were certainly special, it has not been previously recognized or reported in personal or scientific accounts that the idea of using the paraffin substance actually did have at least two specific emotional or emotionally tinged roots. One of these, which had scientific and perhaps partially cognitive components, was that both of Fermi's predecessors in the same field, the Joliot-Curies and James Chadwick (discoverer of the neutron), had used paraffin wax in previous experiments related to radiation and particle bombardment. The Joliot-Curies had let gamma radiation fall on paraffin wax to produce ejection of protons; Chadwick smashed alpha particles into beryllium and allowed the released radiation to hit paraffin wax. The second and more distinctly personal emotional root was that Fermi's mother, Ida de Gattis, was herself a schoolteacher-inventor who had invented a new type of pressure cooker when he was a child. As a young boy, Enrico, who reportedly loved his mother dearly, helped her with putting up the preserves she cooked with the new device. This entailed putting paraffin wax as the necessary sealant between the covers and the bodies of the preserve jars. Two salient emotional factors, his beloved mother as an inventor and user of paraffin wax, along with the emotionally imbued use of paraffin wax by his known scientist predecessors, must surely have entered significantly into Fermi's intuition.

Another instance of an emotional factor fueling an important scientific intuition comes from two widely separated parts of the extensively documented autobiography of Hideki Yukawa. Early in his work on discovery of the meson, Yukawa had the following intuitive idea: "The atomic nucleus is made of protons and neutrons; the forces that act between these particles are stronger than electromagnetic forces. Then, if one visualizes the nuclear force field as a game of 'catch' between protons and neutrons, the crux of the problem would be the nature of the 'ball' or particle.... When I began to think in this manner, I had almost reached my goal."[33] Although the intuitive idea of the game of catch continued to play a role in his considerations, he says nothing following about what brought it about. Much earlier in his autobiographical account, however, when describing his early school years in Osaka, he writes wistfully about his loneliness and his wishes to play the specific game of "catch" for escape with his two younger brothers. The game idea was clearly emotionally charged. That the otherwise unathletic adult scientist intuitively derived the thought of a game of catch in the development of his discovery must at least have had a connection with his early emotions of loneliness and hoped-for relief. Both in Yukawa's and Fermi's cases, forceful emotional factors must have played a role in their intuitions. These charged intuitive ideas provided some of the substance and content of their creative work but they did not in themselves produce the creative discoveries.

Aesthetic considerations and motivations, outside of their importance in the arts, have been alleged to have an important role in scientific creation. Recently the Root-Bernsteins have putatively derived correlational data (currently unpublished) from the earlier Eiduson research showing significant degrees of aesthetic interests in accomplished scientists. On the basis of these data and other anecdotal historical information, they have concluded that aesthetics are critical factors in scientific creativity. Other historical and biographical data, however, have had an opposite trend, indicating a much lower incidence of aesthetic interests in highly achieving scientists.[34] Like intuition, aesthetic factors may have a peripheral role in scientific creation; they seem to be predominantly important for mathematical scientific theorists. Organizing features of various types of aesthetic conceits, and what has been called elegance in theoretical formulations, may indicate some particular potential influences of aesthetic factors for mathematicians. Paul Dirac was very enthusiastic about the importance of aesthetic influences: "Schrödinger and I both had a very strong appreciation of mathematical beauty, and this appreciation of mathematical beauty dominated all our work. It was a sort of [*sic*] act of faith with us that any equations which describe fundamental laws of Nature must have great mathematical beauty in them. It was like a religion with us. It was a very profitable religion to hold, and can be considered as the basis of much of our success."[35]

Chandrasekhar, the Nobel laureate in physics for his discovery of the maximum mass of a stable white dwarf star ("Chandrasekhar limit") whom I quoted in chapter 2, devoted a series of lectures to "Aesthetics and Motivations in Science." In addition to describing the strong influence of aesthetic factors in his own creative work, he emphasizes a quotation from the mathematical physicist Poincaré, as follows: "This special aesthetic sensibility...plays the part of...[a] delicate sieve...."[36]

The concepts of "aesthetics," "aesthetic sensibility," and "beauty" are very broad and, in science, characterizations have ranged from production of simplicity to extreme complexity. At some point, usually at the end of the creative process, matters of elegance and compositional symmetry, orderliness and, when clearly defined, harmony may be operative, along with the emotional pleasure and passion derived from perceiving aesthetic-appearing phenomena. Despite the appealing idea of such connections of science and the arts, almost a poetic idea in its own right, the applications are essentially limited. I believe and shall show that the creative cognitive processes I have described, not aesthetic substance and form, are the factors operating generally for creative success in both areas.

Empirical Design: Methodology and Subjects

The purpose of this research was to determine empirically the developmental and psychological processes leading to creative achievement in science and scientific discovery. The hypotheses to be tested, as indicated in chapters 3 to 7, were derived from detailed autobiographical and primary document accounts of those processes leading to outstanding creative achievements of early Nobel laureates and the pre-Nobel scientist Charles Darwin. In this extended controlled empirical research, the primary investigative tool was a semistructured research interview or interview series. Experimental-group subjects were living scientists who had been awarded a Nobel Prize in Physics, Chemistry, or Physiology or Medicine. They were recruited from university settings in the United States and from university settings and research institutes in England, France, Germany, and Switzerland. All subjects spoke English fluently. Comparison control subjects were engineers on the faculty of an Eastern US technology university.

Twelve early-interviewed Nobel subjects also participated in a controlled word association experiment designed to measure tendencies toward rapid opposite response and, by extension, janusian process cognition.

A developmental investigation that focused on family background variables was also performed. Life history information was collected from all Nobel laureates in the sciences, including the current interview group, starting with the Nobel inception year 1901 until 2003. Documented data for this investigation were procured from an overall total of 435 Nobel laureate subjects.

The primary study was designed to use the semistructured interview procedure because, in all fields, the creative process is multilayered and takes place over different lengths of time. It is necessary when investigating this process to separate out the various layers—mental, physical, environmental, and social factors and influences. Correlational studies may miss crucial intervening creative variables, and personality tests do not necessarily apply to the ongoing creative process. Ideally, an investigator would want to sit beside a person during the process of creating, or else find a way for the creative person to record his or her ongoing thoughts without interference from the recording procedure. As such approaches have not yet been adequately designed, nor have highly or clearly creative people been heretofore recruited to participate in creative-process studies,[1] the retrospective reconstruction of the process, as produced by the following semistructured research interview protocol, provides a basis for illuminating unfolding events and factors in the creative process. This same interview protocol was used with both the Nobel and the engineer comparison groups. The designed procedure is not the same as journalistic, sociological, historical, or psychological or diagnostic psychiatric interviewing focused on personality and behavior.

Published scientific reports require sequential and tightly logical presentation of hypotheses, data, and results, which do not necessarily correspond to the actual sequences and thinking leading to discovery. The semistructured interviews were designed to elicit the most reliable data about production of specific discoveries and the nature of past or in-progress creative work. They were therefore geared toward maximizing free discussion and trust in order to allow for reporting actual sequences, including any possible private or unusual modes of thought and behavior. The disadvantage of the approach is possible investigator bias and absence of direct refutability. In the interview protocol to be described hereafter, the procedures for minimizing biases are spelled out. The application of the same interview protocol with the comparison control group with high-level scientific intelligence but less or absent creative achievement provides an empirical basis for identifying significant factors and of refutability.

The experimental-group interviews were all carried out, with two exceptions, at the Nobel laureates' working or home location. Supplemental interviewing with the French Pierre-Gilles de Gennes and Jean-Marie Lehn was also done in other academic locations during their later United States visits. All sessions were recorded on tape or as MP3s, and in every case the circumstances and thinking connected with Nobel Prize designated discoveries as well as ongoing work was discussed. As the subjects were all aware that the research project findings would be published, they were encouraged to stipulate any confidential information during the session. The comparison control group interviews were all carried out at the technology university offices. Confidentiality assurances and interview conditions were identical to those employed with the experimental group.

Issues of clarity, error, competition, public scrutiny, and interviewer or subject dominance or submission were all potential risks for this sensitive description and assessment, whether a subject was a member of the publicly visible Nobel laureate group or a less well-known engineer. A good interviewer–subject alliance was vital for facilitating frank and open discussion of potentially biasing factors. Also, it was quite essential that the subject's memory be both clear and reliable for accounts of the discoveries. Almost invariably, in the course of interviewing, the subjects in both groups indicated that they remembered everything about the events minutely, whether or not they had written them down or if they had occurred remotely in time. Scientific rigor accounted for some of the accuracy of memory; for the Nobel laureates, the crucial importance of the designated discoveries accounted for another part of the memories' accuracy. Nevertheless, some distortion due to hindsight was possible. In each case, an expert memory assessment was performed.

The section to follow details the semistructured scientific interview procedure that I, as sole interviewer, followed with both groups.

The Semistructured Research Interview Protocol

The Nobel laureate subjects, I anticipated, would all be willing to describe their early achievements as well as their later ones because of previous public acknowledgment and description of their work in Nobel award proceedings, which sometimes included the process of discovery. Also, all were university-level professors; they had an interest in and capacity for teaching as well as trust in me as a colleague and professional with some scientific credentials. Furthermore, they were interested in creativity. Although the engineers' work had less public exposure, their teaching, collegial motivations, and interests would be similar.

The phases of the investigative protocol represent the overall emotional and conceptual flow of the interview. Although the content described in all of the phases is invariably touched on or covered at length, the actual topic sequences within and between phases sometimes varies, as do whole phase sequences. All shifting is based on the subjects' interests and priorities. The first phase is oriented toward gaining a subject's confidence as well as imparting information and getting a broad view of the subject's thinking and beliefs. Inquiry about background and personal or family information is avoided at that point and left for later in the interview. With every subject, after asking permission to record and assuring confidentiality, the interviewer starts with an extensive description of the background and goal of the research project: many years of creativity investigation had already been done; the research previously focused on literary and artistic creativity; the current investigation is being carried out to assess whether the same factors operating in artistic modes of creativity also appear in the creativity of science and technology. Following this introduction, the subject is asked, "Have you thought about creativity? What do you think it consists of?" Common subject comments regarding popular conceptions of the importance of serendipity and of motivation in scientific achievements are discussed and the varying opinions noted.

In this phase, the subjects often begin to talk about some element in their past or present work. All will be alert to whether the interviewer knows about such work and possesses any appropriate scientific or technical knowledge. Absence of scientific pretentiousness or competition is important here, and the interviewer briefly indicates familiarity. When necessary for proper comprehension, more extensive scientific knowledge may be introduced or requested.

In the second phase, a collaborative orientation is maintained and facilitated. Recognition of the subject's emotional reactions as well as the ups and downs of the conceptual course begins at this point and is continued throughout. Adequacy of memory, according to routine psychiatric procedure, is first assessed here. Attention is paid to memory for both remote and recent events and experiences, and requests are made for detailed exposition of scientific, technical, and social matters both past and contemporary. Tendencies toward discussing general matters such as the state of science and scientific education instead of the specifics of the subject's own work and discoveries are noted as potentially representing or covering up memory deficit, especially in older subjects. Memory omissions, stipulated both voluntarily and on request, are heeded and assessed.

The third phase is the longest and most elaborate portion of the interview. Sometimes the subject begins the description of his or her work early and, as the session progresses, fills in and clarifies many aspects. Also, many different discoveries are described at different points. The comparison engineers refer to findings and solutions, rather than creative discoveries, and among their major productions are patentable devices or technical procedures. For both groups, once the topic of a specific discovery or solution is raised, subjects elaborate spontaneously and at great length. The interviewer determines the choice of the particular scientific activity or type of problem and, after that, limits his interventions primarily to modes of thought and emotions. An especially important question at the culmination of this discourse is, "Did the discovery [etc.] come as a surprise?" or simply, "Were you surprised?" Answers to this question furnish a good deal of information about the path to discovery; they point to possible deviance, feelings and ideas about breakthrough, changes of direction, mode of thought, and intention to create. Another productive question is, "What do you do about errors along the way?" This yields information about the subject's perseverance and applications of standard methodologies such as repeating experiments and experimental or mental testing of the error as a negative against a positive. Also, it reveals the possibility that they adopted the content of the error to go in a fruitful new direction.

Following and intermixed with the third phase, the fourth phase concerns the subjects' evaluations of the discovery or solution for their own work, for science and technology, and for society at large. Specific potential and known applications of the discovery or solution are requested. Here, investigation also turns to more personal and possibly sensitive matters of internal and external project collaborations and competitions, and individual effects of the discovery and the recognition (including emotions and changes of modes of cognition). Subjects are asked about or spontaneously report other work, more or less ambitious, they have accomplished or plan for the future. The question, "What are you working on now?" is always included. Although all of the Nobel subjects' prizes are documented in various publications, and the engineers' patents and other products are recorded in government and commercial documents, brief reference to these usually elicits personal and professional comment and elaboration.

The fifth phase, late in the session, focuses on not previously volunteered personal characteristics of the subjects themselves. Earlier collection of personal and background information, rather than inducing confidence and a professional investigatory atmosphere, tends to set up a social or journalistically oriented interchange. Exploring personal factors and influences is, however, ultimately important. Information regarding family background, religious beliefs and practices, aesthetic and leisure activities, modalities of thought, and elements of life history are all discussed together. Opportunities to pay attention to this information follow a subject's spontaneous reference (usually at this point) to a previous work location or mentor. Also, parents' influence or lack of influence may be discussed in connection with questions of choice of an investigative scientific or technological field and problem.

The final or sixth phase consists of the interviewer's gathering comparative evidence that might pertain to various major theories and formulations regarding creativity and the creative process. Many of these theories have already guided questions asked, and they have been implicitly and explicitly assessed by the interviewer throughout. In this phase, to reduce experimenter bias further, specific formulations and theories are presented, some of which are already familiar to the subjects, such the Root-Bernsteins' conception of the importance of aesthetics and aesthetic interests in scientific creativity, Koestler's bisociation, connectivity and combinatorial mechanisms, and deBono's lateral thinking. The subject's direct opinion and experience regarding these theories and known or unknown others is elicited. If general issues such as serendipity were not discussed at the beginning and the factor of mental imagery not later explored, both the questions, "What do you think about serendipity [or luck] in yours or others scientific discoveries?" and "What was the role of mental imagery [any sensory modality] in your work?" are always posed at the end.

PHASE I Focus and Alliance

- Background: description of previous project research
- Interview conditions: recording, confidentiality
- Subject's views of creativity: general and specific; importance of capacities, serendipity, motivation
- Interviewer knowledge of subject's work: correct but nonintrusive or competitive
- Subject's general beliefs, scientific biases, and preconceptions: effects of age factors, parents and siblings, education, mentors, psychological factors, society (details obtained generally in Phase IV)
- Avoidance of early personal probing

PHASE IIA Collaboration

- Report ongoing impressions and request feedback
- Recognition and labeling of feelings (e.g., pride, gratification, irritation)
- Acknowledgment of conceptual strivings and achievements
- Question mode: supply reasons for inquiries, especially unusual or seemingly challenging ones

PHASE IIB Memory Assessment and Facilitation

- Systematic assessment by both interviewer and subject's report
- Possible written documentations: notes, articles
- Interviewer facilitation procedures: work backward from the present—"What are you working on now?"
  - Temporal evocation: "When was the last time you thought about or did something similar?"
  - Spatial evocation: "Where were you when you thought that?"

PHASE III Description of the Discovery/Discoveries

- Sequences, events, background
- Choice of problem; first conception
- Direction of changes and revisions (theory or applications)
- Associated feelings and emotions: disappointment, relief, confidence, excitement, aggressiveness, happiness, need for order
- Anticipation and surprise

(continued)

PHASE III Continued

- Nature of labor and perseverance
- Role of error/errors
- Nature of short- or long-term scientific or personal influences
- Deviation and compliance: theoretical or experiential approaches, relation to accepted canons
- Clarification: issues of fact or meaning
- Modes of thought:
  - visualization (mental or written)
  - auditory or other sensory
  - inductive or deductive
  - dialectical processes
  - pattern recognition, focus on design
  - imagination, hunches
  - aesthetic considerations (symmetry and asymmetry: aesthetic versus mathematical)
  - use of physical models, mental constructions
  - other thought patterns and sequences
- Scientific and technological reports: difference and similarity with actual procedures and thinking

PHASE IV General Considerations

- Applications: usefulness, value, recognition
- Collaboration with mentors, colleagues, assistants
- Later conceptions, formalizations, naming or other types of contributions
- Competition with peers
- Effect of the discovery or solution and its recognition on one's subsequent thinking, orientation, personal life
- Other prizes or patents

PHASE V Background and Personal Information

- Confidential and nonconfidential supplements to public information
- Family background, including siblings, spouse, and children
- Aesthetic and leisure interests and practices: literary, artistic, music, sports, travel
- Characteristic thought modalities: visual, verbal, sensory
- Religious beliefs, feelings, and practices
- Switches among professional fields

- Specific guiding aesthetic ideas or principles; analogies to reasoning factors in art, literature, music
- Connectivity, combination, blending
- Figure-ground theory
- Chance-configuration theory
- Serendipity
- Unconscious regression
- Bisociation, remote associations
- Risk taking, courage, idiosyncratic lifestyle
- Rebelliousness, divergent production
- Mental imagery
- Lateral thinking

Subjects

The 34 Nobel laureate subjects interviewed are listed in Table 8.1.[2] In the United States, they were located in Berkeley, Palo Alto, and Pasadena, California and Cambridge, Massachusetts. In Europe, they were located in Paris and Strasbourg, France; Freiburg, Martinsried, and Tübingen, Germany; Basel, Switzerland; and London, United Kingdom. Ages ranged from 43 to 84 years at the time of the interviews; 33 were male and 1, Christiane Nüsslein-Volhard, was female. All were members of university faculties or research institutes. The criterion for inclusion was the recognition by the Nobel Prize committee together with an independent positive assessment of each subject's creativity by a panel of eight scientist experts, administrators, and technologists. Rating categories were based on a subject's both new and valuable conceptualizing and/or production. The judgment of value consisted of possession of distinct positive social, instrumental, or scientific integrations and benefits. Categories were (1) neither new nor valuable, (2) independently either new or valuable, and (3) both new and valuable. All conceptualizing and/or productions of members of this Nobel group were rated in Category 3.

Comparison Control Subjects: Engineers

The comparison control group consisted of 12 faculty members in the Mechanical Engineering Department at an Eastern US technological university. All subjects in this group were informed that they were being interviewed regarding creativity and the creative process, and the same research interview protocol used with the Nobel laureate subjects was followed. All

TABLE 8.1 Nobel Laureate Subjects

Nobel Laureate	Year	Award	Award Area	Country
Luis W. Alvarez	1968	Physics	Particle resonance states	US
Werner Arber	1978	Med/Ph	Hereditary mutation in bacteria	Switzerland
David Baltimore	1975	Med/Ph	Genetic change	US
Baruj Benacerraf	1980	Med/Ph	Genetically determined cell-surface structures	US
Konrad Bloch	1964	Med/Ph	Cholesterol and fatty acid metabolism	US
Nicolaas Bloembergen	1981	Physics	Solid-state maser and electron spectroscopy	US
Paul Berg	1980	Chem	Recombinant DNA	US
Owen Chamberlain	1959	Physics	Antiproton	US
Elias J. Corey	1990	Chem	Organic synthesis	US
Allan M. Cormack	1979	Med/Ph	Computed tomographic scanner	Australia/US
Pierre-Gilles de Gennes	1991	Physics	Liquid crystals and polymers	France
Max Delbrück	1969	Med/Ph	Genetic replication of viruses	US
Ivar Giaever	1973	Physics	Tunneling in superconductors	Norway/US
Walter Gilbert	1980	Chem	Base sequence of nucleic acids	US
Donald Glaser	1960	Physics	Bubble chamber	US
Sheldon Glashow	1979	Physics	Weak and electromagnetic interaction between elementary particles	US
Dudley Herschbach	1986	Chem	Dynamics of chemical elementary particles	US
David H. Hubel	1981	Med/Ph	Information processing of the visual system	US
Robert Huber	1988	Chem	Structure of large molecules involved in photosynthesis	Germany
John C. Kendrew	1962	Chem	Protein structure	UK
Georges J. F. Köhler	1984	Med/Ph	Monoclonal antibody production	Germany
Arthur Kornberg	1959	Med/Ph	Synthetic DNA	US
Joshua Lederberg	1958	Med/Ph	Bacterial reproduction	US
Jean-Marie Lehn	1987	Chem	Supramolecular chemistry	France
William Lipscomb	1976	Chem	Borane structure and chemical bonding	US
Salvador E. Luria	1969	Med/Ph	Genetic replication of viruses	US
Edwin M. McMillan	1951	Chem	Transuranium elements	US
Joseph Murray	1990	Med/Ph	Kidney transplantation	US
Christiane Nüsslein-Volhard	1995	Med/Ph	Genetic control of early embryonic development	Germany
Edward M. Purcell	1952	Physics	Nuclear magnetic moments	US
Norman Ramsey	1989	Physics	Atomic precision spectroscopy/cesium clock/hydrogen maser	US
Glenn T. Seaborg	1951	Chem	Transuranium elements	US
Emilio Segrè	1959	Physics	Antiproton	Italy/US
Charles H. Townes	1964	Physics	Gas maser and laser	US

Note. Chem = Nobel Prize in Chemistry; Med/Ph = Nobel Prize in Physiology or Medicine.

engineer subjects were identified as creative achievers by the chairman of the department. As an impartial investigator of creativity, therefore, I adopted this judgment at that point. Afterward, however, I obtained assessments from the expert panel (see preceding section) regarding the creativity or creative production of all of these subjects on a three-category scale. The work of one of the subjects (designated here as *Creator*) was rated in Category 3 (both new and valuable), that of two others was rated in Category 2 (either new or valuable), and the remainder were all in Category 1 (neither new nor valuable). Only *Creator*, therefore, met the criteria for creativity comparable with the Nobel laureates. Some of these subjects were potential inventors who had obtained patent protections and honors. All patents were reviewed by the expert panel, however, and determined to be essentially different and variant but neither novel nor new. They were all for potentially useful mechanical products and procedures, but according to the criteria of bringing forth both genuine value and newness, they were not at all comparable with the experimental Nobel laureate group. Although some ideas and methods arguably may have possessed some relative newness together with usefulness, they were considered creative to a very low degree. Separately, the judges, including expert professional technicians, commented that these subjects were generally problem solvers but not creative. All were engaged in technical problem-solving work, and the single woman in the group, also a problem solver, was the only theorist. Ages at the time of the interviews ranged from 40 to 68 years; there were 11 men and 1 woman; 8 were of US origin and 4 were born and raised in other countries (Italy, Korea, the United Kingdom, and Austria). All are identified here by pseudonyms (see Table 8.2).

My overall impressions from interviewing the two groups were that neither one was overall stereotypical. None of the Nobel laureates were unconventional

TABLE 8.2 Comparison Control Engineer Group

Engineer	Area	Country
Visualizer 1	Aero-elasticity	US
Visualizer 2	Wear particles	Italy
Reverser	Contact mechanics	UK
Connector	Mechanical design	US
Analogizer 1	Thermal science	US
Theorist/Connector	Radiation heat transfer	US
Analogizer 2	Solid surface lubrication	Austria
Creator	Superplasticity	Korea
Visualizer 3	Friction and wear	US
Visualizer/Collaborator	Acoustics and noise control	US
Administrator	Bearings and lubrication	US
Theorist/Collaborator	Engineering theory and piezoelectric resonators	US

in clothing, speech, or emotional reactivity. None were careless, preoccupied, personally domineering, or especially egocentric. All members of both groups had recognizable although untested high to exceptionally high intelligence. All were thoroughly knowledgeable about their own and other fields of science or technology and, given the clarity of their explications of theory and data, they all would be considered as having superior teaching abilities. None of the subjects were unconventional, noncommunicative, or unsociable. Both groups had high academic status. Subjects were all quite forthcoming about their work, thought, and whatever elements of their personal lives seemed pertinent to the investigation. High levels of motivation and involvement regarding their work appeared in both groups; some from both appeared overly conscientious and driven. I did not conduct a detailed mental health evaluation with any subjects in either group, but from my extensive contact I can say there was no evidence of disabling mental illness: no pervasive schizophrenia, bipolar illness, anxiety disorder, borderline personality, or organic and addiction disorders. One of the Nobel laureates showed mild to moderate signs of clinical depression, as did one of the engineers. One engineer showed some degree of manic disorganization at times, which did not interfere with his research or teaching. In both groups, there were subjects with obvious compulsive personality characteristics. Problem solving was important for both groups, with a focus on applications of technological knowledge by the engineers and a concentration predominantly on pure science by the Nobel laureates. With respect to memory, all assessments of the subjects including their techniques of embodying and retaining information, as well as their references to details of long-past events related or unrelated to their work, indicated, except for one or possibly two subjects in the Nobel group, excellent to superior short- and long-term memory. All other subjects, especially as predicted for the Nobel group, were able to recount details of the processes leading to important discoveries and solutions.

All of the Nobel subjects considered themselves creative, although a few pointed out that the prizes are given generally because of the impact of discoveries and therefore not necessarily their ingeniousness. When asked about their own theories of creativity, several volunteered that it had something to do with making or seeing connections. Many of the engineers, however, stressed good problem-solving techniques and technical skills. Almost all of the Nobel laureates were interested in and knowledgeable about music, and several of the laureates competently played a musical instrument. Overall, such interests and activities were lacking in the engineer group.

Janusian Process in Creative Discovery

The results of the investigation reported in this and the succeeding chapters consist of detailed and verbatim descriptions of significant processes involved in scientific creation as well as test and family background data. In addition to the use of the janusian process described here, several subjects, as indicated in succeeding chapters, also applied two other cognitive creative processes. In each case cited, the application of the specific process designated was creative or led to a creative result.

Both in the early interviews accompanied by experimental word association tasks and in the later ones not accompanied by a test, the janusian process—actively conceiving and using multiple opposites or antitheses simultaneously—was found to operate in the creative achievements of all types of Nobel laureates in science (Chemistry, Physics, and Physiology or Medicine). These instances are outlined on the accompanying chart (Table 9.1).

The component opposites used by each Nobel laureate are indicated in the second and third columns. These were in each case actively postulated as simultaneously true or valid or as simultaneously operative. The fourth column indicates the resulting janusian formulation, and the fifth indicates the pure or applied discovery.

American chemist Edwin McMillan was a tall, mustached, and distinguished-looking man in a hexagon-patterned tie, white shirt, and gray suit. He sat comfortably straight in his chair, speaking in a relaxed but authoritative manner. The Nobel Prize was awarded to him for contributions to the discovery of the elements neptunium and plutonium. These discoveries helped lead to the theoretical understanding and application of the trans-uranium element series, which played a critical role in the development of nuclear energy. An important basis for his achievement was his formulation of the concept of "phase stability"; this led to the construction of an extremely effective particle accelerator and identifier of elements, the synchrocyclotron or, as it is now called, the synchrotron.

TABLE 9.1 Janusian Process

Nobel Laureate	Opposite Factor	Opposite Factor	Janusian Conception	Discovery or Discoveries
Edwin McMillan	Too high energy	Too low energy	Phase stability	Synchrotron
Pierre-Gilles de Gennes	Hydrophilic	Hydrophobic	Janus grains	Surfactant interchange
Walter Gilbert	Bacterial genome	Human genome	Reverse evolution	RNA world hypothesis
Edward Purcell	Nuclear spins	Inverted nuclear spins	Negative temperature	Negative temperature
Charles Townes	Positive temperature	Negative temperature	High energy source	Ammonia maser
Nicolaas Bloembergen	Negative temperature	Low temperature	Solid-state energy	Solid-state maser
Elias Corey	Putting together	Taking apart	Organic chemical construction	Retrosynthetic chemistry
Arthur Kornberg	Enzyme action on the substrate	Substrate action on the enzyme	DNA polymerase and synthesis	DNA synthesis
Joshua Lederberg	DNA input	DNA output	Genetic effect	Bacterial conjugation
Jean-Marie Lehn	Concave	Convex	Supramolecule	Supramolecular chemistry
	Pure-mixture	Impure-mixture	Instructed self-recognition	Instructed mixture paradigm
	Heterocycle	Opposite-faced Heterocycle	Janus molecule	Janus molecule

McMillan described his process of formulating "phase stability" as follows:

It was the problem of beaming high energy particles accelerated in a cyclotron. The problem with the cyclotron is maintaining resonance, maintaining the correct timing, because of the increase of mass—very energetic—the particles get heavier and you're watching a field that's proportional to the mass of the particles. So, they fall out of step.

People were proceeding with the design of a big cyclotron, a 184-inch cyclotron, which had a limitation, and they were trying to figure out ways of beating this limitation. One [unproductive] way of beating it was seeing that the thing doesn't take very many turns and then it doesn't have much time to fall out of step. It was an error in the timing that's cumulative and if you make many, many turns it'll accumulate to more.

So, after some time I wanted to see if I could think of some clever method of getting high energy. In other words, I was going to try to create something.... So I did some design work on paper on the air corbe betatron and it was an exceedingly brutal way to do the job. Then one night—it was in the month of July, I think it was the month of July, I did not put down the date, I should record these things—I was lying awake in bed and thinking of a way of getting high energy, thinking of the cyclotron and the particle going around and encountering the accelerator field. And I sort of analyzed in my mind that it's going around, being accelerated, and it's getting heavier, therefore it's taking more time to get around and then it would fall out of step. It gets behind and gets the feel of the opposite sense. It gets pushed back again, so it will oscillate. If the timing is wrong, it's not going to completely run out of steam, it's just going to oscillate back and forth, be going at too high and too low energy. Once I realized that, then the rest was easy. All you have to do is to vary your frequency or vary the magnetic field, either one or both, slowly, and you can push this thing anywhere you want. That all happened one night, and the next day I started writing down the equations and proved it would work. Critical phase stability—if conditions are wrong to accelerate, they're not going to fall completely out of step but the particle will overshoot and come back. The very next day I called it "phase stability"—phase is the time relation of what you're worried about; stability implies that it clings to a certain fixed value.

In this verbatim account (some technical language is omitted where specified), McMillan described his application of the janusian process with all its predicted phases described in chapter 4. He indicated his motivation to create "something"; a deviation from his colleagues regarding the approach to the cyclotron design limitation; his focus on the opposite senses of the accelerating particles; and the formulation of the simultaneous operation of the opposites of too high and too low energy. This led to his discovery of "phase stability," the new and valuable product of the janusian process applied to the function of the synchrotron.

French physicist Pierre-Gilles de Gennes was also tall but strikingly thin with a narrow, classically Gallic face. He had a slightly breezy manner steeled with consistently rational disquisition. The phenomena of wetting and adhesions were his primary scientific interest. This has involved work with liquid crystals that has been characterized as operating on the borderline between order and disorder—that is, crystals have perfect order, whereas liquid atoms move in completely irregular fashion.[1] Liquid crystals, in his hands, have been electrically or mechanically transformed from a transparent to an opaque state. As a result, pixels or screen elements could be applied for lettering, colors, designs, and moving images on computer and TV screens as well as digital watches and calculators. de Gennes was also responsible for advances in polymer chemistry consisting of the use of structurally repeated large molecules to form important new substances ranging from types of proteins, starches, and the components of genetic blueprints to the plastics used in modern aircraft and automobiles.

As part of his work with polymers (repeating structural units), he developed a new product that he christened "Janus grains." These double-function particles are applied in building stable carriers used for rate change in chemi-cal reactions and drug delivery. As a result, a plethora of polymer research has been possible with macroscopic, microscopic, and especially nanoscopic particles employed in the biomedical, optical, and electronic fields. Prior to our sessions, de Gennes did not know of my janusian process hypothesis. He described his initial conception for the namesake Janus grains in the follow-ing manner:

> Soaps and detergents are frustrated molecules of which one half likes water, hydrophilic, and one half likes oil, hydrophobic. That gives them very strange properties. A single molecule will want to live at the interface between oil and water or water and air. I was looking for a new object in nature and one of my challenges was whether there could be a way to get something which would be useful in metallurgy [making metals mix better in alloys], a Janus object which would have one part liking metal A and one part liking metal B, at very high temperatures. Two opposite sides—opposite tastes, that's really what it is—at the same time. If you want to establish large interfaces between one liquid and another liquid, you put in these Janus grains, they facilitate the buildup of interfaces so you can mix better. At the same time you want some molecular exchange to be maintained between the two sides. If you only act with the old trick of surfactants [surface-active agents that lower surface tension or resis-tance between liquids], the surfactant makes a very dense opaque inter-face that doesn't allow for interchange of signals or molecules between the two sides. If, however, you put in these particles which leave some little holes between them, you have a very good protection that still allows for interchange.

deGennes engaged in the phases of the janusian process: first, his creative motivation; then the challenging deviation from nature to produce a new metallurgical entity; his focus on opposed hydrophilic and hydrophobic sides; and last, their simultaneous applications. His janusian process conception of simultaneously opposite predilections or "tastes," led directly to a scientific creation of independently and appropriately named Janus grains.

American Nobelist Walter Gilbert was a physicist who later became a biologist. In this second field, he determined the exact sequence of building blocks in DNA and the bacterial chromosome regions of DNA that control transcription of the genetic message in the cell. These chromosome regions involving both gene coding and expression are called *exons*, and regions that do not involve either are called *introns*. Gilbert, very soft-spoken, dark-haired, with piercing and highly intelligent bespectacled eyes, spoke right away about the creativity of his wife, a poet and visual artist. Her knowledge and interests, he volunteered, covered broad intellectual and creative ranges. As for himself, he spoke also of having abiding desires to be creative in science. Discussing, at one point, one of his creative achievements, he added that he "enjoyed the perversity of turning evolution on its head."

Outlining the steps in that achievement, he said he was a strong proponent over the years of the idea that the exon/intron interrelationship was a powerful way of making new genes. The theory he proposed was that, at the beginning of evolution, the very first genes were made this way and that most of the organisms of the world had subsequently lost the complicated structure and functions. "It's a reverse way of looking at evolution," he said. "Bacteria, rather than simple organisms, are very highly evolved and we [humans], while we are looking like we are the very pinnacle of evolution, have nuclei that look like, in some ways, the very first organisms." His theory, aspects of which had been proposed by previous scientists[2] as well as Gilbert's graduate students, has come to be known as the *RNA world hypothesis*. It derives from his own work on introns and exons and consists of his extensively elaborated proposal that life based on RNA (ribonucleic acid) predates the current world of life based on DNA (deoxyribonucleic acid). In this proposal, DNA, RNA, and the protein world of today evolved from the original RNA. His idea, which came all at once, consisted of the nonexpressing or noncoding introns (of bacteria) as involved in creating novel genes. Therefore, the least type of organism, bacteria, were at the highest pole of genetic advancement and, at the same time, the greatest of organisms, humans, were at the opposite, lowest pole—a janusian process formulation. In this conception also, spatially opposite exons and introns were simultaneously operative. Present were the janusian process motivation to create, deviation, choice of opposites, and simultaneity.

In full-blown scientific theories following from a creative janusian process, component oppositions are often modified in varying degrees. The RNA world hypothesis has been controversial and oppositional elements have been to some extent modified,[3] but there has been continuing evidence of its overall validity.[4] A further elaboration is that the first genetic elements were actually simpler components that predated exons. Mixing and matching of these early components of exons made possible by interrelation with introns then led to long chains that made increasingly larger genes.

Three critical scientific discoveries recognized by the Nobel Prize involved the discovery and applications of the quantum phenomenon of "negative temperature," temperature measured as negative on the Kelvin thermodynamic scale of absolute temperature. An independently conceived and differently structured janusian process containing all phases led in each case to the creative achievement. The discovery of negative temperature itself was primarily the work of the American physicist Edward Purcell. Norman Ramsey and Robert Pound had respectively made prior and concurrent valuable contributions.

Edward Purcell, despite his important discoveries and leadership in the academic and international worlds of physics, was quite modest about his work. He had a candid, forthright facial expression and sandy brown hair that enhanced his good looks. Right off, he spoke at length and with enthusiasm about the research on stereovision of another scientist, Béla Julesz. That researcher's cognitive science experiments and theory of "cyclopean perception" had, Julesz thought, important applications for understanding vision and brain function. Purcell's own extensive research was in nuclear magnetic resonance and imaging used for determining the quantum magnetic properties of atomic nuclei and the structure of molecules. A phenomenon originally discovered in molecular beams by Isadore Rabi, Purcell had expanded the Rabi imaging technique to apply fully to liquids and solids. His imaging work had the significant technological result of developing nuclear quadrupole resonance (NQR), which, in crystals and fluids, applies to the measurement of the interactions—so-called relaxations or returns to magnetic equilibrium—between the tiniest particles of matter. Among other uses, NQR has been employed for detecting explosives in military and police-work circumstances as well as for the commercial and noncommercial measurement of various oil-well outflow products of water, gas, or oil. It also has been extended to the development of masers (see Charles Townes section hereafter) and lasers. Today, the results of Purcell's studies with magnetic imaging are applied in medicine to the highly valuable diagnostic procedure of the MRI (magnetic resonance imaging), and are widely used in chemical research.

With respect to the janusian process, Purcell's discovery of the phenomenon of negative temperature came out of a key formulation of employing simultaneously opposite states of regular and inverted nuclear spin. Nuclear spin, an energy-producing property, is angular movement around an elementary particle nucleus. As he told me:

> Bob Pound, my assistant, was working on nuclear quadrupole resonance in crystals and I started thinking about nuclear spin temperature. I got the idea that if we had both regular spins and spins at inverted levels, that everything would go on with no trouble, it could be described as negative temperature. So, when Bob found a crystal with a long relaxation time—a return to regular energy equilibrium—I said to him, "Let's invert the spins and show that they behave as if they were at negative temperature." It worked. This beginning with negative temperature was one of the ideas that moved us out of the conventional realm of upper energy states always having lower numbers of particles than lower energy states. [Note: Negative temperatures are even hotter than infinite temperature, not colder than absolute zero as might be supposed.]

An important application of the developed concept and nature of the negative temperature phenomenon was conceived by another American physics laureate, Charles Townes. Son of a lawyer, and himself a former provost at Massachusetts Institute of Technology, Townes's voice and appearance was that of a friendly minister (he had, in fact, won the Templeton Prize for "Progress Toward Research or Discoveries About Spiritual Realities"). He was responsible for the first production of stimulated emission by what was called the maser (microwave amplification by stimulated emission of radiation) through amplification of electromagnetic waves. This was elaborated later into the optical maser or laser (light amplification by stimulated emission of radiation). His original ammonia-driven maser continues to be used for astronomical investigations as well as for atomic clocks. Townes later derived the concept of the functional and widely used laser in collaboration with his brother-in-law, Arthur Schawlow. Both shared Nobel Prizes in Physics for their discoveries.

In the course of creating the maser, Townes initially had been working on microwave spectroscopy used to study the behavior of molecules and the shapes and spins of nuclei. This led to an interest in developing high-frequency (millimeter) radio waves, and he became a member of a committee of engineers and scientists with the same purpose commissioned by the US Office of Naval Research. As he told me, during one of the meetings of this committee in Washington, DC, he woke early in his hotel room and, not wanting to wake his then-roommate, Arthur Schawlow, went outside to nearby Franklin Park. There, "sitting among the azaleas," as he vividly accounted, he gradually conceptualized the keys to the production of the very short electromagnetic waves on which the maser was based. First, he pondered the theory that radiation could stimulate an atom or molecule excited to a higher level energy state at positive temperatures to emit photons. Considering the energy situation further, he said to himself, "But according to the second law of thermodynamics, atoms or molecules produced at any lower energy levels would absorb the energy photons, because the substance is in thermal equilibrium."

In an excited way, he told me, "Then, all at once I realized that the second law of thermodynamics did not need to apply, all systems did not need to be in thermal equilibrium. I could use, together with the positive temperature, a negative temperature, which inverted the relative excess of lower-level over upper level energy states in equilibrated systems. Then, in a few minutes, I actually calculated, on the back of an envelope, the critical conditions that led to the construction of the first ammonia maser."

Notably, the critical idea included deviation and breaking away from a classically accepted law, the second law of thermodynamics, and the daring choice of opposites of positive and negative temperature (temperature inversion, Purcell's discovery). These would be applied simultaneously to produce a high energy state. This janusian process construction was Townes's breakthrough, leading him to produce the first gas maser. In the developed apparatus, a molecular beam of ammonia is passed through a small orifice into a vacuum chamber. Going through both a uniform and nonuniform electrical field, the molecules become excited and serve to amplify microwave radiation. The designed temperature system produces high-energy amplified wave emission.

Another creative discovery using negative temperature in a different way was independently made by Nicolaas Bloembergen. A Dutch-born American physicist, Professor Bloembergen was a tall, wiry man with a soft voice and a light trace of accent. He had a steady, businesslike manner—steadiness that may very well have been a holdover from a previous time in his life. During the Second World War, as a Jew in the Netherlands, he had hidden in densely planted fields to escape the occupying Nazis. He survived there by eating tulip bulbs. Later, he managed to leave his homeland and get to the United States, where he landed a prestigious job at Harvard working with Edward Purcell. Among the creative accomplishments for which Bloembergen was later awarded the Nobel Prize were his development of the field of nonlinear optics and the invention of the distinctive solid-state maser. This form of maser differs from Townes's gas maser both in practical function and Bloembergen's accompanying precise conceptual advances. Solid-state masers are regularly used for amplification of radio waves at low temperatures. In radar and communication, they have been applied for amplification of usually very weak signals in space returned from distant satellite targets. These masers made possible the measurement of faint radio waves emitted by the planet Venus, giving the first indication of its temperature.

Bloembergen's initial work with Edward Purcell was in the field of nuclear magnetic resonance, and he had continued to use that detailed analytic technique for providing information about the molecular structure of solids and liquids. He described his focus on solid-state materials and his development of the solid-state maser in the following way:

> There was the first maser by Townes, and people were excited about that. So then they wanted to do it in solids. They had things that you can just flip for a little while but they really wanted to do it in a continuous way. And I asked Woody Strandberg [his colleague], "Why is it so important to do that?"
>
> "Well," he said, "then you can use that [apparatus] as a very low noise amplifier."
>
> So, I thought, there was a practical application worth thinking about. Solid materials, especially ones of low temperature, would have some advantages.
>
> I got the new idea of applying low and negative temperature together in order to stimulate the emission. People in molecular and atomic physics, [William] Giauque and the low temperature people, never liked negative temperature. It is, of course, just the opposite of low [because] you have to go to infinity; it's hotter than hot. [Note: The thermodynamic temperature starts off positive, and approaches positive infinity as maximum entropy or

energy disorder is produced. Then, as a quantum phenomenon, it becomes negative infinite, coming down in magnitude toward zero, but always negative as the energy increases toward the maximum.] Using negative together with low, I developed the three level pumping scheme for the maser, the first solid-state maser.

With his intent to create this form of the maser, Bloembergen used electron-spin resonance consisting of the motion of charged particles that spin around their axes to act like a tiny bar magnet. Unlike Charles Townes's idea of using positive and negative temperature simultaneously, Bloembergen deviated from then-prevalent "Giauque" premises regarding low temperature and conceived the different janusian process formulation of simultaneous use of the opposites of low and negative temperature. These were derived in the solid state from electron motion in a field of magnetized atoms or molecules producing continuous energy.

In chemistry, a broad and effective approach to organic chemical construction and synthesis was created by an American Nobel laureate of Lebanese background, Elias James Corey. A medium height, slightly balding man, Corey, wearing large spectacles, had a wise-owl look that conveyed great interest and curiosity. He was a very well-organized person and managed to follow active interests in Asian art, classical music, outdoor activities, and an intense devotion to teaching organic chemistry to graduate students. He was tireless in his work, saying he enjoyed dealing with complexity and problem solving, "sitting at a desk or at a beach," he said, "somewhere with a complicated problem and just thinking about the problem." At one point, he confessed to me that he even spent 2 to 3 hours away from his family in the afternoon on Christmas Day to do some work alone in his home office.

His major contribution was his technique of retrosynthetic analysis, a strategy for reproducing naturally occurring chemicals as well as previously undiscovered functional types. A few chemists had previously used aspects of this approach, but no one had formulated the constructs of his fully developed creation. His pioneering conception consisted of both detailed disassembling and synthesizing of a target organic molecule, specified as enantioselective (*enantio-* = opposed) synthesis. "You simplify the typology," he said, "by disconnecting the structure, that's the reverse of synthetic, so I knew I was doing things reversed synthetic." He conceived simultaneously opposite procedures of taking apart and putting together molecular sequences—the use of a janusian process construction. As a highly effective derived operation, the procedure has been applied with numerous molecule-synthesizing techniques and methods. He and his colleagues have achieved the successful laboratory synthesis of more than 100 natural products including the molecules of the medically important prostaglandins (the class of biologically active leukotriene fatty acids) and gingko (the Chinese medicinal). Retrosynthetic analysis is now widely used by chemists throughout the world for chemical reproduction and generation.

In the field of chemical dynamics, another type of use of a creative janusian process was indicated in an influential discovery by American chemist Dudley Herschbach. Fringe-haired, thin-lipped, and grinning slightly, he looked more like a simple shopkeeper than a man who was both a Nobel laureate and an exceptionally good former football player. He had the unusual background for a chemistry laureate of having won, at a San Jose High School, both academic and football scholarships to Stanford. Then, after playing and studying at Stanford, he was invited to try out for the Los Angeles Rams professional football team, but decided instead to pursue scientific training, where he carried out extensive research in experimental chemical kinetics. Deceptively brusque when the interview started, he became softly eloquent and enthusiastic when speaking directly about his investigative work. He incisively explained complex mathematical factors and I recognized he was accustomed to providing clear explications and guidance to students and other inquisitors. He was very much a professorial presence.

His successful research on the dynamics of chemical elementary processes had included the development of a particular "crossed molecular beam technique" as well as the production of fundamental data with importance for research on combustion. His work also provided knowledge about the troposphere, the lowest region of the atmosphere, and the chemical stratosphere. As stated at the Nobel Prize ceremony by Professor Sture Forsén, Herschbach helped paint a detailed picture of actions and events regarding molecules and atoms in chemical reactions, including properties such as chemical composition, angular distribution from a place of collision, speed, and rotational and vibrational energies.

His approach to molecular chemical reactions involved the mathematic algorithm called dimensional or multidimensional scaling, a system of analytic techniques that display the structure of distantly related data as a geometric picture. Here he indicates his use in this work of the creative janusian process formulation, simultaneous operation of a minimum and maximum in a range of nuclear charge:

> I conceived of a surface where there was a deep minimum dimension and then another surface where that minimum had become a maximum. Then the two opposite surfaces operated together. Recognizing the nature of this relationship made it possible to formulate a treatment that allowed a much more comprehensive discussion across the full range of nuclear charge, from very large to very small. So I could unify the description of the electronic structure of all of these atoms and show that in fact the influence of this region where you had this dramatic switch from one kind of character topology, if you like, to another in this thing that I've been referring to as a

minimum going to a maximum and operating together. This had very far reaching influence on the behavior of things far away.

He applied the janusian formulation of the simultaneous operation and function of the opposites of maxima and minima to processes of change as well as to other factors involving nuclear charges. Significantly, the change in the nuclear charge of an element produces a different element.

Short, broad-shouldered, and energetic, with heavy black eyebrows, thinning hair, and a smooth well-molded face, American biochemist Arthur Kornberg, was, he put forth, a devotee of tennis, travel, music, and time with his family. He stated early that his son, Roger, was a very able, even great chemist. Some years later, Roger Kornberg did become a rare filial Nobel laureate in Chemistry.

Kornberg himself was the first to synthesize what has been called "the 20th-century chemical," DNA. Alternately affable or unashamedly aggressive, he spoke freely about the need to compete with other scientists. With regard to my exploration, he was one of the participants in the combined interview and word association experiment (see Experimental Evidence section later) I carried out. With respect to that experiment, although he frequently referred in the discussion portion of our session to opposites and contrasts in biochemistry investigation, he said later he was especially surprised that, on the word association test procedure, he found he had a tendency always to give opposites as the first word that came to mind. Overall, he was quite forthcoming and helpful, but at one point he stated he was a little diffident about psychological approaches to creativity and offered to have me do blood and urine chemistries on him. I informed him, however, that such physical assessments done with respect to creativity had, at that point, been uninterpretable and unsuccessful.

With regard to his discovery of DNA synthesis, he was very specific and clear about the mental events. "It was apparent," he said, describing many trials and failures, "that we couldn't make this DNA unless we had all the building blocks that DNA required. You just couldn't make it out of one building block. Then, all at once, I thought of adding preexisting DNA to serve as [an enzyme] primer for growth of a DNA chain. And it worked." The idea that an enzyme or protein catalyst (DNA polymerase), always thought by scientists at that point to be absolutely dependent on a substrate (underlying substance), could also be acting as a template for instruction was unprecedented. His decision was, nevertheless, based on the conception of an enzyme operating on the substrate and the substrate simultaneously operating on the enzyme, both determining the synthesis of DNA. The preexisting DNA therefore served simultaneously opposite functions, both affecting the enzyme catalyst and being affected by it. This janusian process formulation was his necessary creative step to the DNA synthesis.

an important messenger chemical in the brain. He has in addition carried out supramolecular investigations of chemical self-recognition, an organizing chemical's identification of its correct and conforming aspects and parts, and the corollary principles of molecular self-assembly. His work has opened new fields of chemical exploration, which have in turn contributed to the development of important new therapeutic drugs.

Describing his first formulation of the idea of cryptands within the molecular crypt, he said his goal was to "transform an inorganic ion, something which is water soluble, into a big ball which is organic outside [non–water soluble]. If one tries to build these objects—receptors which are supposed to recognize a substrate—you must bring together at the same time, the convex and the concave, because the concave is the negative to the convex image. Those are distinct opposites." To build the supermolecules, therefore, he had proceeded with the janusian process operation of simultaneously bringing together these opposites of the concave and the convex.

A more extensive janusian process led him to another creative discovery. He called this "the instructed mixture paradigm." It began with his diverging investigations of the binding properties and self-recognition of chemical substrates; at that time these were not the factors usually studied. He learned, he said, that there were complex but orderly principles. One could, for example, generate self-assembly of a structure resembling a double helix from two equivalents of a particular chemical molecular strand and specific metal ions. Another modification would produce a triple helix where three strands wrapped around. As he elaborated,

> This led to the idea that one can do molecular programming. With this information, one can build one's molecules so that they contain a program which, when it's in the right condition, necessarily gives the double strand. With other types of molecules, a little bit more defined, one can allow for the formation of a triple strand. I refer here to something chemists usually don't do. And this mixing generated well-defined objects, those one could expect. That led to a change in paradigm.
>
> Chemists have always been looking, and rightly so, to get pure substances. It's an insult to a chemist to tell him his substance is impure. But here the idea was intentionally to mix substances and use an "impure" system, but to inform it. In other words, the change in paradigm is from the search for pure substances to the search for mixtures of informed or instructed substances. This is the "Instructed Mixture Paradigm." In the future, we still will, of course, have to make clean "pure" molecules to know what we do, but we will look for complex systems. These substances will contain all the programming needed to generate the final thing. It's not really making connections, but turning around the way you look at things—both multiple/diverse and simple/unique. It was exactly the opposite....

What we planned was the self-recognition, the sorting out of a "correct" partner from a mixture. The added thing was this change in concept to the realization that this property was obviously self-recognition but it required "instruction." It was also a change of the entire way of looking at things.

Yet another instance of the use of the janusian process by Lehn was his creation of so-called double-headed molecules he named *Janus molecules.* In an independently conceived construction from his physicist country-man de Gennes, who used the term *Janus* for oil and water pairs (Lehn was also unaware of my general janusian findings), he produced Janus molecules with hydrogen bonding sites on both sides. The units, in addition to being double-faced heterocycles (compounds containing a closed ring of atoms, at least one of which is not a carbon atom), were complementaries—that is, they had simultaneously opposite faces. They are now used in molecular self-recognition and colloid research.

Clearly, janusian formulations, labeled or unlabeled, entered frequently into Lehn's creative work. At the end of our sessions, he confirmed his intentional use of the process with a general observation, "It's often my position to say, 'Let's try what I have accepted all the time. Then, let's sort it out and turn things around totally, knowing that, of course, what has been taught is still correct.'"

Experimental Evidence

Twelve of the science Nobel laureate subjects participated in a word association experiment at the time each was interviewed: Luis W. Alvarez, David Baltimore, Owen Chamberlain, Allan M. Cormack, Max Delbrück, Donald Glaser, Arthur Kornberg, Joshua Lederberg, Edwin McMillan, Edward M. Purcell, Glenn T. Seaborg, and Emilio Segrè.

Experimental instructions were to give the first word that came to mind in response to a standardized (Kent-Rosanoff Word Association Test[7]) using 99 of the word stimuli. This psychological test, originally developed by C. J. Jung, has been standardized for identifying psychological complexes and also for measurement of "paradigmatic" or conceptual and "syntagmatic" or linguistic dispositions in thinking. Opposites are a specific type of paradigmatic response, and protocols for opposite responding on the Kent-Rosanoff Word Association Test have been independently determined empirically.[8]

Both speed and content of word responses were electronically recorded. Control groups consisted of both Yale College students independently rated as high or low creative and matched high-IQ psychiatric patients. Results indicated, for the most creative subjects (first the Nobel laureates and next the high-creative students), a statistically significant incidence of extremely rapid, virtually simultaneous, opposite responses in comparison with the low-creative and high-IQ psychiatric patient groups. Any tendencies toward giving primarily popular responses were factored out in all groups. Nobel laureates gave a mean of 0.5980 opposites, high-creative students a mean of 0.5035, low-creative students a mean of 0.4059, and high-IQ patients a mean of 0.3775, all statistically significant differences. The significantly more rapid opposite responses given by the Nobel laureate and high-creative groups averaged 1.1 to 1.2 seconds. Although primarily relevant to associational (not directed) thinking, the tendency to very rapid opposite formation supports the proposition of the potentiality and disposition of creative subjects to make janusian process constructions.[9]

Homospatial Process in Creative Discovery

The homospatial process—actively conceiving two or more discrete entities occupying the same mental space or spatial location, a conception that leads to the articulation or production of new identities—was a frequent and necessary factor in creative discoveries of the science Nobel laureates. A concrete representation of the mental image consists of superimposition or interposition of the constituent discrete entities. Although any of the sensory modalities may be involved, and the possible incorporation of each was checked in the interviews, all of the following instances of the homospatial process in creative work involved only visual or spatial mental superimpositions and interpositions. Frequent use of spatial and visual imagery and thinking in various ways not connected with the homospatial process was reported to me by seven Nobel subjects (20%): Corey, Giaever, Glashow, Herschbach, Benacerraf, Delbrück, and Townes (comparison control group = 81%). A few spoke of employing three-dimensional spatial formations at times, and two stated that they needed to draw images on paper in order to use them. Though only one chemist was in this non-homospatial visual and spatial group, several other scientific subjects expressed the opinion that visual thinking was very likely generally important for work in chemistry. Although use of discrete entities, usually mental imagery, is necessary for the homospatial process conception, application of visual thinking or imagery alone without superimposition or interposition, as stated earlier, has not been shown to lead to creative results. The accompanying chart (Table 10.1) indicates the Nobel laureate subjects' uses of the homospatial process. For each subject, the second and third columns designate the discrete entities, the fourth the contents of the mental homospatial process conception, and the fifth the resulting specific and general creative discoveries.

American Donald Glaser, a physicist who became a molecular biologist later in his career, resembled a highly competent and well-organized business executive. He was smiling and genial and impeccably well-dressed. He soon became quite brisk, with a careful and open explanation of the course

TABLE 10.1 Homospatial Process

Nobel Laureate	Discrete Entity	Discrete Entity	Homospatial Conception	Discovery
Donald Glaser	Bathtub	Self, taking pictures	Superimposed in orbit—superheating	Bubble chamber
Joshua Lederberg	Self	Bacterial cell	Superimposed self and cell	Bacterial conjugation
Owen Chamberlain	Velocity-determining counter	Threshold determining counter	Superimposed—reduced material	"Pickle barrel" or "secret weapon" particle counter for detecting the antiproton
Walter Gilbert	Roll of soiled toilet paper	DNA molecule	Continuous replication	Rolling Circle Model of Genetic Replication
Glenn Seaborg	Uranium	Rare earths	Subshell characteristics	Actinide concept of heavy elements
Luis Alvarez	Large meteor fragments	Volcano eruption	Coal-smoke cloud of darkness	Dinosaur extinction
Dudley Herschbach	Energy transfer	Non–energy transfer	Wave node	Bond breaking and making
Robert Huber	Symmetrical protein crystal	Unsymmetrical protein crystal	Protein crystal structure in photosynthesis	Photosynthesis reaction center
Pierre-Gilles de Gennes	Snake	Noodle	Movement of clusters in a cell	Reptation
Joseph Murray	Grand piano	Old upright piano	Transfer location	Kidney transplant
Jean-Marie Lehn	Individual shapes or forms	Other individual shapes or forms	Superstructure	Chemical self-representation
William Lipscomb	Hydrogen atom Diborane	Three-center bond Boron hydride	Chemical bondings Filled levels with energy gap	Borane structure Stabilty
Norman Ramsey	Atoms in a box	Atoms in a tube	Atoms in a bottle	Hydrogen maser

ot his inventing the bubble chamber for detecting particles emerging from high-energy acceleration experiments.

A popular story among students and scientists at the time Glaser won the Nobel Prize in Physics was that he had gotten the idea for the bubble chamber from watching bubbles rise in a large glass of beer. Confessing surprise at how widely that story had been spread, Glaser wryly set the record straight. He explained that after his discovery he did demonstrate, at a local university bar hangout, to some graduate students and faculty colleagues how his bubble chamber worked by showing them the rising bubbles in a glass of beer—but it wasn't how he got the idea. He added that after, not before, he developed the idea of using a supersaturated liquid in the bubble chamber to produce bubbles, he had briefly tested bubble production in beer as well as other fluids.

The actual sequence of thoughts and events leading to the creation was the following: Reasoning from the model of the Wilson cloud chamber, which used streaks in supercooled and clouded gas to detect ionizing radiation such as electrons and alpha particles, he decided he needed a detector of instability in a denser medium such as a liquid or a solid. "Liquids and solids," he said, "have about a thousand times the density that gases do, so you had a thousand times better chance of seeing what you want."

Detailing his key thought leading to the bubble chamber, he said:

I was interested in what are the elementary particles that make up the universe. And what would be the ideal situation in which to see that? You go to the cosmic rays. Somehow outside above the atmosphere but, in an orbit, there would be a tubful of hydrogen. I thought of that bathtub full of liquid hydrogen in orbit and myself over it in the same orbit with a candid camera taking pictures as things happen in it. That was actually before Sputnik.

How do you know whether to take each picture? It's all very fast and there are too many of them, so pretty soon it becomes a computer with a television camera that looks at the picture, keeps a dossier on several million of them. With respect to the tubful of hydrogen, I decided on super-heating rather than supercooling because of being in orbit with the cosmic rays; I wanted to be able to keep up with a modern accelerator which gives a burst of particles every five seconds.

Glaser's description of his development of the bubble chamber illustrates his motivation to create, his focus first on observation and the cosmic rays and a resulting vivid homospatial conception of himself as a cameraman tracer and an orbiting tubful of hydrogen superimposed. This produced mental interaction of the elements and mutual modifications of each. In his mind, the imaged camera was changed to a computer with a television camera, and the liquid hydrogen became superheated because of the effect in orbit of cosmic rays. The entities conceived in the same mental spatial location led to the articulation of the new identity—the bubble chamber.

In the bubble chamber, particles produce an ionization track of charged particles—particles with electron loss or gain—in a superheated liquid. Microscopic bubbles are formed that can be seen or photographed. This creation, which enabled the accurate tracing and identification of subatomic particles, was important for the development of the field of nuclear physics. It also made possible the discovery of weak neutral currents supporting the influential electroweak theory—the particle theory that explains both the electromagnetic and the weak atomic nucleus forces. This led to the specific discovery and theory confirmation of the subatomic particles known as W and Z bosons.

Biologist Joshua Lederberg, who used a janusian formulation in the discovery of bacterial conjugation, later applied a creative homospatial process conception for further findings of mechanisms in the conjugation phenomenon. He conceived of himself superimposed upon a bacterium. "If," he said, "I am thinking about what's going on in bacterial conjugation, I'll think of myself as being a bacterium and of what and how I am going to sense other organisms, and what is it that is going to be a signal to me to start unrolling DNA and send it through and so forth. There is a good deal of imagery involved."

He frequently used homospatial conceptions in his later enzyme work, too. "It is," he said, "a well-tooled procedure, essentially quite self-conscious. I imagine myself as an atom in the molecule I'm thinking about and I try to visualize all of the environmental circumstances that would be impinging on me, what could happen to me if I were living there, and what therefore could an atom in that molecule know about the outside world."

American physicist Owen Chamberlain, tall and soft spoken with a thin, angular face, comfortably enjoyed continually smoking his pipe. Together with Emilio Segrè, he had been awarded the Nobel Prize for the identification of the subatomic particle, the antiproton. This achievement confirmed, along with the prior detection of the positive electron by Anderson, the existence of the world of antiparticles. At the very beginning of our session, Chamberlain asserted that Segrè, not he, was the creative one of the two. "Some physicists are great idea people," he said. "Segrè is one. He is all the time making suggestions: would it be worthwhile to do this? Or is that connected with something else? And so forth."

Nevertheless, while Segrè undoubtedly made very important contributions to the antiproton project (see collaboration account in chapter 13), Chamberlain was the creator of the actual counter mechanism providing for the identification of the particle. Necessary for the production of presumed antiprotons was a giant particle accelerator named the Bevatron located at the University of California, Berkeley. Inside the Bevatron, particles were accelerated and mass and charge were measured by the Chamberlain counter. The measurement served to achieve the first recognition of the antiproton and its nature.

Deviating slightly from his previous, somewhat adulatory description of Segrè, Chamberlain stated:

> There was an occasion in which Segrè came back from the East Coast describing a new velocity selecting counter made by Samuel Lindenbaum. But he got some of the details wrong, so his description didn't make much sense later on. His drawing of the apparatus, however, was very close to the correct one so that I could rework what he said and come up with what I thought was the original counter. I then took the design of another threshold determining apparatus and mentally superimposed it on this original one.

He conceived of particles continually going through the mingled images:

> I made a design from this which had as little apparatus material in the way of the particles as possible, only thin things in the way of the beam. I conceived of the particles going quickly down through our vacuated tubes and through a magnet bending their trajectories. This turned out later to be very important to the success of the experiment; antiprotons had been eaten up much faster as they went through heavy materials. Mine was a new counter and it served our purpose very well. The fellow that designed the threshold counter had trouble with it because he put too much material in the way of the beams.

On the basis of a homospatial process conception, the mental image of a reworked Lindenbaum velocity apparatus superimposed on a threshold determining one, he developed a new and effective counter that led to the identification of the antiproton particle. The counter was later dubbed the "pickle barrel" or "secret weapon" by his scientist colleagues. It especially allowed for the passing of antiprotons through thin and therefore nondestructive materials.

The antiproton has a -1 electric charge, opposite to the $+1$ charge of the proton; all other properties match those of the proton. It is now known to be composed of two of the elementary particles called up antiquark and down antiquark. The meeting of a proton and antiproton results in elimination; important questions that are still unanswered today include what role the types of antimatter played in the presumed Big Bang origin of the universe, and why so little antimatter currently exists in our solar system. Also, antiprotons are used in collision experiments in the very large particle accelerator Tevatron at the Fermilab, and they have been shown in laboratory experiments to have the potential to treat certain cancers.

Chamberlain's account demonstrates four phases of the homospatial process: the motivation to create a counter (the first phase), deviation from the accepted selecting counter of Lindenbaum (the second phase), and choice and superimposition of discrete images (the third phase), and the construction of the new identity, the "pickle barrel particle counter" (fourth phase).

Another finding of the use of the homospatial process comes from the creative achievements of Walter Gilbert, the physicist turned biochemist whose work on exons and introns and the RNA world hypothesis I described in chapter 9. Gilbert was also motivated to create in another application, where he deviated from an accepted construct. He set out to create a new replication model for DNA.

Gilbert's Nobel Prize–winning determinations of base sequences in the nucleic acids DNA and RNA involved constructions of both theory and methods. As one aspect, he developed a model for the determination of the exact sequence of DNA building blocks as well as the bacterial chromosome transcription of the genetic message of the cell. Here is his description of the homospatial process conception leading to what he called the "Rolling Circle Model of Genetic Replication":

> One idea that had a period of development, the "Rolling Circle Model" for replication of DNA, was the particular conception about how one might actually copy DNA. Since DNA occurs in circles, the general notion was just to copy around and around and around. It seemed, however, that only some organisms use that just to construct a circle and start in a place and copy DNA once around. There then was the curious emergence of sort of an idea that came gradually, in a sense, that there was something there, some idea around me. "Only have the patience," I told myself, "it's almost there." There was a certain amount of exponential input from the way experiments with circular viruses containing DNA were going, but they didn't actually suggest a conception of continuous replicating around the circle. I remember the actual idea as emerging—a toilet paper roll model, in which there was stripping off sheets of this long roll, and each sheet was then going to hold up pieces [fecal matter] which were superimposed on a little of the virus itself. It was a very exciting time. It provided an explanation for continuous DNA replications and an explanation for what were otherwise very obscure sorts of experimental results that didn't make any sense.

Gilbert's frank description of the elements in this homely but meaningful creative idea involved a homospatial process conception. In a third-phase choosing of discrete entities and superimposition, fecal matter and virus were conceived within the same space. The soilages on a roll of toilet paper radiated out together with images of pieces of viruses in the DNA replication cycle. Interaction of the images led to articulation of the new identity, continuous replication of DNA in the Rolling Circle Model. This model provides for and explains the synthesis of multiple copies of circularly structured molecules of DNA. In an operation involving phages, a protein—the enzyme DNA polymerase or another derived DNA-acting enzyme, helicase—first nicks one strand of either of these molecules as a primer, and replication proceeds in continuous circular fashion around the molecule to complete the synthesis.

American physicist Glenn Seaborg, the son of immigrant Swedish parents, had a flat-toned, deep voice, a heavily rounded face, and large shoulders. He deceptively resembled a lumberman or a boxer rather than the intellectually powerful investigator and leader he was. He had been chancellor of the University of California and head of the Atomic Energy Commission, and had participated in the discovery of what ultimately became a key nuclear energy element, plutonium. His creative development of the actinide concept of heavy-element electron structure allowed for discovery of the elements americium and curium, and by extension, identification of an additional 24 heavy elements as well as a number of isotopes. Element 106 was named seaborgium in his honor.

In the 19th century, Swedish scientists had discovered 14 different but closely associated chemical elements named *rare earths* or *lanthanides*.[1] The Royal Swedish Academy of Sciences, which awards Nobel Prizes in Chemistry, expressed acknowledgment with gratitude that Seaborg, a scion of Swedish parents, had followed these scientists up with his own notable element discoveries, his work on plutonium, and his contributions to identifying the structure of numerous heavy elements. Before him, other scientists, especially Niels Bohr, had thought that any kinds of newly found elements would be arrayed in a closely associated series with well-known elements; the accepted idea was that new elements discovered would be related to uranium, in what Edwin McMillan called an "uranide series." That hypothesis, however, did not yield any results and Seaborg instead developed his productive actinide concept. He described that achievement as follows:

> The biggest idea I had came all of a sudden. I'd been thinking for a couple of years about how to correlate all these transuranium elements into the periodic table. Then, one morning in my office, I mentally put all of a sudden images of the rare earths and their characteristics on top of uranium, neptunium, and plutonium and thought, "Oh God, it's got to be this way." The next two elements would not be either the same or sort of like half rare earths but you go a little further up. Because of newly formed shapes [the filling of an atomic subshell] the series would start right after actinium [number 89] with thorium, and the elements would be homologs of [rare earths] europium and gadolinium. Then I just called in my secretary and dictated the paper that first put it all together that way.

Seaborg's solution involved the formulation of an element series containing the newly discovered uranium, neptunium, and plutonium, and a reorganization of the periodic table of elements. He described his motivation to create (a deviation) and his focus on the transuranium elements and the rare earths. His homospatial process conception consisted of mentally putting images of the structures of the already known rare earths "on top of" or superimposed on structures of the new heavy elements. Mental interactions between superimposed mutual atomic subshell structures within this homospatial conception led to his determination of new structural identities and places further up on the periodic table where the series of heavy elements would begin. His resultant actinide concept of heavy elements stipulated that actinium (element number 89), was the basis of a new series, and that the characteristics of the to-be-discovered new elements would not be comparable to the superficially similar rare earth cesium (58), but to the rare earths europium (63) and gadolinium (64). He later extended the concept to a transactinide and superactinide series, all of which eventually led to later investigators' identification and discovery of an additional 24 elements. Many of these additional elements are used in operations ranging from medical imaging to powering spacecraft. After describing the process of constructing his theory, Seaborg added, "I was warned at the time I propounded it that it was professional suicide to promote this actinide idea. I luckily stuck to my guns and it has now been called one of the most significant changes in the periodic table since Mendeleev's 19th-century design."

Stocky Luis Walter Alvarez, bespectacled and gray-haired with a genial but sharp-eyed look, was very enthusiastic about the topic of scientific creativity. He spoke of being very pleased to be interviewed and tested (in addition to the word association test I administered, he had previously been given psychological tests by Anne Roe[2]) because, as he said, "I've read a lot of junk by people who apparently never met anybody who was creative and who wrote down what they thought a creative person should be like." He was very proud to be diversely creative, having worked on nuclear physics and radar, participated in the Manhattan Project on the atomic bomb, and helped to develop a large hydrogen bubble chamber for the determination of a number of resonance states. For this last achievement he was awarded the Nobel Prize in Physics. He later developed important theories of dinosaur extinction, determined the structure of Egyptian pyramids by the use of cosmic ray photography, and traced forensic factors involved in the assassination of President John F. Kennedy. Described by some of his colleagues as a "wild idea man," his work has generally been successful and his theories accepted. His explorations have also extended to his recreational time as he spent many adventurous hours in his airplane as a licensed aviator.

His father, Dr. Walter Alvarez, was a widely known physician who wrote a useful and homely newspaper column about medical problems. During the same period, Dr. Alvarez worked late in the mornings in his own physiology of gastroenterology laboratory, and then became employed, for a period during the Second World War, in full-time research at the Mayo Clinic. This background had an influence on Luis's own interest in science. Not until he took physics in college, however, did he become really curious about the way things worked in the real world; at that point, he "started calculating things in my head like centrifugal force when doing a giant swing on the horizontal bar."

For his work on the hydrogen bubble chamber and the identification of resonance states (usually short-lived subatomic particles), he had served as administrator to a large staff using the Bevatron particle accelerator at the University of California, Berkeley. Of his many discoveries and accomplishments, however, Alvarez spoke most enthusiastically and in detail about his now famous dinosaur-extinction theory. He had gotten involved in the project when his geologist son, also named Walter Alvarez, found during excavations in a gorge near Gubbio, Italy, a narrow but extensive layer of clay bounded by different colors of limestone. This layer was, according to Walter's calculations, laid down underwater at the end of the Cretaceous period of geological history, during which the dinosaurs of the world were known to have become extinct.

Luis became interested in the layering and collaborated with his son to determine their rates of sedimentation (settling of matter). Together with nuclear chemists Frank Asaro and Helen Michel, Luis determined that the extensive layer was primarily composed of the element iridium, a metal related to platinum. Soon, a similar layer was found near Denmark. From that point on, they all attempted to find an explanation for the laying down of the extensive iridium layer that might connect it with the dinosaur extinction. Luis considered possibilities such as radiation from a supernova, an iridium-containing comet from Jupiter passing over the earth's atmosphere and spreading enough hydrogen to do away with all oxygen, and other variations of these phenomena. His key idea, the one that became what is today accepted as the most valid cause, was derived from a homospatial process conception. He mentally superimposed an image of a comet entering and breaking up in the earth's atmosphere upon an image of the well-known 19th-century eruption of the volcano on the South Seas island of Krakatoa. As he described it:

> [An iridium bearing] comet or asteroid passed through a fairly long segment of the atmosphere and fragmented into bits. Superimposed on these fragments at the top of the atmosphere, was an image of lava and rock coming up from the volcano. From this, I vaguely visualized the spreading of a floating layer of dust then industrial smoke like coal smoke. The coal smoke was thick and although I knew it would cover a very small number of milligrams per square centimeter of the earth's surface, in my mind I could hardly see the sun through it. What emerged was an image of spreading darkness where there would be just too much absorption of the light by fragmented asteroid and rock bits. The floating fragment layer would, I considered, stay at the top of the atmosphere for a long time. So my idea was that it was going to chop out all of the visible light from hitting the surface of the earth and that had the very important consequence that photosynthesis would stop instantly.

Iridium is not ordinarily found in the earth's crust, so his postulated break-down of an iridium-bearing comet and the eventual settling would account for the iridium in the clay. The layers above and below the iridium layer, Alvarez speculated, were produced by the extinction of limestone-producing underwater protozoan-like "worms" called foraminifera. After making his coal smoke formulation, Alvarez used a book his father gave him regarding the effects of the catastrophic eruption of the Krakatoa volcano. He found that 18 cubic kilometers of material were blown up from the island and that 4 of them actually ended up in the stratosphere and remained there for a period of 2 to 2½ years, blotting out light for long distances. He calculated that a collision with the earth of an asteroid of the Apollo class (large asteroids with earth-crossing orbits), therefore, would produce ascendant light-blotting particles throughout the earth's atmosphere for several years, enough to interrupt all photosynthesis and subsequent plant growth. This would deprive first the foraminifera worms, then the herbivorous dinosaurs, of food. Spreading fires from the collision and the destruction of other animals, trees, and large plants would also kill off the carnivores.

The theory, proposed together with his son Walter, at first provoked a good deal of controversy among geologists. However, the 1991 discovery of an immense crater near the Yucatán Peninsula in Mexico measuring 180 kilometers in circumference, a size predicted by the theory, has now been accepted as evidence for their formulation of the mechanism of dinosaur extinction.

In taking the critical step regarding the blocking out of photosynthesis by an asteroid collision with the earth, Luis Alvarez had, early in the homospatial process, deviated from such theories of dinosaur extinction as climate change and creature competition. In a key formulation, he superimposed mentally constructed images of the Krakatoa eruption and fragments of a disintegrating asteroid. This led to the conception of the blotting out of light needed for photosynthesis, and then the fully developed creative theory of an asteroid collision with the earth causing massive particle debris at the top of the atmosphere, the subsequent blocking of sunlight, and the cessation of photosynthesis. Plant and large animal life, including the non-avian dinosaurs, was extinguished and only small underground animals and roots survived.

Dudley Herschbach, Nobel laureate for his findings about the dynamics of chemical elementary processes, was studying the making and breaking of chemical bonds when he noticed that a family of reactions in which one or more electrons transferred were similar in distribution, angle, and velocity of products to reactions in which electrons were not transferred. In the course of trying to understand the discrepancy, he brought the two types of reactions into the same mentally conceptualized space as follows:

> I had a sense that I was trying to organize an electron transfer reaction
> like arranged blocks or something and then a chute opens and another

load of blocks of nontransfer reaction comes down before I've got the first one arranged. It knocks those around and then I start reorganizing again. The images were abstract and interposed and from the way the transfer and nontransfer blocks moved I got the idea that the key thing for both was the placement of a lump or node which kept them apart or sometimes connected them. This led me to the idea that the placement of a [quantum] node in a wave function produced the attractions and repulsions. I recognized that, in the case of ions, when electrons transferred, you got a positive ion [an atom minus an electron] reacting with a negative ion [an atom plus an electron], and a node was introduced that led to the strong repulsion. And, depending on the position of the node in the very different situation with no electron transfer, there was also a way you could have strong repulsion, so I felt sure that the node and its interactions must be the key thing.

The interpretation was very lovely as well as exciting, and I knew it had to be right even before we did any further work. So I could go right ahead and design an experiment that would test that. I was totally sure how it would come out, and it did come out. I was excited because I realized this kind of situation actually appeared in a great many situations where you're breaking one bond and making another one.

Herschbach constructed a key formulation of node behavior from a homospatial process conception of an energy transfer reaction and non–energy transfer reaction superimposed. The resulting chemical reaction explanation has been especially applied to the so-called noble gases—helium, neon, argon, krypton, xenon, and radon—which form no bonds with each other. Diverse uses of these gases have thereby been facilitated in particular areas such as nuclear magnetic resonance imaging, aerial blimps and balloons, lighting, lasers, and anesthesia.

German Nobel laureate in chemistry Robert Huber looked, with his open shirt, smooth, unlined face, and loosely combed hair, boyishly younger than his middle-aged years. Born in Munich, he took regular advantage of the nearby mountains and was a lifelong avid skier. Regarding his molecular crystallographic work, he spoke enthusiastically and at great length. Crystallography is a method of passing a beam, usually an X-ray beam, through a constructed or natural crystal; molecular crystallography is used to determine the arrangement of atoms in a solid substance. As a very young man, Huber had not been sure of working in chemistry, or any aspect of it, rather than in some other scientific field. His decision to take up crystallography came after he, as a science diploma student, discovered an important error committed in the research literature by two famous scientists (one a Nobel laureate). This error concerned the molecular weight of an insect-molting hormone, ecdysone, that Huber had been working on. "It was," he said, "a relatively large organic molecule and my excitement about the discovery was because I had found out it was related to the mammalian sex hormones; their incorrect molecular weight had instead pointed the famous scientist to a very different molecular class. I was excited that I, a diploma student, had discovered a miserable mistake made by such important scientists."

From then on, he spent his career in molecular crystallography and he, together with Hartmut Michel, Johann Deisenhofer, Opp Epp, and Kunio Miki, discovered, through the study of the protein of purple bacteria, the three-dimensional structure of the photosynthetic reaction center.[3] This led to an understanding of the functional photosynthesis reactions—the conversion of carbon dioxide into organic compounds that is necessary for all aerobic life on Earth—in the transport of nutrients within cells, hormone actions, and nerve impulses. The discovery also gave theoretical chemists a tool to understand how biologic electron transfer occurring in as little as a trillionth of a second takes place in the reaction center.

In his own participation in the crystallization aspect of the research, Huber reported, he began with a mental conception of an unsymmetrical purple bacteria protein crystal superimposed upon a symmetrical one. Then, he decided to average the patterns of the two images and apply specific construction steps: "I put a protein crystal with regular shapes, clear faces, sharp edges and color, under polarized light. It was very beautiful and a great joy. There was symmetry, not only within the crystal but also within the molecular structure. We got independent pictures of 60 variants containing symmetrical crystals superimposed on blurred unsymmetrical ones. We averaged the diffraction patterns and a true structure emerged. What was a complete blank box then suddenly was illuminated in bright light, and we were the people to see it for the first time."

With this ardent account, Huber indicated his application of an initial homospatial process conception of superimposed symmetrical and unsymmetrical crystals, then the resolute mathematical calculation of the interactions between the resulting diffraction patterns, and last the determination of the photosynthetic reaction center's structure. This center is a complex of proteins, pigments, and other cofactors producing the energy conversion of photosynthesis.

In the course of his groundbreaking work with polymers, physicist Pierre-Giles de Gennes, whom I previously described as a liquid-functions investigator, created the mathematical concept of "reptation" (snakelike motion) regarding the actions of very long polymer chains. This theoretical concept has been used to explain the sequential movement of clusters of subunits in a polymer chain. It also applies to the behavior of DNA within a polymer solution and genetic mapping, and contributes significant factors in plastic action and construction.

de Gennes described his formulation of reptation as a result of a homospatial process conception consisting of a snake and an elongated noodle moving in the same spatial location. The extended mental experience he described and the mental interaction between the two images, serpentine and culinary, occurred during an afternoon in clear consciousness. As he said:

> I conceived of snakes trapped in a tube and upon them superimposed images of noodles in broth. I thought of the broth boiling and bubbles which agitated the system. Then, the snake noodle assemblages threaded their way around. These little objects moved backwards and forwards just as well, and also they were agitated, not by the voluntary sort of snake motion, but by thermal agitation around them. The snake elements were required to move both headward and tailward, in very unsnakelike fashion, and they in fact had to commute back and forth because they had to choose exit gates when they moved.

The movements were due to the interaction of the imaged snake with an imaged noodle in boiling water. By translating these interactions and movements within the extended homospatial process conception of snakes and noodles in the same mentally conceived spatial location into mathematical terms, de Gennes created a widely useful model named the reptation model of polymer dynamics.

Joseph Murray, the American surgeon who received the Nobel Prize for his performance of the first successful type of organ transplantation, the kidney transplant, insisted that a number of collaborators played an important role in his accomplishment. In addition to other surgeons at the Peter Bent Brigham Hospital (now part of the Brigham amd Women's Hospital in Boston), the hematological and pharmaceutical developers of the immunosuppressant azathioprine had supplied crucial supporting factors for the successful operation (see chapter 13). Tall, white-haired, upright, and distinguished-looking despite his advancing years, Murray proposed early in the session the theory that creativity and disease were somehow connected. He cited especially the presumed motivational and facilitative effects of the illnesses of Keats, Renoir, and Klee as described in books on creativity he had read. He himself had suffered from serious diseases, including pericarditis, encephalitis, and a cerebral thrombosis, all of which he had successfully overcome to go on to outstanding achievements. As for the collaborative development of kidney transplantation, one of his own early creative contributions consisted of a critical determination about the placement of the transplanted kidney. As stated in the Nobel ceremony, Murray designed "a reproducible operation using intra-abdominal vascular anastomoses [communicating openings] and a ureterocystostomy [bladder connection] for urinary drainage by placing the kidney in the lower abdomen. This has become the universal renal transplant procedure since that time."

Early in his career, Murray had performed many skin graft operations on burn victims. When he turned to organ transplantation, he practiced first on dogs. In deciding where to place a kidney transplant, he told me,

> While I was out taking a walk I thought first of a grand piano, I guess because my wife is such a good musician and because the piano top is sort of kidney shaped. Well, I quickly visualized the grand piano with an accompanying stool overlaying an old upright in a room. I vaguely saw the grand piano legs and stool on top and sticking out over the sides of the old one and I also realized I couldn't set them both together near the door of the room because then I couldn't open the door. The old piano, an upright diseased kidney, could stay in the room and, I conceived, could still be used to tune up [provide immunity] the new one. The grand piano, with its jutting out stool or ureter and its circulating anastomoses legs needed to be put in a corner somewhere where it was protected and there was good accessibility. I figured I'd put the big piano with the ureter piano stool and the jutting-out leg anastomoses in the abdomen not too near the bladder and away from the diseased kidney where it could easily have a good blood supply and drainage. I could also leave the old diseased and interacting kidney piano in place.

His conception of an old and new piano superimposed and representing kidneys was a homospatial process conception of two discrete entities occupying the same space. This conception led him to articulate a procedure of placing the transplanted healthy kidney in the front bottom of the abdomen where he could provide it a good blood supply and drainage. The diseased kidney was to remain at first in place, where it still provided some immunological protection. Murray's success at kidney transplantation, supported by the work of the surgical, hematological, and pharmacological teams, opened up the entire field of organ transplantation, making it possible to transplant the pancreas, liver, heart, lungs, and others.

Jean-Marie Lehn, creator of supramolecular chemistry, described the use of a homospatial process of mentally visualizing two chemical structures with their properties interposed in his studies of self-recognition and self-organization of chemicals: "Two objects which have individual structure, when I put them together they have it again as a resulting superstructure, and this I visualize. The first representation of the superstructure is purely geometrical, just shapes, forms, but I ask myself to go a bit further to see what properties could result, and how do individual structures perturb each other, and then you can, on the basis of what you know, try to predict what's going to happen."

Kentucky-born chemist William Lipscomb—thin-faced, starkly white-haired, and wearing a looped string tie—looked like the classic "colonel,"

as he was affectionately called by his students and friends. He had also offi
cially received the same appellation from the Honorable Order of Kentucky
Colonels. A competent tennis player and professional clarinetist as well, he
spent a good deal of time describing and speaking proudly of the innovative work of his second wife, Jean Evans, a lettering artist. The Nobel Prize in
Chemistry was awarded to him for his extensive work on the structure of the
chemical family of spare boranes, with special applications to the nature of
chemical structural composition.

Borane compounds, which do not occur in nature, are composed of the
chemicals boron and hydrogen. They are electron deficient and do not bond
with covalent (electron-shared) pairs. Lipscomb had expertly used them
to illuminate factors and provide solutions regarding chemical bonding
that extended the pioneering chemical work of his mentor, Linus Pauling.
Describing the X-ray derived work on bonding, Lipscomb talked of his characteristic creative use of visual superimposition of elements in a chemically
detailed homospatial process: "I have images in my mind and I superimpose
molecules. I'm used to it; I don't remember if I learned it or whether it came
naturally." He elaborated the experience with a specific example: "I literally
took diborane [boron and hydrogen, B_2H_6] and superimposed it on a region
of one of the boron hydrides, and then there was that kind of reproducibility
which led me to the idea that the boron was really making tetrahedral [trian-
gular base and three sides] bonds. With that idea I was able to draw structures
for all the other boron hydrides, and with the molecular orbitals that showed
that these were stable, filled levels with an energy gap between the unoccu-
pied orbitals. This is the criteria for stability."

He described another particular instance regarding a hydrogen atom
and a three-center chemical bonding: "I put in a hydrogen bridge over the
three bonds and it would be diborane, but what I mean by superimposition
is that I move the hydrogen around and it interchanges with a vacancy. The
three-center bond then comes loose and twists around. I did all that in my
head and it became perfectly clear in the nuclear resonance study I published.
I had the right structure. Those things, they occur in the head."

Lipscomb's discoveries were widely applied to the understanding of the
nature of bonding and chemical structures. In particular, boron hydride
(boron and hydrogen combined) compounds have been studied as potential
fuels for rockets as well automotive functions.

Born in Washington, DC, Norman Ramsey had an unusual background
for a Nobel laureate scientist, being the son of a brigadier general in the US
Army Ordnance Corps. He was awarded the Nobel Prize for his creations of
the separated oscillatory field method and (with Daniel Kleppner) the atomic
hydrogen maser (as distinct from gas and solid-state masers). Both of these
creations were applied to atomic clock development. The clocks have provided
the precision required for the most advanced astronomical and subatomic

particle discoveries, and for assessments ranging from derivatives of relativity theory to space probe launches, the Global Positioning System (GPS), and the Internet.

Ramsey had sparse, graying hair and an elongated face with a strong chin, and he sat with a perfectly erect military-looking posture. The hydrogen maser he developed consists of a small storage bottle of molecular hydrogen (pairs of atoms bound together) that leaks a controlled amount of gas into a discharge bulb. This uses the intrinsic movement properties of the atom to measure frequency precisely. Ramsey described his creation of a key step in the following way:

> I thought I could put in an atomic beam from one end of an apparatus to another. First, I thought of putting the atoms in a box to circle around. But then I realized that if you had abrupt bumping of the atoms on a surface and bouncing off, the collision and frequency would be short. I thought then I should make a circular tube around the beam and have the atoms rattle down this pipe. Thinking of the trapped atom bouncing was an important factor but I wasn't satisfied about the speed. I remember that I put the pipe spatially together with the box of atoms in my mind and realized that the correct shape would be a bottle with a one-side neck opening because the beam then would not be confined in three directions and bounce excessively. The pipe tube interposed with the box gave me the bottle idea.

Ramsey used the homospatial process of conceiving the tube or pipe superimposed in the same space upon a box of bouncing atoms to create the important bottle structure of the hydrogen maser.

Sep-Con Articulation Process
in Creative Discovery

The integrating cognitive creative process, sep-con articulation, consists of actively conceiving and using separation and connection concomitantly. In this process, functionally separate entities retain their identities and functions while they are connected with each other. Table 11.1 lists each Nobel laureate's conceptions of functionally separate entities, designated as <sep'> and <sep>, in the second and third columns, and the concomitant connection <con> in the fourth column. The sep-con articulation constructed is shown in the fifth column and the resulting discovery in the sixth.

Norman Ramsey, creator of the hydrogen maser, was also the creator of the separated oscillatory field method, the basis of the first atomic or cesium beam clock. These atomic clocks are the most accurate time and frequency standards currently known. Narrating the steps in his creation of the separated oscillatory field, Ramsey said he had first worked on a magnetic beam-measuring apparatus while at Columbia University. When moving after the Second World War to Harvard University he devoted himself, he said forcefully, to making a better functioning one. By making it longer, he believed, it would be at least 10 times better. According to the Heisenberg uncertainty principle, the longer the time one spent making such a measurement, the narrower and better the measurement would be. At Columbia, however, he and his colleagues had tried to make a somewhat longer apparatus and, disappointingly, it came out worse. The reason for that, he concluded, was that the magnetic field was not sufficiently uniform. Trying to use a uniform field, however, had also not been working well.

"This was a worry; it sort of nagged me a lot of the time," Ramsey said. "I worried about falling flat on my face. And then actually the idea, the first idea that provided the way of overcoming this came while I was giving a classroom lecture in physics." Lecturing about optics, he was also thinking about the variable nature of optical and magnetic fields. Then, he said, "the first thing

TABLE 11.1 Sep-Con Articulation Process

Nobel Laureate	Functional Separate (Sep')	Functional Separate (Sep)	Connection (Con)	Sep-Con Articulation	Discovery
Norman Ramsey	Beginning bit	Ending bit	Oscillation	Separated oscillatory field method	Atomic precision spectroscopy/cesium clock/hydrogen maser
Georges J. F. Köhler	Antibody lymphocyte cell	Myeloma cell	Joining	Unitary cell	Monoclonal antibody
Max Delbrück	Physics / Bacterial host / Minimal error	Biology / Phage virus / Investigative factor	Phage study / Interaction / "Nailing down"	Phage genetic replication / Resistant bacterial variant / Principle of limited sloppiness	Molecular genetic biology / Genetic replication / Phage biology
Salvador Luria	Resistant bacteria	Nonresistant bacteria	Uniform agent	Genetic probability distribution	Lurian distribution
David Baltimore	Virus DNA	Tumor cell RNA	RNA polymerase	Messenger and genic replication	Reverse transcriptase
David Hubel	Stimulus	Visual cortex cells	Line of orientation	Orientation selectivity	Functional organization of the visual cortex
Werner Arber	Restriction	Modification	Enzyme	Restriction/modification	Hereditary mutation in bacteria
Allan Cormack	Inside measurements	Outside measurements	Connected images	Axial tomograph	CAT scan
Paul Berg	DNA molecule	Complementary DNA molecule	Sticky end	Connected DNA molecules	Recombinant DNA
Sheldon Glashow	Fourth quark	Up quark (also leptons)	Eliminating interactions	Charm quark	Electroweak theory
Ivar Giaever	Aluminum	Lead	Electron waves	Tunneling phenomenon and energy gaps	Solid-state tunneling
Jean-Marie Lehn	Inside molecule	Outside molecule	Surrounding cavity	Three-dimensional negative image	Supramolecular chemistry
Baruj Benacerraf	Peptide series	MHC complex	Ir genes	Genetic control	Genetic immunity
Christiane Nüsslein-Volhard	Segment	Even or odd segment	Pairings	Even and odd genetic pairings	Genetic contributions to early embryonic development

that came to my mind was, 'I want to do something that's two separated bits. One was one side and the other was the other side.'" After the lecture, he conceived that the method would involve an oscillating magnetic field that induced connecting transitions all the way throughout the region. "It would be a short, much stronger field at the beginning," he said, "and a short, much stronger field at the end—the separated oscillatory field method."

In a sep-con articulation process he had conceived that the distinct and functionally separated regions, the beginning and end, were concomitantly connected by an oscillatory magnetic field. The method, he realized, would have the great advantage that it could operate at very high frequency. If there were a long field region, there would be a limitation that the wavelength of the radiation could not be shorter than the total distance of the region, because then it would get out of phase.

In the unfolding sep-con articulation process, Ramsey, with a strong motivation to create, had shifted from the accepted idea of uniformity of the field to focus on the functionally separate "bits," which were the beginning and ending. His solution consisted of the concomitant connection through oscillations between the functionally separated and independent regions.

For the creative discovery of the immunity elements known as monoclonal antibodies, the 1984 Nobel Prize in Physiology or Medicine was awarded to Georges J. F. Köhler (together with César Milstein). Ordinary production of immune-reacting antibodies in the human body is stimulated by antigens— introduced foreign substances including viruses and bacteria. In the natural state, these antibodies are impure. Preparation and use of pure monoclonal antibodies (identical immune cells that are clones of a unique parent cell), which allow for identification in the body of specific foreign substances or antigens, has revolutionized the field of immunology. Not only can these antibodies be used therapeutically to protect against disease, but they can also help diagnose a wide variety of illnesses and detect the presence of par-ticular drugs, viral, and bacterial products, as well as other unusual or abnor-mal substances in the blood.

At the age of 38, Georges Köhler was, along with Joshua Lederberg, James Watson, and David Baltimore, one of the youngest scientists to be awarded the Nobel Prize. He developed the monoclonal antibody while working in César Milstein's laboratory, and the latter shared the Prize because of his mentorship and facilitation. But the initial idea was Köhler's own. During 1993, when I interviewed him, Köhler was 48 years old; he died from unde-termined causes two years later.[1] Born in Munich, Germany, he received his biology diploma and his doctorate at the University of Freiburg, went on to the Basel Institute for Immunology in Switzerland and then to a postdoctoral fellowship with Milstein's laboratory at Cambridge University, England. At the time of the interview, he was the Director of the Max Planck Institute of Immunobiology at Freiburg, Germany. A tall man with streaked blond and brown hair and a heavy, untrimmed, brownish-black beard, he was friendly and strikingly self-effacing. He asserted right away that creativity was not a special capacity in his own case but rather was a universal function. Nevertheless, he described an intense personal happiness when he got the idea that developed the monoclonal antibody.

At the Basel Institute, he had become interested in somatic mutations—mutations (gene change) occurring from a single-body gene rather than from developing germ (sexual reproduction) cells. He decided that the best way to pursue his interest was through a study of antibodies. At that point, however, antibody preparations from blood serum necessarily contained many kinds and could not be used to find specific antigens. When he moved to the Milstein laboratory, therefore, he attempted to develop antibodies with the necessary specificity for his somatic mutation exploration. First, he worked on mouse myeloma tumor cells having separate so-called heavy (long amino acid chains with several parts) and light (shorter ones with fewer parts) genetic chains. Connections between these chains did not suppress chromosomal gene co-expression or produce a single cell line.[2]

He continued to search for a method to make a specific cell line for his study of somatic mutations. One night, he was thinking about the problem in bed before going to sleep, as was his characteristic. All at once, he got the idea that he could use functionally separate normal antibody lymphocytes and myeloma tumor cells. A single antibody-secreting cell would die out, but the myeloma cells reproduced indefinitely in what, as he described to me, was "immortality" (unlimited growth potential); together with them, the antibody immunity would produce a specific cell line. Myeloma cells would interact with antibody cells and result in fixed cell and antibody specificity.

"I said to myself," he continued, " 'Yes, that could work. Right?' "

> So I was very excited and I was telling that to Claudia, my wife, the next morning. She listened and calmed me down because I have come with ideas the next morning, or next day, or next week, and I later say, "Forget it, it was nothing." So she knew already that ideas were only ideas, right? And they are important only if they work out. She said, "Okay, don't worry,"[3] but I was still excited and I talked to César Milstein. He listened and took it seriously. He tried to find out whether it was feasible and then we came up with some calculations and, "yes, maybe it was feasible."

Köhler had considered two types of functionally separate cells, those of abnormal myeloma tumors, which were chromosomal-gene co-expressive and immortal; and normal B-lymphocyte antibodies, which develop against antigens and die both in culture and the body. He conceived of concomitantly connecting these functionally separate cell types in order to produce a specific antibody cell line. Bringing the two types into a single cell structure with resulting multinuclei would, he thought, retain separate properties that would interact. The lymphocyte antibody cell would express specificity and the myeloma cell co-expression and immortality when joined together in cell lines. The sep-con articulation process conception consisted of functionally separate entities retaining their individual characteristics while concomitantly connected. Application of his conception led to pure antibody cell lines, designated monoclonal antibodies. These recognized and responded to a single antigen, and could be cloned and manufactured in sizeable quantities for identification of specific bodily antigens.

Although the creation of the cell line did not directly forward Köhler's initial somatic mutation interests, it became very important in medical and pharmaceutical applications and research. Antigens are always factors in diseases and growths. As stated by Hans Wigzell in his 1984 Nobel Prize presentation speech:

> In less than a decade the development and production of monoclonal antibodies revolutionized the use of antibodies in health care and research. Rare antibodies with a tailor-made-fit for a given structure can now be made in large quantities. The... cells can be stored in tissue banks and the very same monoclonal antibody can be used all over the world with a guarantee for eternal supply. The precision in diagnosis is greatly improved, and entirely new possibilities for therapy have been opened up. Rare molecules present in trace amounts in complex solution can now be purified in an efficient manner using monoclonal antibodies. In all, it is therefore correct to describe the... technique... as one of the major methodological advances in medicine during this century.[4]

Monoclonal antibodies have been especially used to target antigens in cancer growth and stimulate the patient's own immune system against the cancer. It is the most widely used form of cancer immunotherapy in current practice.

German born physicist-biologist and Nobel laureate in Physiology or Medicine, Max Delbrück, was very ill with heart disease and only a few months from his death when I interviewed him. Tall, bespectacled, with cowlick-arranged gray-black hair, he was warmly friendly and strikingly forthright as he sprawled weakly on the couch in his living room. He interspersed personal information about physical problems in his early life, relationships with colleagues, and both philosophical and technical matters regarding his work. His initial and famed career in physics, he said, developed in earnest when, as a refugee from Nazism, he worked at the Niels Bohr Institute in Copenhagen. There, Delbrück became devoted to Bohr and his investigations, and throughout the rest of his scientific career he attempted to apply Bohr's broadly applied theory of complementarity (described in chapter 3) to all his explorations. The irreducibility of elementary quantum phenomena and of life and the interaction between the two fascinated and occupied him. "The theory became," he said, "the turning point in my entire career, why I switched from theoretical physics to biological investigation and more specifically to the study of genes and genetic replication."

His creative work and ideas then consisted of a broad type of sep-con articulation process with several particular applications. He conceived of explorations that involved strong concomitant connections among the functionally separate content, methods, and identities of the fields of biology and physics. Not simply a matter of combination or association, Delbrück pioneered, as extolled by Schrödinger,[5] connections producing specific theoretical and empirical interactions between the two fields. Later, together with Salvador Luria, he created a foundation for functionally separate but concomitantly connected new fields of molecular genetics and microbiology. "You never thought of genes at all in those days," he said, "they were arranged like a pearl string. What else did you know about them? They determined, in some complicated way, characters. And they multiplied. Every time the cells divided, there must be duplication. So what else goes on? Are there molecules that make copies of themselves? Molecules don't ordinarily do that."

Delbrück first studied the genetics of the fruit fly, *Drosophila melanogaster,* at Indiana University; later, at the California Institute of Technology, he worked on bacteriophage viruses in a laboratory basement with Emory Ellis. These virus organisms provided him the means to follow his new interest in genetic replication, a problem, as he stated, "that no-one else working in biology was interested in." Similar to other creative scientists, Delbrück's choice of a specific and functionally separate element at the beginning of a sep-con articulation process deviated from a scientific mainstream. As he said:

> The merit that I had was to go after the bacterial phages [viruses attacking bacteria], back in the late 30s, from the point of view of really finding out how replication works. Now you would think that this was an obvious problem; it's the basic problem, it's a universal problem in biology. So, everybody who was anybody, and ambitious, should have been after that problem. The fact is that not one damn person went after that problem. They were just not naive enough to consider it as a solvable problem. For me it was the fundamental problem because it was the most likely situation in which Bohr's complementarity might come in. Nobody—the physicists were busy with their physics, and the biologists hadn't heard of quantum mechanics. So between the two, I zeroed in on that. I could change both.

He taught a famous course on bacteriophages to scientists at Cold Spring Harbor Laboratory on Long Island. Later, as interest in bacteriophage or "phage" research became more widespread, he founded and developed a Phage Group consisting of eminent scientists including his Nobel co-laureate Salvador Luria as well as students working in that area. This group met with him frequently and a good deal of fruitful collaboration and advance in molecular genetics resulted. Here, too, he saw himself following in another way the model of Niels Bohr, who had surrounded himself with outstanding physicists at Copenhagen, including Delbrück himself. "The Phage Group was open," Delbrück said, "for anybody who wanted to join. We talked freely to each other and exchanged information freely, with disregard for any personal claims of priority or whatnot. Not allowing any kind of possessiveness was my contribution, I would say. And that was an imitation of the spirit of Copenhagen." A particular principle for creativity that Delbrück advocated to the group was what he called "the principle of limited sloppiness." This principle he described as follows: "If you are too sloppy, you never get reproducible results and can't draw any conclusions. If you are just a little sloppy, then when you see something different and potentially new and worthwhile, you nail it down."

I have independently described a similar application of the sep-con articulation process. The sloppiness or production of minimal or chance error that Delbrück advocated results in the separating out of a deviant but related factor in an investigation. The "nailing down" may lead the investigation in a new direction, but to be creative it must involve concomitantly connecting of that functionally separate factor with one or more other functionally separate factors in the inquiry or procedure that produces an integration of something new and worthwhile. Such a sep-con articulation process using sloppiness or error is characteristic of creative achievement in a number of other fields such as literature and the arts. Separating out and subsequent connecting of errors to a project is an important factor in the free-thinking, deviance, and risk-taking characteristic of all creative processes. I have described such a creative application in some detail and earlier named it "articulation of error"[6] (N.B. sep-con articulation of error) in which errors and mistakes such as the stray or unintended dripping of watercolors, shifts of plot, a musical riff, and what Delbrück called a little sloppiness are articulated into a creation.

Delbrück's collaboration with Salvador Luria resulted in their creative discovery of the principles of viral mutation in bacterial fluctuation or secondary growth. Delbrück's contribution was based on an experiment by Luria from which he theoretically formulated the genetic factors involved. He conceived that the experiment showed that interaction of phage with bacterial organisms resulted in the growth of a resistant bacterial variant ("secondary culture" or "secondary growth"). This conception was based on the sep-con articulation process formulation that functionally separate phages were concomitantly connected and interacted with functionally separate bacterial organisms to induce the variant. Fluctuations in the number of the resistant bacterial mutants were the result of spontaneous mutations and genetically induced change from virus sensitivity to virus resistance. Viral replication was based on adaptation.

The continued investigation of bacteriophages has also led to a better understanding of viral disease. "Your imaginative approach," said Professor

Sven Gad on presenting the Nobel Prize to Delbrück, Luria, and phage worker Alfred Hershey, "succeeded in making the impossible possible. The realization that bacteriophage after all is a respectable representative of all living matter was slow in coming."

Physician Salvador Luria was a naturalized American born in Italy. Like Delbrück, he also knowingly worked in a largely neglected biological area of bacterial genetics. Along with being partially responsible for the beneficial impact of the field of molecular biology on vital human processes, and the eventual elucidation of the nature of phage viruses, he also contributed significantly to the understanding of and subsequent combat against virus diseases.

Tall and swarthy, he was soft spoken, eloquent, and self-assured. Although married to a psychologist, he was quite doubtful about assessments of his own or others' mental processes. Nevertheless, he was very detailed in describing the mental steps in one of his earliest and most important discoveries regarding the genetics of microphage resistance. "It's the one," he said, "that started what is called molecular biology today."

Recounting the events in his achievement, he said that the traditional wisdom among bacteriologists as well as a prominent physical chemist at the time was that bacteria had no chromosomes and no genes. Together with Delbrück, however, he believed that the phenomenon of bacterial resistance against bacteriophages was due to gene effects. Colorfully citing his deviance from the mainstream, he told me, "I was an arrogant David pitted against the Goliath of physical chemistry." For several months, he struggled because he could not conceive of a way to investigate or test his ideas. Then, one of his achievements was setting up a creatively designed phage experiment that served to provide the results for Delbrück's previously described theory of viral replication. "My problem," he said, "was to decide whether phage-resistant bacteria were spontaneously arising mutants or were cells that became resistant as a result of an action of phage on otherwise normal bacteria." He first focused on the mathematical probabilities. If phage-resistant bacteria resulted from random unconnected actions on normal nonresistant bacteria, he hypothesized, discrete events would be produced according to a Poisson or random distribution. Instead, he conceived that the functionally separate resistant bacteria would be concomitantly connected through the action in a medium of a uniform agent on functionally separate nonresistant ones. This would produce an experimentally determined genetic probability distribution. He set up a critical experiment to test his formulation and, after two days, he had successful experimental results indicating that "a spontaneous uniform agent," which Delbrück identified as a mutation, "was exactly what it turned out to be." The positive experimental result based on his own correct sep-con articulation process formulation led him to calculate the so-called Lurian distribution. He conveyed the result and distribution to Delbrück, who then formulated the broader theory regarding viral replication.

Short, bearded, relaxed, and clearly authoritative, American biochemist David Baltimore discovered what came to be called "reverse transcriptase," the enzyme producing interactions between tumor viruses and the genetic material of the cell. The possibility of such an intermediate between the messenger RNA of an infecting tumor virus cell and the genetic DNA of a host cell had first been suggested by Baltimore's Nobel co-laureate, Howard Martin Temin. Close to the time of Baltimore's discovery, the latter had also independently identified the enzyme, and both were given equal credit for the achievement.

Baltimore, who started his work at the MIT laboratory of Salvador Luria, was, at the time he made the discovery, relatively quite young at age 32. Sometime after he received the Nobel Prize, Baltimore notably applied his broad scientific knowledge, administrative brilliance, and considerable personal charm first as president of Rockefeller University and then as president of the California Institute of Technology. Discovery of reverse transcriptase has led, through subsequent use, to an understanding of RNA viruses, or retroviruses. These viruses are involved in certain types of cancer and the disease of acquired immunodeficiency syndrome (AIDS) as well as others. Both AIDS/HIV treatment and gene therapies have employed reverse transcriptase.

Baltimore's selected path to the discovery of this significant enzyme was an independently creative one. Working with his biochemist wife on a lipid virus while at MIT, he had discovered that solitary strands of RNA did not produce virus infection in a host cell. He knew that Temin's suggestion at the time of some type of DNA intermediate in the production of tumors such as Rous sarcoma by viruses had been widely rejected—"anti-supported," Baltimore reported, "throughout the scientific world." Therefore, motivated to create and, like Temin, decidedly deviating from the accepted beliefs, he turned, taking his own path, to the study of RNA-producing tumor viruses. He found that there was only a single genetic transcription strand in the virus RNA, and he conceived that therefore, "it was necessary to have biological coding" for both infection and tumor to occur in the cell. This code would likely be that a single strand of the DNA would be formed from the RNA that could develop into genetic double helix DNA; from this, new RNA would then be produced in the tumor cell. "Maybe," he hypothesized, "there was a specific connecting and converting DNA polymerase enzyme in one of those viruses."

Next, after obtaining an unexpectedly sizeable amount of RNA-containing tumor virus, he carried out an assay procedure and found a very large output of the DNA polymerase. Excited by this result, he did further experiments to determine the biochemical nature of that polymerase. The particular type of RNA-dependent DNA polymerase he had discovered was later named *reverse transcriptase* because the enzyme reversed the sequence of RNA to DNA instead of the usual transcription of DNA to RNA. In the final portion of a sep-con articulation process, Baltimore had formulated and found a DNA polymerase enzyme concurrently acting on and connecting the functionally separate RNA in the virus and the functionally separate replicating DNA in the host tumor cell. The RNA, in his conception, would produce the DNA, which would in turn produce more RNA; the functionally separate RNA retained its messenger function and the connected DNA continued as the functionally separate genic replicator.

Canadian-born American physician David Hubel, together with Nobel co-laureate in Physiology or Medicine Torsten Wiesel, determined information processing as well as structures in the visual system of the brain. Hubel, a balding, scholarly-looking man with a slight twinkle in his eye, was, he smilingly offered, the grandson of a pharmacist who invented the first process for the mass production of gelatin capsules. Hubel himself also had a passion for music; he played piano, recorder, flute, and later the oboe, and remarked that he kept instruments in his office in case any visitor might like to play a duet. Regarding his own creative investigations with Torsten Wiesel, he spoke enthusiastically and said the two of them frequently worked into the night and together had a great deal of fun in the course of it, especially in their early collaboration. Before they started, he had worked at Walter Reed hospital in Washington, DC and developed a microelectrode to record cat brain and eye activity. This proved to become an important part of the duo's visual system exploration. A detailed description of the columnar structure and functions of the neurons in the cat visual cortex was the culminating achievement of the work.

Their success began with a discovery that others have sometimes described as due to an accident. The two, however, had worked long and hard with Hubel's microelectrode within what he called "a very elaborate ophthalmoscope." They used this to watch the retinal ganglion cells connecting to the visual cortex of an anaesthetized cat, and then recorded cell responses. Constantly, they put black circles on a glass slide and moved the slide in front of various areas of the retina to produce a visual response. None came. Then, one night, after several hours of work, they found that the shadow of the edge of the moving glass, rather than the effects of the black circles, was making the visual cortex cell respond. It fired, Hubel said, "a tremendous barrage of impulses."

"It sounds like an accident," he went on, "but if you play around for nine hours straight the chances are pretty high of having some fortunate accident occurring, so this wasn't entirely accidental. We were just stubborn enough to wrestle with this stupid cell until we got it to do something, and had we started and stopped off after the sixth or seventh hour we only would have tumbled to the way the cells tend to work in the cortex maybe weeks or months later."

As I pointed out earlier in the discussions of accidental discovery (chapters 4 and 7), and indicated regarding the sep-con articulation process of error, so-called accidents and serendipity in science usually occur to seeking and prepared investigators. Successful interpretation of such complex events as these typically has been creative. In this case, Hubel himself formulated the important principle of "orientation selectivity," which he later stated was "the most striking attribute of cells in the primary visual cortex." He postulated the new idea that a fine shadow or input line connected and thereby produced responses only in a certain range of orientations to a visual cortex cell group. These responses would in turn affect perception of the stimuli. Having this postulation in mind, description of aspects of the columnar functional organization of visual cortex cells was then possible.

The conception of orientation selectivity was derived from the sep-con articulation process. A fine shadow line was conceived as concomitantly connecting the functionally separate range of orientations with a functionally separate group of individual visual cortex cells, producing optic interaction. Changes in the separately perceived placement and the separate reaction of the cortex cells affected each other. Tracing the orientation selectivity of a group of three neighboring cells indicated that they were lodged in somatosensory columns. This contributed to these investigators' overall formulation that visual responses were integrated by orientation in complex columns. The visual physiology advance produced an understanding of how the retinal image was interpreted by cortical cells and also applied to general modes of sensory processing in the brain.

Swiss molecular biologist Werner Arber, the son of an inventive farmer, was short, straight browed, and keen eyed. Passionate about doing science and developing scientific education in Switzerland, he held sharply honed convictions about proper procedures. He spelled out his highly complicated scientific investigation rapidly and precisely. This concerned his theoretical formulation of the nature and action of restriction enzymes, for which he was awarded the Nobel Prize in Physiology or Medicine.

Subsequent identification of these enzymes, the endonucleases, has been very significant for genetic knowledge, genetics, and the biotechnology industry. They are the basis for the recombinant DNA technology that has made possible the large-scale production of insulin for diabetes using *E. coli* bacteria as well as human factor VIII for the treatment of hemophilia. Insertion of genes during cloning or copying and expression of important proteins, distinguishing alleles (alternative gene forms on the same chromosome), and identifying the number of gene copies present in an individual's genome are other specific applications and developments from the recombinant DNA product.

Arber said he was interested in bacterial defense systems that could destroy, to a large extent, invading so-called foreign nucleic acid—that is, "foreign" genetic information. ("Whatever foreign is?" he asked laughingly). He studied the matter with bacteriophage viruses and focused on the specific functions of cellular DNA. Bacterial strains marked or coded virus cellular DNA for their own, and any entering viruses without that particular separate mark would be destroyed. When the virus went from one bacterial host to another, the separate mark would come through each time; but when the virus eventually returned to the initial bacterial strain, the mark would become lost. A small number of roving viruses, however, got progeny that remained and grew in the bacterial cell, and these then retained the mark of that cell. At the time he considered this, other researchers following the process said that it could all be due to mutation. He wondered instead if the mark was due to a functionally separate methylation, the addition of a methyl ion on the DNA that forestalled enzymatic cleavage and was later lost. The other researchers insisted methylation could not be responsible. They believed that it was not due to anything on the DNA itself but that the virus would pick up a host protein. Once it picked up that host protein, it could go back into the same host but not into others. "Everything was logic," Arber recalled.

Motivated to create and deviating from the mainstream, he decided, rather than growing several different cycles as usual, to do a one-cycle experiment with the bacteriophage viruses and inspect the results. In this experiment, he saw that the resistance pattern of the bacteria indicated that the code was on the DNA molecule. He conceived therefore that host-controlled modification of DNA by methyl ions, not spontaneous change or mutation of the virus or bacteria, led through enzyme activity to the returning loss or "restriction" of the virus DNA. "Then," he said, "we made some experiments to prove that. This was done against a general belief, but in this particular instance, of course, the experiments were so convincing that people accepted it rapidly." He went on to develop the theory that restriction is the result of "restriction endonucleases" producing methyl modification of specific DNA sequences by bacterial enzymes. This group of enzymes both methylate and protect bacterial DNA (modification enzyme) and cut or cleave (restriction enzyme) unmethylated invading viral DNA. This mutual operation he called *recognition*. Using the sep-con articulation process, he had postulated that the functionally separate operations of DNA protection and restriction were concomitantly connected in such a recognition operation. Elaborating this theory of enzyme recognition and the joint operations of modification and restriction, he applied it to mechanisms of cleaving or cutting DNA at particular sites by the restriction endonucleases. Experimental discovery of several types of such restriction enzymes, used later in recombinant DNA technology, both in his hands and that of other scientists, followed later.

As stated by Peter Reichard in his presentation speech for the 1978 Nobel Prize in Physiology or Medicine, "The application of restriction enzymes has revolutionized the genetics of higher organisms and completely changed our ideas of the organization of their genes.... With their aid we can selectively remove parts of the genetic material and transplant genes into a foreign [recall Arber's own wry question regarding "foreign"] background. In this way genes from higher organisms have been transferred to bacteria, and in certain cases such bacteria can be used to produce human hormones. In the near future we can expect many products of medical importance to be synthesized."[7]

South African–born American physicist Allan Cormack was the conceptual inventor of the CAT scan (computed axial tomography); his Nobel co-laureate Godfrey Hounsfield of England built the first commercially viable CAT scanner. Cormack, a large, teddy-bear-shaped man with round horn-rimmed spectacles upon a rugged face, had a warm, amiable manner and spoke often of his love of music, statistics, and science. He also expressed pride at being the only Nobel scientist who came from the African continent. Describing the circumstances leading to his original conception of producing three dimensional X-rays, he said:

> It was a stroke of luck in a way, because I had studied at Cambridge in England and I was primarily interested in nuclear physics. Then, I went out and got married and, returning to South Africa, I got a job at the University of Capetown. I was the only nuclear physicist in Capetown at the time—I think maybe in Africa. Anyway, at the Groote Schuur Hospital nearby, the resident consultant physicist got fed up and quit.... So, I was asked to go spend a day and a half a week to keep the radiotherapy program going. Otherwise, they would have had to shut it down because the South African government at that time required a competent physicist to supervise the use of radioactive materials in the hospital.
>
> I was working at treatment planning with radiation therapy. Up to that point, they had only isotope charts and things that should have been considered barbarous. I figured there must be a better way of improving treatment planning. I got the idea that they could do a series of X-ray measurements made at points outside as well as within the body. The images would be interconnected and the information from that interaction would be what was needed to produce what could be considered a tomogram [a two-dimensional image representing a slice or section through a three-dimensional object]. It took me many years, however, to work out the prototype.

The resulting CAT scan (now called a *CT scan*) produces a three-dimensional image of the inside of an object from a large series of two-dimensional X-ray images. Applied to the human body, it demonstrates various bodily structures based on their ability to block the X-ray beam. This procedure is especially applicable for conditions affecting the head and abdominal cavity, but used broadly it is generally considered to have revolutionized the practice of medical diagnosis. Cormack's initial conception of the three-dimensional

X-ray scanning consisted of concomitantly connecting functionally separate exterior and interior body images. Mathematical calculations based on complex interactions of these separate and independent images in the sep-con articulation process resulted in his desired axial tomograph and the steps to eventually producing a fully developed CT scan.

American biochemist Paul Berg was the first scientist to construct the transfer recombinant-DNA molecule, the molecule that contains DNA from different species such as genes of humans joined with bacterial chromosomes. Looking much younger than his 60 years at the time I interviewed him, the small-featured, light-haired, and athletically built Berg strongly emphasized the importance of his discipleship in the laboratory of Arthur Kornberg, where he worked for many years. It was also rather easy to visualize him as a young, enterprising boy who, as he said, was attracted to science after he read of the adventurous scientists in Paul de Kruif's *Microbe Hunters* and Sinclair Lewis's *Arrowsmith* as well as being inspired by his high school teacher, Sophie Wolfe. He was at first quite modest about the recombinant DNA achievement, attributing recognition by the Nobel Prize generally to the wide influence of particular discoveries rather than personal outstanding prowess. In his own case, he emphasized the seemingly obvious aspects of his procedure. However, as we pursued the detailed steps, his motivation to create and his deviance was clear. The resulting creation was distinct. He described the process as follows:

> At the time nobody conceived of trying to make recombinant DNA molecules outside of the cell. You could make recombinant DNA molecules within the cell but you were constrained by what the cell was able to do. What we set out to do was devise a system by which we could transfer genes from one cell to another and construct main cells that were models for genetic experimentation.
>
> What was known is that you could take DNA molecules and join them together if they had natural cohesive ends, "sticky ends." But the idea of actually building sticky ends onto the ends of DNA molecules had not occurred to anybody. All that had been recognized was if you had DNA molecules that already had sticky ends, they would come together and pair and you could join them. The question then was if you took DNA molecules that didn't have sticky ends, how could you get them to join together?
>
> The idea of constructing tails that were complementary to each other, and using those to join DNA molecules together was my own distinct one. What nobody seemed to recognize was that you could build synthetic tails onto the ends of molecules and have them join just as the natural ones do.
>
> After doing that, I was able to take any two DNA molecules and, with an enzyme, join them together to make a recombinant DNA molecule, then

put them into a cell where they could propagate inside. That had never been done before and I don't know that it ever was conceived of before.

Berg had conceived of a connection of a functionally separate complementary DNA molecule tail with another functionally separate and complementary one to form what became transfer recombinant DNA. The independent DNA molecules retained their functional identities and were concomitantly connected into a new and integrated molecule to be used in other cells.

DNA molecules from all organisms differ in the sequence of nucleotides—building blocks consisting of bases and other chemicals—within that structure. When a genetic-replication-linked DNA is introduced into an organism, both the introduced DNA and the organism's own DNA are replicated. This differs from genetic recombination in a test tube and is designated recombinant DNA. This recombinant DNA is used in the mapping of the human genome and other applications involving identifying, mapping, and sequencing genes. It is widely applied in human and veterinary medicine, agriculture, and bioengineering to produce diagnostic tools, crop resistances, growth hormones, and many other products.

American physicist Sheldon Glashow was a large man with a round, smooth-skinned, and also young looking face topped by a forelock of dark hair. Together with his later Nobel co-laureate Steven Weinberg he had attended the well-known Bronx High School of Science, where the two of them learned physics on the way to school on the New York subway. He was mentored in particle physics much later by Murray Gell-Mann, and was also a faculty member successively at Stanford University; the University of California, Berkeley; and Harvard University. Along with Steven Weinberg and Abdus Salam, he was responsible for the development of the so-called electroweak force theory, the unification of electromagnetism and the weak force (responsible for radioactive decay of subatomic particles), for which they received the Nobel Prize. The electroweak force, a critical feature of the Standard Model of particle physics, has been important for modern cosmology, among other applications, particularly determination of the long history of how the Universe has evolved.

Early in our discussion, Glashow expressed deep attachment to his father. He spoke movingly of feeling sorrow that his father, a plumber who was very inventive and had a deep interest in science, did not live to see his son's greatest accomplishments. On his own side, Glashow still felt a pride that, in New York City, one could still see numerous trucks circulating with his father's logo, "L. Glashow, Plumbing," on their panels (the business is now run by the former foreman). With respect to current ambitions, Glashow had become disappointed with a long period of lack of theoretical progress in his so-called subparticle field (action based on quantum wave behavior), and had turned to astrophysical work, where he was quite successful.

Early in his career, in collaboration with James D. Bjorken, he had identified a special type of quark that he called "the charmed quark." The name
charmed was not at that time derived, as popularly espoused, from the idea
that it "worked like a charm," although later, when he developed a successful comprehensive theory, it seemed to do so. "It was a play on words," he
said, "a play on 'charge,' an attribute that particles have when not charmed."
Gell-Man had developed the original idea of the quarks as basic constituents
of nuclear particles such as protons and neutrons. He defined three species or
"flavors" of quarks designated as "up," "down," and "strange." These particles
interacted with one another by means of the strong force, the force holding all
the components of the atom together.

Together with Bjorken, Glashow focused on the three separate quarks, and
they conceived a separate fourth quark which they then called "the charmed
quark." The conception, Glashow told me, came from the idea that there
existed "two doublets of quarks." One of the doublets, electrons and muons,
interacted with each other; therefore a newly conceived subatomic particle
in the other doublet would also have to have an interactive quality and be
functionally separate with "charm" and concomitantly connected with its
counterpart. Eventually, they considered that all four quarks would interact
with each other. In an ongoing creative process, the qualities of this newly
conceived and significant quark played an influential role in Glashow's contribution 6 years later to the electroweak theory.[8]

While working on this theory, Glashow had confronted an interfer-
ing problem, the factor of strangeness-changing neutral currents (SCNC),
which prevented electroweak unification. It was theoretically necessary to
predicate suppression of these currents, but no SCNC effects at all had ever
been observed in the laboratory. Together with John Iliopoulos, and Luciano
Maiani, he developed the conception of an interaction of his functionally separate charmed quark (which is subject to the weak and strong forces, gravitation and electromagnetism) with other quarks as well as with leptons. Based
on the connections and interactions of the charmed quark, the SCNC effect
would be removed. This has since become known as the GIM (authors' initials) mechanism.[9] The qualities of the charmed quark served theoretically to
restore unperceived relationships between quarks and leptons. These allowed
a theory that has flavor (subatomic particle quality) conserving mediated
weak interactions but no flavor-changing ones. The charmed quark was initially conceived in a sep-con articulation process based on the existence of
four quarks, and the qualities of functional separation with concomitant connection later became critical factors in the creative production of the electroweak theory.

Norwegian-born American physicist Ivar Giaever developed a procedure
for superconductor or solid-state tunneling—the passage of quantum or
wave-state electrons through a barrier—and contributed significantly to an

understanding of the nature of superconductors. The phenomenon has been used in a wide range of electronic applications such as quantum interferometry involving measurements of temperatures near absolute zero, strength and direction of large objects such as submarines, detection of gravitational waves, ore prospecting, communication through water and in mountains, radio astronomy, and the investigation of the electromagnetic field around the heart or brain. Naturally occurring tunneling is in part responsible for the dispersion of light by the sun.

Giaever was a chisel-featured, good looking, and soft-spoken man with an excellent sense of humor. He laughingly spoke about being one of the least educated persons to have won the physics Nobel Prize, referring to his having done poorly in his early schoolwork including a course in physics. He was, however, deeply interested in creativity in science and he spent a good deal of time with me at one point rating the degree of creativity of each of the individual Nobel laureates in physics up to that time (he has agreed to be identified as one of the members of the evaluator group for this investigation). He described his own creativity as arising from his childhood in Norway during the Second World War when, due to the scarcities imposed by the Nazi occupiers, he had to fix everything himself, including bicycles, shoes, and other needed objects. As a professor at Rensselaer Polytechnic Institute, he cotaught (with Charles Bean) a course on creativity. In that course, as well as in general lectures, he asserted one of several general principles in doing great science—the need to avoid, as he did in his own work, the use of big machines, "because," he said in an affirmation of creative deviation," lots of people have big machines." He insisted instead on inventing subtler methods oneself.

Giaever developed an interest in tunneling while he was working at the General Electric research facility early in his career. He tried tunneling procedures in semiconductors, but they produced an equivocal result. He then decided that superconductors (materials that lose no energy to resistance) would be more reliable for studying the phenomenon. He spent the next six months, day and night, trying to develop the procedure. He described his motivation to create and a decision to deviate at that time with, I thought, a good deal of feeling: "It was up to me what was going to happen," he said. "I went to meetings about tunneling. The first meeting I ever went to they talked about tunneling between normal conductivity levels and nobody asked me about superconductors. I couldn't believe that they didn't think about it."

In quantum mechanics, tunneling occurs when an electron is allowed to escape from a metal without acquiring energy. Therefore, Giaever decided to study both tunneling and the so-called BCS (authors' initials) theory[10] of energy gaps (bands where electrons do not have energy) in superconductors. To produce the tunneling phenomenon, he focused on using of extremely thin films of the metals aluminum and lead. "I conceived of a 'sandwich' of metal insulator material," he said. "Between the two metals I would produce a quantum superconducting tunnel juncture by vapor-depositing aluminum on ordinary glass slides and allowing the surface of the aluminum film to oxidize. After a suitable oxide layer had formed, I put it between the aluminum and lead to form the metal-oxide-metal 'sandwich.' As far as I know I was the first to conceive of using aluminum oxide for such an effect."

The metals would not be touching but would be just a few atoms' distance apart. By passing an electric current through the "sandwich" he produced the connecting tunneling phenomenon in the solid-state superconductor and was able to measure the dimensions of the energy gap. In a sep-con articulation process, Giaever chose two operative and functionally separate strips of aluminum and lead film, and then, through a tunneling charge, he concomitantly connected them through an aluminum oxide juncture. In the Nobel Prize ceremony, Professor Stig Lundqvist said, "Through…work by Giaever and others the tunneling method has developed into a new spectroscopy of high accuracy to study in detail the properties of superconductors, and the experiments have in a striking way confirmed the validity of the theory of superconductivity."[11]

Jean-Marie Lehn, as I stated in chapter 9, was the founder of the field of supramolecular chemistry. The development of this designated field has had many interdisciplinary sources in physics, chemistry, and biology. Used effectively for the advance of nanotechnology—the control of matter on an atomic and molecular scale—it has also applied significantly to the design and understanding of catalysts and catalysis—the increase in the rate of a chemical reaction. Supramolecular chemistry includes production of most industrially important chemicals and, as previously stated, the understanding and construction of new pharmaceutical therapies.

In addition to the earlier described uses of both the janusian and homospatial processes in creative aspects of his supramolecular work, Lehn applied the process of sep-con articulation in his creation of the specialty of supramolecular chemistry itself. He described the basic formulation of functionally separate and individual molecules operating as concomitantly bonded and connected and subsequently interacting as follows:

> Along the years, an enormous amount of knowledge has been accumulated allowing chemists to construct more and more complex molecules on the basis of knitting together—really, holding together—strongly, by strong bonds, so-called "covalent" bonds [shared electrons], atoms to build large molecular architectures.…
>
> This chemistry is not intra-molecular any more, not internal to the molecule, but inter-molecular, happening between them. And the fact that you may build up a whole chemistry which is not any more built on the strong bonding which defines the molecule on the basis of atoms, but by weak,

so-called non-covalent bonding which allows molecules to interact. To use a language which is more descriptive, I would say even a sociological language; it's the population of molecules you talk about. Those interfere, because if molecules were to sit in the same flask next to one another, "talking" to each other, so to speak—talking, meaning without interacting—they would be just isolated, there would be nothing else. The whole would be the same as the sum of the parts [not integrated]. But because they interact new features and properties appear and this is then this supramolecular part which results from the fact that molecules, when in a collection, in a collectivity, have interactions. These interactions will determine the formation of super structures of larger units, which are more or less well-defined, depending on how they are constructed. This supramolecular chemistry is the chemistry which has then to do with the designed manipulation and use of those weaker interactions among molecules, which, compared to the intramolecular ones, glue the molecules together and allow you to construct large architectures.

Lehn's explanation that the chemistry has to do with the "designed manipulation and use of those weaker interactions among molecules" indicates a sep-con articulation process with functionally separate molecules concomitantly connected and interacting. Instead of the supramolecular compound being the same, as Lehn declared, as the sum (or sums) of its parts, it is integrated through applications of the sep-con articulation process; the wholes then become greater than the sum of their parts.

With regard to the creation of specific new supramolecular structures, he indicated that ordinarily chemists looked at molecules from the outside. Motivated to create and deviating from most others, however, Lehn thought about inner cavities and tried to imagine what was inside, how other molecules might fit in. He focused on the functionally separate inside and outside of the molecule. Then, he visualized the three-dimensional aspects of the inside and the outside—what was front, what was back, and what were the different sides. Immediately, he thought of having as many points of contact, information transfer, as possible in these dimensions. "Therefore," he said,

> having a three-dimensional cavity which surrounds a molecular object should be better than having something of lower dimensionality, something which would only be a ring, or a chain. In other words, what you would really want is conceiving a three-dimensional negative image, as one says, in space. The idea came at once—I remember that quite well—from the moment I realized that you must build something which is three-dimensional, it seemed like it would work. I was thinking that one should have a word which would be understood in many languages, not only in English, but French, German, so on. "Crypt" is a word rooted in

Greek as well as Latin. Everybody understands "crypt," people will easily remember.

It's a cavity, so there are cryptons, cryptates, and so on. Crypt is the empty cavity of the molecule and cryptate is the result when the substrate is inside; so cryptate is the joining of the substrate with its receptor [a binding substance]. The crypt is the receptor. The hidden aspect is an important aspect because the interactions of the outside species with what is hidden determines both the properties of what is inside (in some ways, depending on how well they are hidden) and also what's outside.

The creative sequence here consisted first of his focusing on the functionally separate inside and functionally separate outside of the molecule. He conceived the "cryptate" joining or connection in all three dimensions. The result, which he said, came all at once, was a rich and productive sep-con articulation process conception consisting of concomitant separation and connection. The joining of the substrate with its receptor provided for interaction between the functionally separate entities, which determined the properties of both. Because the entities were necessarily weakly connected as microscopically distant inside and outside structures, rather than strongly connected, the interactions instigated by the concomitance of the functional separations and connection were quite numerous (as discussed in chapter 6). Moreover, the articulated structure was unsymmetrical and unidirectional, with the hidden, inside aspect determining the interaction modifications. The phases of the process of sep-con articulation produced the supramolecular creation.

Although born in Venezuela, biologist Baruj Benacerraf spent his entire scientific career in the United States. With slicked-back graying hair at his temples and a commanding presence, he had the looks of a successful industrial executive. In contrast, his black eyebrows imbued his face with the vitality of his Latin background together with a clearly very sharp intelligence. In addition to his discoveries concerning genetic immunological response structures, for which he was awarded the Nobel Prize in Physiology or Medicine, he had worked actively as the president of the Dana-Farber Cancer Institute. Although impaired by the condition of dyslexia (a language learning disability) since childhood, he ultimately became, as he smilingly said, "the most famous person suffering from dyslexia." He was president of the American Dyslexia Association at the time I saw him. Bouts with other conditions, such as his bronchial asthma and intestinal allergies as a child, however, had stimulated and advanced his interest in allergies, allergens, and immunity.

Benacerraf's discoveries regarding the genetics of immunization, particularly on the cellular level, have had an important impact on all forms of tissue and organ transplantation as well as the understanding of diseases and conditions such as juvenile diabetes, multiple sclerosis, a wide range of allergies, and chronic dermatological disorders. The molecules in the cellular immune system he had investigated are known as the major histocompatability complex (MHC); this complex includes T cell (thymus-derived lymphocyte white blood cells) immunity receptors. Presented to such T cells are various types of antigens (extrinsic substances), and the MHC functions to determine tissue type and transplant compatibility. Benacerraf discovered and defined the specific immune responsiveness (Ir) genes within the complex that govern the thymic development of the T cell receptor immunity.

Describing the sequence leading up to his creative discovery, he explained that in the decades of the 1950s and 1960s all that was known about immunology was the action of protein antibodies. He and other researchers, however, had recognized there was another form of immunity caused by cells. That immunity, which turned out to depend on the T cells, was responsible for tuberculin resistance and for contact sensitivity, and the general assumption was that it was similar to the antibody immunity function.

Earlier, Benacerraf had worked on identifying specific protein antibodies by immunizing animals. Finding that some yielded the antibodies and some didn't, he concluded there must be something genetic that controls the process. Then, a long time later, he studied T cell function by investigating cellular protein antigens and antibody reactions, using both folded (organized) proteins in a characteristic three-dimensional structure and unfolded proteins—"the formless form," as he called it. T cells, he discovered, recognized and reacted to the unfolded protein. He described a new conception as follows: "I realized we were dealing with a different immunity recognition system, the peptide amino acid sequence [order of amino acids]. Eventually this came together with the recognition of genes responsible for the immunity. Separate and specific MHC genes, I believed, bonded to the separate whole peptide sequence in the unfolded protein. So out of two different formulations, it took me something like ten or fifteen years until I wrote a paper published in the *Journal of Immunology*, with that specific hypothesis, and for the first time I predicted precisely."

In a gradual long-term creative process, Benacerraf first postulated a functionally separate genetic factor in cell immunity and then much later deduced that the functionally separate peptide order in unfolded or formless proteins was concomitantly connected. The specific functionally separate and connected genes in the T-cell–containing MHC complex he named Ir genes. In this sep-con articulation process, which had an overall biphasic configuration of a long input and gradual output, he had formulated that the histocompatibility complex and the peptide ordering each retained its separate functional identity. The governing by Ir genes of T cell production and immune responses was based in this conception of concomitant interactions and connections between the types of genes operating together with modified or unfolded protein.

The Ir genes in the MHC help different cell types collaborate to bring about a specific response to antigens. Some function to stimulate suppressor T cells and thereby suppress immune reactions such as allergies that would otherwise get out of control.

German biologist Christiane Nüsslein-Volhard was the only female Nobel laureate I interviewed and only one of eight living female scientists who had received the Nobel Prize up to that time. She was awarded the Prize for discoveries concerning the genetic control of early embryonic development. With a tall, sturdy presence and spiraling, diffusely curled hair, her voice was mellifluous, and her manner frank and straightforward. Although, as I noted earlier, most of the Nobel laureates I interviewed had spoken of nonscientifically applicable interests in music and, to a lesser degree, the other arts, Nüsslein-Volhard particularly emphasized her own strong aesthetic orientations and values and related them at several points to her thinking in science. Her father was a successful architect, her maternal grandmother a painter, and both of her parents played a musical instrument and painted. Although Nüsslein-Volhard herself made no artwork, she was an art enthusiast and a serious flute player. Her scientific work involved the identification and classification of genes that governed early embryonic development. She first primarily investigated the embryos of the fruit fly, *Drosophila melanogaster*, and later on the zebra fish. This work has had widespread application for the understanding of general embryogenesis as well as for specific advances in development of vertebrates.

"I think," she said, "the creativity came after we had the material, established the method, found all these mutations, and then made a picture out of what we had seen. Interpreting the patterns was the creative step, I think. You look at this, and then you play around, and you do something in the meantime. Then you dream and the next morning you've got an idea and you say, 'Oh, let's check that,' and so on. Then, someone comes into the discussion and says, 'But have you looked at this?' And you say, 'Oh, no,' and then you do a lot of more systematic thinking which, when done, you write a paper about it."

She went on to describe that the *Drosophila* larvae normally has three thoracic and eight abdominal segments. When she discovered that every other segment was absent, she interpreted it as a regularity indicating that gene expression arose from a pairing of the remaining segments present. "It was necessary," she said, "to recognize the individual segment types. This was creative. The gene was called 'paired' because pairs of segments, both even and odd, were connected. Naming of the pairs was simple but it was interpretative in the sense that it was derived from the type of regular segment skipping and expression, that is: paired, even-skipped, and odd-skipped segmentation. The pair-wise connection of segments was in the back of my head when I [in collaboration with co-Nobel laureate Eric Wieschaus] named them. For each gene type there were several independent mutations."

From her observation of the phenomenon of absent genes, Nüsslein-Volhard was able to postulate, in a self-conscious process of creative discovery, the presence of functionally separate segments paired and concomitantly connected with other segments in either an even or odd distribution. Both even and odd connected segments, she believed, composed interacting genetic pairs that introduced mutations. The sep-con articulation of separate and concomitantly connected gene pairs, either even or odd, proved to be correct and was the breakthrough formulation that resulted in the development of an extensive classification system and the elucidation of the interactions of mutants. These extensions of her creative discovery led to an understanding of the stepwise embryonic development of *Drosophila melanogaster* body segments. One of her joint discoveries also has recently led to the development of an anticancer drug. A gene pair that she and Wieschaus named "hedgehog"—when mutated the resulting flies had a coat of spines all over their undersides—was identified by other researchers in humans and vertebrates. Investigative work regarding this gene pair, widely called "Hedgehog Research," has produced a anticancer drug named vismodegib or "vismo." This drug has been an effective modifier of a number of types of cancers.

Creative Emotion in Discovery

The predominant emotions connected with or accompanying the scientific creative process directly reported in the Nobel subject group were the motivation to create, problem interest and problem finding, deviance from the mainstream of their scientific field, aggressiveness, openness and a wish for learning, risk taking, courage, and passion. These emotions or emotional predispositions characterized all members' work, but as they varied in expression and degree, I shall primarily give clarifying examples. As all cognitive processes have affective or emotional components, subjects using the janusian, homospatial, and sep-con articulation processes invariably experienced opening up, surprise, radical change, and the sense of creating. All of the scientists in the group spoke, in a manner similar to Einstein, Darwin, Bohr, Yukawa, Planck, and Heisenberg, of passion connected with their investigations. There was exceptional devotion to creatively solving chosen puzzles and enigmas. All reported a great sense of relief and elation at the realization of completion and success.

Initiating the creative processes was the emotional drive or motivation to create. As for factors of chance and serendipity, versus conscious motivations to create, Hubel, the discoverer of cat cortical vision (chapter 11), made his defining remark in the following detail: "People might conclude that the discovery was a matter of luck. Although I would never deny the importance of luck, as in any success, I would say it was the refusal to give up. It would be more correct to say that we would have been unlucky that day if we quit working a few hours earlier."

Conscious motivation to create was clearly attested by Christiane Nüsslein-Volhard, who spoke explicitly about the creative activity of establishing the method, finding the mutations, and making a picture of what she had seen. "That [last] was the creative step I wanted," she said. "I remember distinctly when I came down with this and said 'This is something.'" She also spoke later of deviating from the approaches and conceptions in a previous laboratory where, painfully and against much opposition, she adopted her own path.

Kornberg, the synthesizer of DNA, described his motivation to create and his necessary deviation in the early phases of his work as follows: "I designed experiments to see if the building blocks could be put together by an enzymologist in some ways. It was bold, because people who were doing nucleic acid chemistry, DNA chemistry, would have assumed it couldn't be done, or wouldn't be done in their lifetime. But I didn't approach it that way." In chapter 9 I reported Kornberg's telling me of another emotional matter, his passion and elation when, at the moment of the successful synthesis, he said to himself: "Why should it happen to me? I mean, what have I done to deserve this? It's extraordinary. But still, there was no other way to interpret it. It was great."

Kornberg elaborated on the passion and also described his and others' aggressiveness and competition as follows:

> What matters most is the enthusiasm to find it. And I want to mention this to you—that I've worked in the laboratories of people who have been very successful in science and I remember at the time being puzzled by two things which now, thirty years later, I see myself and they don't puzzle me. There was great enthusiasm and competitiveness, despite their advanced age in science—they were in their forties—and despite their great success. What made them run, I mean, why should they feel impelled to keep on working hard and being competitive? I understand it now, if you're in this game you compete.

Luria, cofounder of microbiology, was motivated to create quite early in his career. He proclaimed his deviation, as I reported in chapter 11, in such vibrant terms as, "I was an arrogant David pitted against the Goliath of physical chemistry."

His fellow microbiology cofounder, Delbrück, told me of his sustained motivation to create in a more extended and detailed way. He spoke of shifting from working exclusively in the field of physics, where he had gained a good deal of eminence, to explore jointly the field of biology primarily because of his philosophical concerns. He was interested in the origin of life and of mind and was convinced he could apply Niels Bohr's concept of complementarity creatively to these matters in the field of biology. With respect to his studies of genetic replication, he elaborated that "not one damn person went after that problem [replication]" and his deviation (see chapter 11) from the mainstream as follows:

> ...they were just not naive enough to consider it as a solvable problem.... [My colleagues at the California Institute of Technology] were amused that this young naive theoretical physicist [Delbrück] thought he could solve a fundamental problem in biology by diddling around.

Deviation together with the motivation to create involved shifting into other fields for two other subjects, Alvarez and Gilbert. Gilbert described the shift as follows:

> I was in physics as a practicing theorist for several years before I started to go into biology. Changing your field is actually a good way to find yourself in a position in which you don't know as much and you're learning everything new for the first time. Two elements of that: you're both seeing the material that everyone else thinks is standard with possibly new eyes and you also may not realize that certain things are not known or impossible because everything you're learning is new and given to you.... I have a constant desire for novelty. I am expressly creative because in the sort of science I do, we're constantly looking at new things and new findings and new discoveries.

Alvarez, who was motivated to create in many different fields, described his divergent approaches as follows: "That's one of the things that makes me tick; I will get into a field about which I know absolutely nothing, I don't even know the words. I read the books, get the programs for the computer, learn in the school of hard knocks and make creative discoveries."

Giaever was strongly motivated to create in his own field when he was working at the General Electric research facility and taking courses early in his career. "If you're creative," he observed," you're really dying to do something different but the 'professor' doesn't want to do that. He wants you to take this problem, solve it and give it back. 'It'll take three days to do it, but I want it back,' he says."

Baltimore knew early in his work on reverse transcriptase that geneticist Howard Temin had made the suggestion that there was a DNA intermediate in the production of tumors such as Rous sarcoma by viruses. Although the existence of this intermediate was "rejected throughout the scientific community—'anti-supported,'" as Baltimore said, he was motivated to creative discovery. He turned with aggressive opposition to the study of ribonucleic acid–producing tumor viruses. With this approach, he discovered that the DNA intermediate was reverse transcriptase.

Arber spoke of his motivation to create and the need for deviation, courage, and aggressiveness:

> If you are a scientist and realize, as I have, something is wrong, how could I change that? First of all, I have to convince all my fellow scientists that my ideas are better than many of the things that are written in textbooks. But it's very difficult. So I think one really strong bind against creativity is that one has to bring up the courage to say, "Well, here is something." But then you ask yourself, "Am I right?' I mean, maybe I am a crazy with these ideas because all the other people think it's different. So here is something to overcome, and I have overcome these barriers, sometimes.

Describing both his motivation to create and deviation, Corey said: "I like to work on things that other people aren't working on but there's so many people in science these days that invariably there are overlaps and lines of research tend to flow together. If I had my preference, I would like not to sort of intersect with the work that others have done. It's almost inevitable that there is some competition, you're working on something you think no one else in the world could possibly even be interested in."

As for problem finding, many of the subjects had worked under the direction of a senior scientist, often one who had been a previous recipient of a Nobel Prize. Harriet Zuckerman, in a sociological study of American Nobel-winning scientists, found that, as of 1977, being mentored by a previous Nobel laureate was statistically particularly common.[1] Nevertheless, those in the group here, whether working in the general area of their mentors or not, all defined their own particular problem or problems to work on. Several had found significant problems early and worked on them completely independently. Even the British John Kendrew, who insisted on another crucial influence, a background of good schooling (by which he meant the British "public" school) as the basis for creativity, and who worked in the laboratory of Max Perutz (who shared with Kendrew the 1962 Nobel Prize in Chemistry), independently found and pursued his own problem of myoglobin structure. The problems that all the Nobel group members individually found were selected for a number of reasons, intellectual as well as emotional. I have already detailed some of the intellectual reasons. With respect to the influence of emotional factors, although personal considerations undoubtedly entered in, the method of investigation I used was not appropriate overall for a fully meaningful elucidation of personal emotional variables. Intensive as well as extensive to some degree, the interviews were not conducted over a long enough period of time or with the kind of exploratory conditions that would reveal underlying emotional content; this applied to the problems chosen as well as other aspects of the creative process.

Personal emotional factors determining individual problem finding, motivation, and passion for creating were nevertheless suggested to some extent by Alvarez, Delbrück, and Nüsslein-Volhard. For Alvarez, there were indications that an emotional factor guiding his choice of and approach to particular problems was the nature and content of his very close and admiring relationship with his father, Walter Alvarez. The real love of that famous physician himself was, according to his son Luis, private laboratory research on human digestive processes that he carried out after hours. As a young boy, Luis had many happy hours by his father's side in this laboratory. That experience knowingly influenced his early choice of investigative research, but more specifically and less in awareness were the influences on aspects of his problem formulations and discoveries, in particular regarding the unknown chambers of the Egyptian Pyramid of Chephren and the extinction of dinosaurs. With respect to the pyramid chambers, he became interested early in the idea of calculating a gas bubble searched by cosmic rays. He conceived, he told me, that "the way a gas bubble would look in the intestine, the more cosmic rays would come through."[2] With respect to dinosaur extinction, his father's digestive interests took a different form. Luis became interested in that problem when his son first told him about the presence of a different kind of layer in the earth's limestone crust; he very early formulated a prospective answer in terms of the digestive processes of undersea organisms. He wondered if the multicolored layers resulted from deposits from the digestive cycle of foraminifera or aquatic worms. These repeated gastrointestinal suppositions may have derived in part from a childhood familiarity, but in connection with his father's strong laboratory interests, they also had emotional roots.

Delbrück's problem finding was also influenced by emotional factors pertaining to his father, but in a very different way. Not long before his death, Delbrück had recounted to me that he had always bitterly hated his father. An eminent historian, the father, according to his son Max, was domineering, belittling, and authoritarian. With striking and meaningful insight, Delbrück said, "I hated my father, highly repressed hatred which I became conscious of only much later. My drive, I felt, was certainly unconscious competition with my father." Although Delbrück chose fields topically different from his father's, namely astronomy first, then physics, then biology—"If I competed in history, I would have been absolutely hopeless. My father knew absolutely everything, from the Egyptians to Bismarck," he said— ironically he chose to work on a problem that actually followed the basic configuration of his father's work. He chose the problem of genetic replication in the bacteriophage, a study distinctly involving history and an historical orientation, in this case the historical unfolding of genetic function and reproduction.

By contrast, Nüsslein-Volhard's problem finding in *Drosophila melanogaster* genetic research was influenced by positive emotional factors relating to her father. Her father was an architect and she, in her work on chromosomal components and transmission in the *Drosophila* fly, focused on structural patterns. This interest in patterns, she told me, was directly related to her feelings about her father, who showed her his work and often worked together with her on drawing. She became emotionally and intellectually disposed to looking for the patterns of closed and open spaces in the chromosome.

As indicated earlier, Kornberg knew that aggressiveness involving competition with peers as well as colleagues was, in science, open and socially acceptable. Bloembergen also stipulated that in his comment about his choice of a profession: "The thing that attracted me to physics has to do with competitiveness. I like to meet challenges." Less acceptable but related to this aggressiveness are the destructive feelings connected specifically with creative scientific achievement. All members of the group, however, either tacitly or explicitly evidenced both aggressiveness and destructive feelings. Together with the motivation to create, these feelings were in a complex way a constituent of the passion associated with creating. Sometimes, the wish to overthrow a theory, experimental finding or approach, or scientific perspective predominated in the subjects' reports. Usually, however, the destructive feelings focused on a particular aspect of a previously held factor or scientific canon. Some destruction was always required to eliminate a critical causal connection with past objects, ideas, procedures, and processes.

For instance, in his quest to create a binary or co-expressed product, Köhler had in mind the intentional elimination of a single or unitary immunoglobulin expression in myeloma heavy chains. This product became the integrated monoclonal antibody. Arber, having obliterated the previous widely held notion of viruses picking up host proteins with his theory of code modification and restriction in DNA, cited awareness of destructive feelings together with the motivation for creation. "With regard to creativity," he said, "it needs actually a kind of courage to overrun a general belief or dogma to get the next step. I think this is important."

Lehn, the creator of the chemical "instructed mixture paradigm," referred to destroying previous contemporary chemists' exclusive goal of working with pure chemicals. "It was an insult," he said, "to tell a chemist his preparation was not pure." He nevertheless proposed the insulting but creative use of "informed" or "instructed" substances in his paradigm.

As in the examples here, the destructive feelings were required to eliminate a critical connection, especially a causal one, with past objects, ideas, or processes. The aggressive aspect of the creative process in all fields is often hidden and is seldom stated explicitly by creators or theorists and investigators of creativity. A related aggressiveness involving competition with peers and colleagues, however, is often open and professionally acceptable.

Risk taking together with courage and ego strength—manifested as self-confidence and belief in one's own judgment clearly characterized all members of this Nobel subject group. As examples, Arber, quoted earlier, spoke explicitly of risk taking and courage, and Seaborg (chapter 10) spoke of sticking to his guns in the face of possible professional "suicide." Courage and risk taking were also conveyed in all accounts of deviation from the scientific mainstream and the frequent standing up to peers' early or late criticism and rejection of their work and findings. Risk taking as a possible overall personal characteristic within and outside of scientific work could possibly be ascribed to Alvarez, who was a recreational airplane pilot. He took many solo flights throughout his home state of California and the rest of the United States.

Curiosity and the wish to learn were universally present and persistent in this group. These were highly significant emotional matters in every subject's scientific work. Dictating both problem finding and motivation to create from the beginning was the opportunity to learn known and unknown aspects of scientific knowledge and function. Love of learning then operated at every succeeding step of the creative process. Opening up and following difficult pathways rich with new enlightenments, including the need to master new techniques, was a constant objective. This learning was gratifying and impelling regardless of the perceived outcome of any work. Some, like Hubel, spoke explicitly of the fun they had in learning while doing the job. Although all sought the accomplishment and gladly received the recognition and compensation of the Nobel Prize, in each case they spoke of the importance of the learning enhancement along the way and the opening up of new knowledge. Creating, because it requires mastery and absorption of the most advanced information in any scientific field, is the most complete particular means to satisfy curiosity and enhance learning. An especially notable characteristic of the research with all members of this Nobel laureate group was their display of superlative clarity and teaching in the interviews themselves. Also, I learned from others in the schools and research institutions in which they taught that all were excellent teachers. Although excellent teaching does not necessarily derive from love of learning, there is a close affiliation.

Unlike literary, artistic, and musical creators, whose love of words, paints, sound, and musical instruments is important for their creating, intense love of materials was not universally expressed by members of the Nobel scientist group. Some did continue long in their career to work in their laboratories and enjoyed the use of apparatus, chemicals, spectrometers, calorimeters, gravimeters, DNA sequences, and growth media. Some used and particularly enjoyed work with optical and electronic instruments in the final formulations of their discoveries. Many of the members of the group instead loved general work with numbers and puzzles as well as pure thinking. Köhler, for instance, said, "Lying in bed, I was trying to solve strange problems. One of the things was how to make a continuously increasing round table. You want to have a table for four persons, six persons, eight persons. And I knew that it is very difficult to increase in size a table which is round." Many of the group spoke of earlier involvement with work materials but later they turned solely to research administration.

In distinction to the claims regarding the importance of aesthetics in scientific creativity of the Root-Bernsteins as well as the mathematicians I quoted (chapter 7), this emotional factor was not characteristically present in the orientation or creative work of the Nobel group. Only two (Lehn and Bloch) had an interest in literature, and only three (Corey, Purcell, and Nüsslein-Volhard), indicated consistent interest in visual art. Music, however, was more generally appreciated. Twenty-two members of the group spoke of enjoying music, particularly classical music, and 14 had played musical instruments at some point in their lives. Glaser had considered becoming a professional musician on the viola before he went into science; Lehn played the piano professionally while he continued his scientific career; and although not a professional, Hubel was passionately devoted to frequent playing of multiple instruments.

Although I systematically inquired of all the subjects who expressed interest in music whether musical aesthetics or auditory, rhythmic, or harmonic factors played a role in their creative work, none could remember any evidence for such an application or influence. As for the other arts, several subjects who were not interested in visual art used visual images and conceptions in their work. Rather than an aesthetic application, however, much of that visualizing applied, as I reported earlier (chapter 5), to the use of spatially based conceptions and special abilities with three-dimensional formulations.

Aesthetic considerations were knowingly applied in the creative work of only one member of the group, Nüsslein-Volhard. In addition to employing the pattern-structure teachings of her architect father, she focused in her work on fruit fly genes on aesthetic pattern relationships and intentionally used productive metaphorical terms to name gene groups. "On the whole," she said, "I think we did perfectly well using this [aesthetics] as a criteria. I think the reason for that is, in biology, when you have very clear deviations from normal development, even with single switches, the outcome usually is something which still looks quite well organized, and you don't get chaos. When things look too much like chaos, that is often where some very general issue was disturbed. Therefore, whether it looked beautiful, or clean, or nice, or aesthetically pleasing was certainly a criteria [for correctness]."[3]

Unlike the mathematical physicists mentioned in chapter 7 who emphasized aesthetics, none of the mathematicians in this Nobel group did so. Although some employed the word *symmetry* in aspects of their work, most—especially Glashow, the highly conceptual symmetry user—strongly affirmed that the symmetry conceived in scientific theories, indicating equality or repeatability, was not the same symmetry as in art or other aesthetic fields. Other subjects de-emphasized the role of aesthetics in the active process of their creation except as a confirming afterthought. Köhler said, "Aesthetics means that you feel well after you had the idea; the idea doesn't have aesthetic properties." Lehn noted, "The aesthetic feeling comes into it but is perhaps very much in the background. It doesn't lead to the concept, but once you have it, you would like to look for a given property—one might as well make photophysical or photochemical properties because that adds another dimension. Of course, it's nice." Lipscomb believed that visual symmetry was an aesthetic factor for him: "One's pleasure in symmetry usually occurs after you have made the discovery, not during, not before. It isn't the driving force for what you have to do because normally when you are in the process of making a discovery, things are sometimes a terrible mess and it's only after that, later, that one sits back and really admires it."

In summary, the predicted emotional factors connected with the creative achievements of the Nobel laureate group consisted of affects connected with the use of the cognitive creative processes, passion and drive involving the motivation to create, deviance from the mainstream, and aggression and destructive feelings. Also, there were the emotional variables related to choice of problems and persistence—problem finding, courage, ego strength, risk taking, curiosity and drives for learning. Although the majority of laureates were interested in music and some played an instrument, aesthetic factors, except in the one case of Nüsslein-Volhard, were not employed in the creative work of the group. Other emotional aspects of the creative cognitive processes such as anticipation, defensiveness, ambivalence, connection and joining, opposition and reversal, displacement, and negation were probably operative, but these, according to the research methodology employed, could not be investigated.[4]

Collaborative Investigators

Science is primarily a highly cooperative enterprise. Not only do researchers and investigators work closely together in laboratories, institutes, hospitals, and universities, but all also depend on swift and complete dissemination of information and investigatory results from other scientists nearby and around the world. Rapid sharing has now become extremely efficient because of regular information transmission via the Internet and electronic journals as well as in print. Throughout the history of science up to the present, however, it has often been difficult to determine the contributions of individuals and the factor of individual creativity in any theory and discovery. For this reason, I have focused on scientists who have been awarded the Nobel Prize because these have been singled out, often with much difficult consideration, as persons of individual achievement. In all of the scientific instances I have discussed, particular forms of individual processes have been described to me or documented in written first-person reports. Nevertheless, they all have been carried out with some degree of consultation and collaboration. Because of the extensiveness, complexity, and need for verification, all the Nobel laureates produced their full achievements in a context of working with other scientists, whether through direct assistance and collaboration from the start, continuing development, or both. This consultation and collaboration came from colleague investigators and many times from science graduate and postdoctoral students as well. Max Delbrück and his mentor, Niels Bohr, are examples of scientists who taught both colleagues and students at all levels and who self-consciously developed groups that worked on the same problem or did interlocking investigations.

The purpose of this chapter is to describe the work of those members of the Nobel laureate group who did not primarily indicate individual achievements but whose creative productions apparently developed through extensive collaboration. Three of the Nobel laureates in science I interviewed—chemists John C. Kendrew and Konrad Bloch, and physicist Emilio Segrè—did not describe individual creative-breakthrough conceptions. This cannot be interpreted to mean that they had none; for various reasons they might have wanted to keep such thinking and constructions private. It is also possible that they largely forgot having the particular conceptions. Two of these three were the oldest subjects at the time of our interviews, Bloch age 84 and Kendrew age 75, and they may have suffered from specific memory lapses.

What definitely characterizes each of the three who did not report individual creative conceptions to me is their degree of collaboration for the achievement. All teamed with other scientists in a very active and frequently intense way in their outstanding discoveries and accomplishments. Kendrew worked regularly in a laboratory with his former teacher, Max Perutz; Bloch had active, substantively detailed correspondence with German biologist Feodor Lynen; Segrè consulted constantly with Owen Chamberlain and others (despite Chamberlain's disclaimer of Segrè's superior creativity over his own; see chapter 10).

In each case, these scientists reported that they were fascinated and excited by their work, and all had the same degree of persistence as the individual Nobel creators I have already described. All, to some extent, were also risk taking and courageous. Could their collaborations be considered creative? Certainly, with respect to the presumably interconnected creative processes necessary and the ultimate outcomes, their joint endeavors were to some degree creative. All of their major collaborators received the Nobel Prize in the same year with them regardless of whether they worked in the same laboratory or, as in the case of Bloch and Lynen, were far apart from each other. If the collaborations as such then should be considered creative, what were the factors in that type of creativity? I have no systematic data pertaining to this question, but it is certain that, in all these cases, as with the preceding individual scientific creators, exceptional intellect, aggressiveness, broad and detailed scientific knowledge, and the ability to identify important problems and areas of investigation played important roles. Deep-seated curiosity regarding nature in general and the scientists' particular problematic sphere, together with their ardent and express motivation for important scientific discovery, characterized each and every one, as it did for the individual creators. All the collaborators had the capacity to stimulate and work conjunctively with colleagues. As Max Delbrück emphasized with his companionate Phage Group, there was also, with these three collaborators, constant openness to other scientists' thoughts and accomplishments.

British microbiologist John Kendrew spoke softly with an upper-class accent as he, the first editor of the *Journal of Microbiology*, sat in the journal's London office. He was gray haired and medium height with fine, regular features and high-styled clothing. He spoke early of being very interested in art, especially Italian art. His mother was an art historian and he, a bachelor, spent much time in museums and galleries, an interest and activity he did not believe was common among British scientists. Creativity in science, as he conceived it, consisted of being able to develop models and theories. To his previously cited comments about the importance of schooling for science, he made this further observation: "Most of the scientists in England came from the upper classes because they had been exposed to university educations at places such as Cambridge. One should look for creativity in the factor of social class and the background education at 'Public' Schools." He himself attended the prestigious Dragon School.

Together with co-Nobelist Max Perutz, in a scientific pursuit Perutz designated as different and courageous, Kendrew was a pioneer in the field of X-ray diffraction and crystallography. He ultimately determined the three-dimensional atomic structure of myoglobin soon after Perutz unveiled the atomic structure of hemoglobin. These proteins are responsible for transport of iron and oxygen to muscle tissue and to the body as a whole, respectively. Determination of their structure paved the way for understanding how body proteins did their jobs and for today's massive storehouse of structural determinations of other important proteins in the body and in nature.

Kendrew's investigative work was arduous. He exposed large quantities of horse heart to crystallographic analysis and then switched to similar studies of a large chunk of whale meat. The problem of determining the structure of myoglobin seemed insurmountable until Perutz, in his work on hemoglobin, discovered that patterns from several crystals, one from native protein and others soaked in solutions of heavy metals, presented metal ions in different, well-defined positions. Kendrew, with Perutz's support, then set out with great persistence to do several hundred myoglobin/heavy metal modifications before obtaining a few with the well-defined structure necessary for X-ray analysis. He was surprised, he told me, when the first outlines of the structure appeared because instead of the neat, symmetrical array he expected, the protein chain was wrapped in haphazard fashion around the central iron atom.

German-born American biochemist Konrad Bloch was also soft spoken but, in contrast with Kendrew's elite diction, his German-accented English was slightly rough edged. A refugee from Germany during the Second World War, he went first to Switzerland for a time before settling permanently in the United States. He was gray haired, tall, and slightly bent, and wore a plaid vest and dark jacket, clothing that conveyed an appearance of an aging country gentleman. In these last retired years of his life, he had followed up on life-long interests in scientific matters appearing in art and literature that he had discovered on his travels. He wrote about them in a then just-published book titled *Blondes in Venetian Paintings, the Nine-Banded Armadillo, and Other Essays in Biochemistry*. In this book, he described intriguing chemical precursors such as the nonscientist Thomas Mann's prescient anticipation in his novel *The Magic Mountain* of the discovery of brain endorphins (opioid inhibitory chemicals), and the use of a rudimentary hair-bleaching agent named "aqua blonda" by early northern Italian blonde women. He was also an ardent lover of music and played two musical instruments well. As a refugee from Hitler's Germany, he had, through a number of intercessions by colleague scientists, been able to spend his entire scientific working career in the United States.

Bloch, together with German biochemist Feodor Lynen, determined the mechanism and regulation of cholesterol and fatty acid metabolism. In addition to furthering the understanding and treatment of arteriosclerosis and heart disease, Bloch showed the role of cholesterol in building sterol substances such as female sex hormones and bile acids. Using his skills as an early pioneer of radioactive isotopes for tracing chemical reactions, he collaborated at Columbia University with Rudolf Schoenheimer and quite closely with David Rittenberg, and together they were all able to demonstrate use of acetic acid in the biosynthesis of cholesterol. "Depending with whom you work," Bloch said, "and whose ideas you either receive or assimilate or whatever, it becomes a major factor, and I say that I was lucky to be associated with Schoenheimer, an absolutely brilliant person. His enthusiasm also was infectious. I think I may have acquired a little of that." Later, when at the University of Chicago, he collaborated with Edward Tatum to use *Neospora* for the production of the fungal steroid ergosterol, and then found that the chemical squalene was an important intermediate in the production of cholesterol. Other steps followed and, on learning that Lynen was also investigating the synthesis of cholesterol, Bloch developed an active correspondence with him. Lynen wrote that he had made a crucial demonstration that an enzyme, coenzyme A, was necessary for the uptake of the acetic acid–related chemical groups in cholesterol. Bloch went on to show that another precursor, mevalonic acid, was also operating. Both men independently persisted while constantly sharing their findings. All in all, the synthesis of cholesterol was found to involve 30 different steps.

Emilio Segrè also emphasized the importance of collaborators in his work. Italian born, this American nuclear scientist was involved with Chamberlain as well as the students Clyde Wiegand and Thomas Ypsilantis in determining the existence of a subatomic particle, the antiproton. Segrè's contribution was largely theoretical but he also emphasized that he and the other members of the "very small group" carried out the creative technical experiments using the Bevatron, a particle accelerator capable of producing 6 million electron volts. This large accelerator used the energy of beams of protons to produce particle collisions that isolated the antiproton.

Members of the group, according to Segrè, associated very closely and were quite willing to accept one another's criticisms. He had many years of experience with scientific collaboration in nuclear physics while in Italy with his idol, Enrico Fermi, as well as with the chemist Carlo Perrier, with whom he had separately discovered a new chemical element, number 43, technetium.

Segrè was silver haired and short, with a venerable, creased face and Italian-accented speech. Despite his anxious, sharp manner of speaking, he was charming and very cooperative. He had a strong literary bent, having written a biography of Enrico Fermi; a textbook titled *Nuclei and Particles;* another physics book, *From X-Rays to Quarks: Modern Physicists and Their Discoveries;* an autobiography, *A Mind Always in Motion;* and other books, both technical and designed to appeal to a lay audience. Although also interested in visual art, he denied using visual thinking to any great extent in his work. His knowledge of physics was wide ranging and both historical and philosophical. When describing the evolution of his endeavors, he struck me as geared toward a good deal of competitiveness with other scientists, coworkers, and others nearby or in more remote portions of the world. Although he was clearly respectful, understanding, and basically trusting, Segrè spoke frequently of challenges, interference, antagonisms, dismissals, and concerns about primacy regarding all of his achievements.[1] He said, "If people collaborate, and somebody, as it always happens, gets more awards, for instance is promoted first and the other is promoted later, it takes a certain greatness of soul not to become enemies." His competitiveness is also manifest, I believe, in the accounts spread throughout his autobiography.

As described in chapter 10, Joseph Murray, using the homospatial process, individually created the stable and important kidney placement in organ transplantation, but much of the previous and remaining discovery work was carried out in active collaboration with his colleagues both in the United States and England. With a different perspective on collaboration than Segrè, he himself emphasized that point: "Honestly it's not false humility, but I get embarrassed when people say I'm a great guy because I did all this, because I didn't do it alone, we've got a team, an institution. Sure I developed the operation...but you're part of a team."

Murray first became interested in tissue and organ transplantation at the military Valley Forge General Hospital in Pennsylvania, where he performed numerous skin grafts on casualty burn patients. His chief of service, Colonel Brown, showed him that patients with close genetic relationships, specifically identical twins, maintained grafts permanently, unlike temporary nonrelated donors. Later, in his years at the Peter Bent Brigham Hospital, under the administration of surgeons Francis D. Moore and George W. Thorne (whose support he constantly cited), he carried out numerous transplantation operations of various organs, especially kidneys, on rabbits, mice, sheep, and dogs. In these, he and his colleagues tried to prevent immune reactions to donor difference from causing transplant rejection; they applied total body radiation as well as available bone marrow transplantation with minimal success. A few effective operations were then performed in human identical twins. The turning point came through the work of Peter Medawar in England and of George Hitchings, Gertrude Elion, Robert Schwartz, and William Dameshek in the United States, who introduced the possibility of using a drug to block the immune reaction in transplantation. Much communication at that time took place with Medawar, who sent Roy Calne to Murray's group in Boston. Calne had tested an antigen-resistant and immune-preventive drug on dogs in England. With the pharmaceutical help of Hitchings and Elion and the hematological and physiological consultations of Dameshek and Schwartz, Calne was able to introduce the group to his successful immunosuppressant drug azathioprine. This drug had originally been used with patients suffering from leukemia, and its use prevented rejection of kidney transplants in humans, initiating the era of organ transplantation.

Collaboration for all scientists involves both cooperation and competitiveness with others doing similar work. In collaborations of individual creators in the Nobel group, there was evidence of some sharp competition. Both Chamberlain and Wiegand wanted to separate from the competitive Segrè and work on their own soon after the antiproton discovery was made. Milstein erroneously disavowed Köhler's claim to having initially conceived the monoclonal antibody despite their jointly receiving the Nobel Prize. Destructive feelings, whether connected with the creative process or not, may spread into relationships.

To specify the complicated components of successful creative collaboration is very difficult. A review of studies of research collaboration most frequently indicates the importance of the following: mutual respect, understanding, and trust; an appropriate cross-section of members; open and frequent communication; sufficient funds; and a skilled convener or organizer.[2] In addition to the four predominantly collaborators I have described, all of the Nobel laureate group collaborated to some degree. In these collaborations, distinctly present were openness to others' work and thought, and shared exceptional knowledge and learning, but there was also particular willingness to deviate jointly from the mainstream, and an extreme persistence as well as aggressiveness applied especially to the content of the problem. In addition, there was interaction based on clear-cut individuation or separateness together with connection, a large-scale, continuing form of the sep-con articulation process; where possible, there were collaborative uses of the cognitive creative processes. A very striking factor that I have mentioned previously in other contexts (e.g., chapter 12) was the superior teaching orientation and communication ability of every member of the Nobel laureate group. This was especially manifest in their willingness and skill in making clear to me as interviewer the nature of their thinking and scientific achievements. As they were all university-level professors, good teaching might be expected, but I found them all to be especially proficient in this regard.[3] Several, such as chemist Elias Corey, were devoted to teaching large numbers of highly competent graduate students. The collaborations with graduate and postdoctorate students, which occurred to some degree even with achievements leading directly to the Nobel Prize, must have been facilitated at least partly by the group's teaching and communication capacities. As I indicated earlier in chapter 7, on creative emotions and motivations, love of learning played an important role in the Nobel-winning creative achievements. Such love of learning and teaching are, as I have suggested, intrinsically connected. Enlightenment and discovery motivate and guide the best teachers.

Further assessment of all factors involved in creative collaboration requires detailed analyses of particular successful collaborations from cognitive, interpersonal, social, and cultural perspectives.

Developmental Background of Creativity and Genius

"Geniuses are born, not made" is a time-honored and broadly held conviction, applied both by sophisticated and nonsophisticated believers. All so-called geniuses are included: persons of high accomplishment in the arts and sciences; those in a wide variety of social, political, and commercial fields as well as those who seem destined for high achievement; and others already manifesting skill and accomplishment but who are quiet and diligent and as yet unrecognized. As most clearly and lexically defined, however, genius is the manifestation of extremely high-level capacity and intellectual accomplishment. With respect to creativity, therefore, use of the literal term *genius* is slightly confounding in that all products of genius—for example, the consistently outstanding performance of a standard surgical procedure, or constant and good problem solving—are not necessarily creative. Contrariwise, all creative products, such as a new and valuable computing program, are not necessarily the work of genius. Nevertheless, genius and creativity may frequently and meaningfully overlap, especially in science. There is also wide consensus that creativity and genius consisting of high skill and capacity, although not necessarily of extraordinary intellect, may overlap in literary, musical, and artistic fields. Therefore, in the assessments to follow, which focus on creative individual prizewinners in both scientific and artistic pursuits, it can be assumed that some features of true genius also will be revealed.

The scientific evidence for the conviction that geniuses are born, not made, or that creativity is inherited, is very meager—currently, in fact, it is virtually nonexistent. In addition to Francis Galton's unreliable study of father-to-son transmission of genius and creativity (described in chapter 2), other studies done since then, based on occupational inheritance and temporal and national distribution, have yielded very variable and essentially negative results.[1] It shall be worth exploring some of the reasons for the widespread persistence of the idea, however, before proceeding further. One important positive reason, I believe, is to give geniuses their due. The relationship between genetic transmission and environmental influences, although today better understood and clarified, remains in specific cases somewhat of a mystery. The designation "genius" is an honorific based partly on that mystery. A belief that someone of very high accomplishment, or even potentially high accomplishment, is "born that way" designates an inviolate capacity. No one else is responsible for the accomplishments—except, indirectly, the parents' genetic makeup—and no person or influence (except poor health or injury) can change or reduce the capacity. The genius-designate is highly endowed, completely special, and worthy of high accolades. On the other hand, a negative reason for holding the absolute genetic conviction is that all persons who know they are not such geniuses can feel reassured. The mysterious piece of luck simply did not occur to them and, moreover, they need not strive for such attainment. Geniuses, they may conclude, don't necessarily deserve a lot of personal credit for exceptional capacities and outcomes; those were thrust upon them by birth.

Although there is no direct evidence for the genetic basis of genius or creativity, one factor deserves distinct consideration, particularly with respect to science. Intelligence, which as Gardner[2] and Sternberg[3] especially have signified consists of diverse forms and different faculties, has been shown indirectly to have strong genetic transmission. This factor, in one form or another, has been important for creative accomplishment in all of the branches of science. Although it is only one of the cognitive factors involved and therefore not causally sufficient in itself, the high degree of complexity and the breadth and quantity of scientific knowledge has required a well-above-average level of intelligence (not empirically determined) for creative accomplishment. The scientific intelligence requirement provides one explanation for the well-established observation that creative achievement in mathematics tends to fall off after the age of 40. High intelligence is particularly vital in mathematics, and human intelligence, as still measured by standard IQ tests, characteristically rises to a peak in the years between 20 and 30 and then begins to recede. All of this does not perforce apply to so-called idiot savants, persons with special capacities in fields such as mathematics or music but with deficiencies in other cognitive areas such as logic and means–end reasoning. Their genetic and developmental patterns are not clearly understood.

Coordinated with genetic factors of intelligence and other undefined types of capacities, developmental factors involving nurture and upbringing very likely play an important role. I shall present evidence that suggests that one of the most important characteristics of both highly creative persons and geniuses, an intense motivation to discover and create, develops from particular kinds of family backgrounds. These backgrounds consist of the presence of at least one influential family member, usually the parent of the same gender, whose occupation was the performance or applied (including technological) equivalent of the offspring's field of scientific accomplishment. Examples among the fathers of Nobel laureates not in my investigative group include mathematician/physicist Einstein's father, who was an electrical engineer; biochemist Linus Pauling's father, a pharmacist; the fathers of chemists Friedrich Bergius, Fritz Haber, and Hans Fischer, who respectively ran a chemical factory, sold chemical supplies, and was head of a dye company; physiologist Ragnar Granit's father, a forester; and physician Charles Huggins' father, a pharmacist. Among the scientists in the investigative subject group, atomic physicist Seaborg's father was a machinist; physicist/ magnetic resonance investigator Purcell's father was a telephone company manager; biologist Arber's father was a farmer; physicist Chamberlain's father was a radiologist; physicist Bloembergen's father was a chemical engineer; and chemist Kendrew's father was a climatologist.

Beyond these examples, I have assessed the pattern of performance/ applied equivalent occupations present among the parents of Nobel laureates in science, starting from the first Nobel Award year to a recent one. Exploring the parental background of these laureates, I was able to procure factual data regarding parental occupations from the biographies of 435 out of all 488 Nobel laureates in the sciences (physics, chemistry, and physiology or medicine) from the award's inaugural year, 1901, through 2003. The number of parents of both genders who were in the same occupation as their Nobel laureate offspring (i.e., investigators, professors, and pure scientists), including parents who had been scientific Nobel laureates, was only 11 out of the entire 488 (2%). In contrast with this result, I found, in a general comparison, that the most recent US Census measurement of parental occupations indicated that 21% of American men were in the same occupations as their fathers.[4]

The findings regarding performance/applied equivalent occupations were, however, markedly different. The types of these performance/applied equivalent occupations of the parents of the documented Nobel laureate scientists are listed alphabetically in Table 14.1.

I found that 53% of same-gendered parents of the entire Nobel laureate group were in one or more of these occupations. Therefore, I compared the incidences in the entire Nobel laureate group of both same and performance/applied equivalent parental occupations with two types of control groups. The first was a comparable nonscientist high-achieving group previously and independently identified by Goertzel and Goertzel,[5] consisting of 548 internationally eminent men and women living during the same period as these Nobel laureates in the sciences. Among this group were persons such as Jomo Kenyatta, Ho Chi Minh, J. Edgar Hoover, Greta Garbo, Hubert Humphrey, Charles Lindbergh, Emma Goldman, vehicle designer

TABLE 14.1 Applied and Performance Occupations (Based on Practice, Materials, and Nature)

Agriculture
Animal breeding
Chemical and dye manufacture and processing
Climatology
Dentistry
Electrician
Engineering (structural, chemical, mechanical, civil, and communications)
Forestry
Geology
Horticulture
Land survey
Machine design
Machinist
Medical supply
Mining
Pharmacist and pharmaceuticals
Practicing physician
Veterinary medicine

Louis Renault, Lytton Strachey, Frank Sinatra, Joe Namath, Paul Tillich, Bob Dylan, Henry Kissinger, Pierre Trudeau, Aly Khan, and General George Patton. The second was a group of 560 very-high-IQ non-Nobel-Prize-winning men and women who were longitudinally and systematically studied under the direction of psychologist Lewis Terman and who also lived during the same period as the science Nobel laureates. For the first group, the proportion of parents in the same occupation as their offspring was 20%, in significant contrast with the 2% of parents of Nobel laureate scientists. This indicated, therefore, that there was no evidence of direct inheritance in the Nobel laureate group based on occupation. For the second group, in a comparison of performance/applied equivalent occupations—the very high IQ persons Terman and his group followed throughout their lives[6]—only 17% were in the those occupations, another statistically significant contrast with the science Nobel laureates.

When I analyzed the biographical data that manifested a statistically significant number of parents of Nobel laureates in science who were the same gender as their laureate children and who worked in applied or performance-equivalent occupations, I found indications that a number of these parents themselves had unfulfilled wishes to have a scientific career. Also, several other same-gendered parents who were in more remote non–performance/applied equivalent types of occupations, such as plumber or small business owner, had similar unfulfilled wishes.

Such unfulfilled parental wishes were also identified among the members of the interviewed Nobel laureate subject group. The physicist Owen Chamberlain told me the following instance:

> My father was a physician radiologist, but he always wished he were a physicist. I think my interest in physics stems partly from the fact that he always had an interest in physics. I don't think he ever really trained as a physicist. After he was in medicine, he realized that physics was an interesting area. And he had lots of applications of simple physics. Not high-brow particularly. Some of his best work was done with hydrostatic models of the human system.... He'd point out things that people thought they were doing that they were doing all wrong. So he had a leaning toward being a physicist. And now and then he owned up to it. I think I got into physics not realizing what the word physics meant. I liked certain kinds of problems and went in that direction.

Another physicist, Luis Alvarez, told me he was influenced to go into scientific research because of his physician father's dedicated interest in his research laboratory (detailed in chapter 12). Also, Nicolaas Bloembergen said that his father, a chemical engineer, was throughout his life very interested in research science. Several other subjects suggested similar but less strong parental proclivities.

As for the entire science Nobel laureate group, the proportion of all same-gendered parents with unfulfilled wishes to be a scientist and/or scientific investigator was 24%. This finding, quite likely underestimated from information available from ordinary biographical accounts, not interviews, is notable.[7] That a considerable proportion of same-gendered parents of science Nobel laureates were in applied/performance occupations, and a large number—in these and more remote occupations as well—had relatively uncommon unfulfilled wishes to be scientists, suggests a specific developmental background inducing strong motivation. Children are frequently strongly influenced by parental inclinations and unfulfilled wishes. The notable incidence in this parental population suggests positive identification with the parents and the living out of their wishes and dreams. Also, there was very likely a greater overall positive vocation-related identification with same-gendered parents in performance/applied equivalent fields. Together with such identifications, an individuating competition with the same-gendered parent often must have occurred. The developing scientist both identified with those parents in a general way and competed to go further and outdo them. Both the loving component of interest and sharing of those parents' applied scientific type of work, and the aggressive wish to supersede in a related field with far greater social recognition, were likely to be present. Living out a parent's wishes was an incentive but all together, the three motivating factors—vocation-related identification, living out the unfulfilled wishes, and competition—would serve as powerful incentives to achieve, and may well account in good measure for the motivation for scientific achievement at the highest level possible.

In addition to the feature of motivation, parental innovative orientations in both related and unrelated occupations also influenced the creativity of their offspring. Data regarding this come from the interviewed Nobel laureate group. Biochemist Werner Arber described the following:

> I must tell you that, when I was still a very small kid, my father, who was a farmer, had large fields of potatoes. We always collected the potatoes by hand and then afterwards we had to sort them out according to size. So my father felt that could be made mechanistic, and he constructed himself a machine to sort three kinds of size—very small ones, medium, and larger ones, and they were sold separately. He made this all-wooden construction with springs. So, you see there was something innovative there. He helped me in that way. I learned not just to accept what I saw or learned from others but—let's make something different.

Theoretical physicist Sheldon Glashow said, "My father was a plumber. He was technically oriented, he invented a device to use a boiler to produce hot water for the domestic home by making a small hole in the boiler and injecting a series of pipes. By pulling a rod, these pipes would spread out and produce a secondary flow of water inside the boiler for the hot water system."

Chemist Elias Corey lost his father at a very young age, but he was brought up by a stepfather, his uncle John. About John, Corey said, "He was a very, very intelligent man. When I was in grade school we used to sort of play games together and he'd invent games; we'd do mathematical things together, adding columns or multiplying. I could never beat him at those things." Biologist Georges Köhler's father spent many nights watching the stars and taught Georges and his other children new ways to study astronomy.

As for members of a large, biographically studied Nobel group, I have already mentioned Fermi's inventive mother. Also, the father of physicist theorist Richard Feynman, had always wanted to go to medical school and he actively taught his son such skills as pattern recognition, both within nature and in academic materials.[8]

Both general and particular scientific skills, it can be assumed, were transmitted from parents in the related performance/applied equivalent occupations. All of these types of occupations involve interests and activities related in some way to scientific work. Given a likelihood of transmission of component skills, it is possible that gene expression, recessive and dominant, may have occurred. Such expression requires interaction with other genes as well as environmental influences, however, for the development of creative potential. It is likely that factors such as direct training, support of interests, and modeling by parents in performance/applied equivalent occupations all combined with whatever genetic factors might have been involved.

With respect to creativity in general, a similar type of developmental background likely inducing strong motivation for creative achievement has also been present for outstanding persons in literature. Together with Grace Wyshak, I carried out another study of the parental background of a group of 50 Nobel laureates in literature, 135 Pulitzer Prize winners in literature, and 31 Man Booker literature prize winners (United Kingdom).[9] In this field, although high intelligence comparable to the Nobel scientists might not have been necessary for creative achievement, many in the group nevertheless would be considered geniuses for their outstanding literary and intellectual prowess. All in this literature group certainly may be considered creative—that is, productive of entities widely considered both new and valuable.

The parental backgrounds of the literary prizewinners were compared with a total of 392 persons of nonliterary eminence from Goertzel and Goertzel's study, as well as 560 nonwinners of literary prizes in Terman's longitudinal study of very high IQ persons. Performance/applied equivalent occupations with respect to literature were defined as those involving language, persuasion, or artisanal skills as follows: bookseller; clergy; educator; journalist or legal profession; linguistics, missionary, or notary; potter or cabinetmaker; publisher or editor; salesperson; scholar, biblical, professorial, telegraph communication, or theater-related activities. Eugene O'Neill's father, for instance, was an actor, and John Hersey's father was a missionary.

In this study also, the proportion of parents of both genders in the literary prizewinner group (2; less than 1%) was statistically significantly less than the proportion of same-gendered parents (61; 16%) of the eminent nonliterary group from Goertzel and Goertzel;[10] also, the proportion of literary prizewinner parents in performance/applied equivalent occupations was significantly greater than among members of a nonliterary prizewinning high-IQ group from Terman et al.[11] Similar to the finding of unfulfilled parental wishes among science Nobel laureates, there was a high incidence of parental unfulfilled wishes for a literary occupation or literary achievement in the literary prizewinner group. For example, the father of novelist and poet Robert Penn Warren relinquished his lifelong ambition to be a poet to support his family. Warren was gratified, he told me, to fulfill his father's ambition and go beyond it. Apparently operative, as with the Nobel scientists, were the factors of identification and competition of the literary prizewinners with a same-gendered parent in a related applied-type field.

Family influences, therefore, seem to play a role in the development of different types of creative persons, including creative geniuses. The operation of the dual forces of identification and competition together, particularly in persons with some degree of genetic endowment, serves to produce strong motivation for creative achievement that lasts throughout life. Extreme persistence, extraordinary motivation to work and explore, willingness to take risks—all of which are characteristic of creative persons in diverse fields—are very likely fueled by the developmental influences. Living out the explicit or implicit parental wishes to become scientists or, in a parallel way, creative writers may be a particularly potent incentive, whether or not the off-spring is explicitly aware of it. When the living-out variable is implicit it may, in fact, have an even stronger influence than explicit directives on choices and behavior. The living-out factor, possible genetic components, and parental inventiveness—and additionally an acceptance of deviant thinking and nurturance of individuality—may, as I shall discuss in chapter 16, play a role during adolescence in the development of the basic properties of the cognitive creative processes.

Other family background tendencies also play a facilitating role. Whether a result of the gratifying recognition of specially developing skills in their offspring, or because of their own independent high valuation of education, or both, parents often provide a great deal of constant support of learning and formal education. The autobiographies and biographies of Nobel laureates and other prizewinners contain frequent references to parents' having provided, despite in many cases being quite poor, uneducated, or themselves displaced, large amounts of preliminary as well as high-level education in the chosen fields. Moreover, many parents in performance/applied equivalent occupations were in the position to exert facilitating influences in work or, when appropriate, academic fields. A salient matter is that, although many of the biographies and autobiographies studied were relatively brief, there was no evidence that any of the parents exerted high pressure or forced achievements at an early age, a factor that often works to stifle adult creativity.

Comparison Control Subjects

A group of applied scientists and technologists, professional engineers, was interviewed according to the same semistructured protocol used with the Nobel laureates (chapter 8). This group was matched with the Nobel laureates in gender, age at the time of the interview, cultural and national background, and professional status. All, like the Nobel laureates, were academic researchers or faculty members. As engineering faculty of a prestigious Eastern US technological university, all had postgraduate training with doctoral degrees or the equivalent. Although I did not apply any intelligence measures, all demonstrated well above average intelligence, in several cases comparable with the Nobel laureate group.

As described earlier, identification of the group as a comparison control group was achieved as follows. At first, the chairman of the Mechanical Engineering Department identified particular members of his department as high achievers or creative persons. I therefore adopted that point of view and undertook the use of the same semistructured interview protocol with those he had designated as I did with the Nobel laureates. All subjects in this group were informed that they were being interviewed regarding creativity and the creative process. Afterward, as I reported, I obtained assessments of creativity by the same expert judges used for the Nobel laureates. One subject's work was rated in Category 3, both new and valuable (social, scientific, instrumental); the work of two others was rated in Category 2, either new or valuable; and that of the remainder was in Category 1, neither new nor valuable. Only Category 3 subject *Creator*, therefore, met the criteria for creativity comparable with the Nobel laureates. Some of these subjects had obtained patents and honors. All patents were reviewed by the expert panel and determined to be essentially different but not new commodities or procedures. Patents are regularly issued by the government for nonduplicated products without any requirement for utility or even applicability. For several members of the group, some of their patented constructions had never been produced or evaluated. All were for potentially useful mechanical products and procedures, but they possessed little or no proven genuine value and newness. Although some of the ideas and methods arguably may have possessed some relative newness together with usefulness, they were nevertheless considered creative to a minimal or very low degree. Separately, the judges, including expert professional technicians, commented that these subjects were generally problem solvers but were minimally creative or noncreative. *Creator* was the only member of the group judged to have made an authentically creative achievement.[1]

Many of these subjects were colorful, interesting people. All were proficient in problem definition and problem solving, often to a very high level of complexity; effective theory construction to some extent; and the production of technical changes with indeterminate or variable degrees of value. Like the Nobel laureates, their memory was detailed and apparently quite reliable. They expressed some degree of positive emotion when describing their technical solutions.

As for gender comparison, there was, like the Nobel group, one woman in the group of engineers. Average age at the time of the interviews was 58 years (Nobel group = 65 years). Although, unlike the Nobel group, all the engineers lived in the United States, 25% had foreign cultural backgrounds, compared with 26% of the Nobel laureates who were foreign dwelling or of foreign cultural background.

Results of this investigation were that the engineer group used many different types of thought processes in its achievements. Emotional factors were also varied but were largely less intense than in the Nobel laureate group. Constructive problem solving based on all or some of various effective approaches were employed: problem framing, gathering information, flexibility, imaging, analogical thinking, combining, and connecting. Often, successful outcomes arose from attempts to think about different rather than routine techniques, theories, and products. No consistent type of content, or psychological or technical structure, characterized this motivation for difference or a different approach. Although some subjects indicated a minimal degree of motivation to create, none of these attempted to deviate from accepted canons or tasks. Only within a narrow problem area or chosen task was there any attempt to move away or reconceive given or customary facts, processes, techniques, or ideas. Except in the case of *Creator*, no instances of employment of the creative cognitive processes similar to those the Nobel group used were found throughout the group of engineers. Through an apparent use of the homospatial process, *Creator* achieved a particular creative solution. In several cases, some aspects of the three creative thought processes without their critical features were used. One subject used reversal or opposition but not, as with the janusian process, the conception and use of multiple opposites simultaneously. All of the subjects described using visualization and visual imagery in their conceptualizing, but none save *Creator* conceived, as in the homospatial process, two or more discrete images or entities superimposed or interposed in the same mental space or spatial location. Many subjects did thoughtful and meaningful separating and connecting in varying ways, both concrete and theoretical, but none, as in the sep-con articulation process, effected concomitant connection of functionally separate components. No use of aspects of the creative thought processes led to integration and creative results, although in some cases the outcomes were otherwise successful. The creative specificity of the cognitive processes was affirmed and illustrated by the differentiation between their effective use by the Nobel laureates and an absence or a restricted-aspect use by the comparison group.

Problem Solving

Almost all of the engineers used straightforward and well-established inductive and problem-solving methods in their work.[2] These methods were often effective in producing useful products. None of the primary problem solvers, however, produced the kind of integrative solutions that problem-solving investigator Maier designated as meaningfully creative.[3]

Chairman of the Mechanical Engineering Department *Administrator*, a tall, well-dressed, and quick-speaking engineer with an intelligent face and helpful manner, was very thoughtful and detailed about the steps in his problem-solving work. He described the sequence and schema as follows:

> I was working on a human-powered machine for invalids and it was necessary to design first a kind of machine that would torque [moment of force] test the shaft when it's loaded. So, I wrote down a specification with geometry, kinetics, forces, energy, materials, signals for control, and including ergonomics, production, assembly, operation, costs, and maintenance. Of course, these all are subject to some extent to change, which one could allow, but there were certain targets. I measured whatever torque that was measurable, recorded the measurements, made them easily accessible and so forth. Then, I went back to look for the essentials and to narrow things down. I established function structures which were the controls and the power supply transmission and structure. I broke it down into blocks and set up feed-forward block diagrams changing the control. Then I started sketching up various combinations, pictures of how I might do it—by dropping a weight or by running a cam [a rotating or sliding piece]. I decided on the weight and worked out its size as well as that of the springs and the loads on the shafts that would allow the brake to work. And I calculated the horsepower required and the problem was solved.

Many of the other engineers also presented similar detailed and successful schemas and problem solving approaches.

Reversal

Reversals and turnarounds appeared in the work of a few of the engineers. Born in Great Britain, *Reverser* sat very erect, sedately dressed in a dark suit and patterned silk tie. He spoke with a soft, cultivated accent, and his voice rose and eyes flashed as he described work that interested him. His field was contact mechanics and he had three patents, one for a type of synthetic surface and two for particular synthetic surfaces applied to piano keys. With respect to his viewpoint on creativity, he knew well and was enthusiastic about deBono's theory of "lateral thinking": the consideration of approaches, as I described in Chapter 2, that were "lateral" or sideways from usual modes of problem solving.[4]

Reverser had developed a theory of frictional heating in connection with a local large-gun arsenal commission to study the friction involved in firing large shells. He began with the knowledge that for any contact between objects, the friction or interface temperature was calculated both from the dimensions and the pressure at the contact points. After considering the effects of rubbing plastic hard and continually on ice, he realized that the friction temperature could possibly rise up to 300 degrees centigrade and the ice would melt. As he told me,

> And then I thought that one could have the idea that if you rub hard enough, something like when on skis or on anything like tires, perhaps you could conceive that the surface temperature would always come to some temperature beyond which it could not go. If you fixed the temperature, you could calculate the heat, which means you could calculate the energy loss and the friction. It was an inverse of the usual way the formula had been applied for fifty years. And it came up with something useful. That was very interesting and very exciting too.
>
> I knew this copper alloy they used at the back end of shells; I knew that it melted at about one thousand and fifty centigrade. So, I used that temperature and worked backwards to find what the friction was. And it seems also to work on brakes and tires as well as guns. As soon as I saw that there was some universality with this idea, I realized that I was onto something. The method was subsequently applied by the local arsenal in their gun manufacture.

Reverser experienced some of the same kind of gratification and enthusiasm in his problem solving as many of the Nobel laureates cited earlier. Conceiving the reverse of the usual is a contrary procedure, but it does not involve mutual contradiction or the conflict of simultaneous opposites as in the janusian process. It therefore does not produce, as in the janusian process, the interaction stimulated by conflict of simultaneous opposites that leads to a breakthrough and a creative result. Instead, going backward or using a reversal produces only a different and possibly useful change of formula. In developing an approach based on a reversal of a classical computation, *Reverser's* formulation somewhat resembles that of Nobel laureate Elias Corey (chapter 9) in the development of retrosynthetic chemistry. A crucial distinguishing factor, however, was that Corey used the simultaneous opposites of reversal of the steps of chemical construction together with synthesis, whereas *Reverser* conceived a reversal alone. *Reverser's* result was different and useful but, on the basis of the experts' judgment, it was not both new and valuable and a creative achievement.

Visualization

Visualization and the use of visual imagery, as I stated earlier, is sometimes thought to be a factor in creativity of all types.[5] Although visual or any type of sensory imagery is often a component of the homospatial process, there is no evidence that frequent use of visualization or of particular types of visualization capacities lead to creative achievements. As engineering especially requires spatial design and visual constructions, it was not surprising that 100% of the engineers used visualization and visual imagery in their work. None of the uses described, except for *Creator's* incorporation of visual imagery in a homospatial process, led directly to creative results. Extensive mental visualization skills, including three-dimensional formulating, were often used in other ways, such as in mentally constructed designs for machines or objects to be drawn and then built by others. Two examples of the engineers' general and productive use of visualization follow.

Casual but neat in appearance, American *Visualizer/Collaborator* was medium height and bespectacled, with dark hair and an impish-looking face. He frequently smiled broadly and elaborated his comments at great length. Proudly he described an effective "trick" he used in his office, the placement behind his head of a dramatically colored painting called *Rhythm in Four.* This, he believed, distracted students from ordinary preoccupations and made them concentrate on their discussions with him. Likewise, in his teaching he used colored images and colored blackboard drawings to command attention. His primary work areas were, somewhat surprisingly, in the primarily sound areas of acoustics, vibrations, noise control, and sensors. He had been able to procure 12 patents for products ranging from types of inkjet printers, hardness testers and special synthetic surfaces to piano hammer and key contrivances, laser Dopplers, and tools. Although he did not give an account of the specific use of visualization with any of these commodities, he described his general visual ability in detail: "I have a highly developed spatial aptitude. I can visualize things in my head and they don't just have to be stationary, they can be moving around. I teach dynamics and I can visualize

things in three dimensions including colors, not black and white but colors
of other dimensions. I can shut my eyes and see this chair in front of us. A lot
of people can do that but then, I can take that chair and I can maybe turn it
around in my head."

American engineer *Visualizer 1* was tall, broad-faced, and heavy-set with a
brooding, anxious quality. He worked in the field of aeroelasticity, the nature
of materials used in flight. Primarily involved with engineering theory rather
than practice, he had applied for a patent for a practical device but had not at
the time received it. "I actually visualize the physical process," he said.

> There are approximate solutions, elasticity solutions within what is called
> the theory of structures. They involve beams which are long slender objects
> like measuring sticks, and plates which are thin objects that are slightly
> curved like the top of an airplane wing. If one pulls in one direction and
> the object contracts, then it might be different than what happens in iso-
> tropic [having the same value when measured along axes in all directions]
> cases. Also, if one pulls a nonisotropic block of material it can also tip.
> I looked at those things and I had this geometrical concept immediately.
> The constants can go into the coordinates [linear or angular quantities]
> and you get back in a different space to something that looks isotropic.
>
> It was a very visual thing for me. If one had some kind of isotropic mate-
> rial, it would, by various shrinkings or stretchings look slightly different,
> but topologically it'll look the same. An ellipse becomes a thinner ellipse or
> flatter in one of its dimensions.

Visualizer 1 developed a theoretical change but not a creative result. In neither case described did the use of visualization involve superimposition or
interposition of visual images in the same spatial location as in the homospatial process; nor were any creations produced. For others in the engineer
group, visualization was facilitative, even vital for problem solving, but also
did not produce judged creative results.[6]

Analogy

Conceiving analogies is a very useful type of cognition, and it may often be
used in various aspects of problem solving as well as at early stages of the creative process. Analogies, however, are comparisons or applications of structure from one domain to another, such as from the concrete to the abstract.
Analogies are not the same as metaphors.[7] Nor is analogy at the root of metaphor creation, although various analogies may be derived from metaphors
as with other suggestive tropes or figures of speech and thought. Unlike the
homospatial process, which produces effective metaphors both in art and in
science, analogical constructions neither disrupt mentally conceived space

nor involve conflict and mutual interactions that lead directly to creative results.

Two of the engineers described an effective use of analogies that helped them construct problem solutions. Both, as is often the case with the framing of analogies, also used observation and visualization to a large degree in applying the formulation to a different domain.

Trimly bearded, of medium height, and comfortably affable and straight backed, the muscularity of *Analogizer 1* clearly showed under his clothing. He loved the outdoors and spent a good deal of time hiking, boating, and lumberjacking as well as at strenuous snow and winter activities. Talking about his love of canoeing, he told me he once perceptively noticed that little drops of water bounced along the surface of the paddle as it went into the lake. "They won't just drop in and splash but they'll bounce," he said. "Each drop will keep its form for a while, then it gets slowed up and just goes back into the water. When I really noticed that, it immediately brought to mind an experiment I could run."

This experiment had to do with a problem in his heat transfer work called entrainment and deposition in liquid and vapor flow. Entrainment occurs when liquid drops form on the walls of a tube containing vapor in the center of a container. The deposition appears when these drops are sheared off back into the vapor core. "The question," he said, "is how you model this entrainment-deposition process. What are the parameters that govern it? When I saw these little drops bouncing along, I thought, right here, here's the deposition problem. I visualized this drop in the vapor core bouncing against the liquid fill on the wall; sometimes it's captured and sometimes it isn't. And I thought if I developed a drop generator I could angle at a liquid film wall at different angles with different-sized bubbles and different velocities and maybe I could get an idea of what this deposition process is all about. What are the parameters that govern the capture process?"

Seeing an analogy between the behavior of the water drops on his canoe paddle and the entrainment-deposition problem, *Analogizer 1* applied it to the formulation of an experiment in heat transfer. He did not create a metaphor of canoe water drop and vapor core transfer, nor did he superimpose images as in a homospatial process, but used a productive comparison and application to another domain. It was not a creation, but he did move toward a successful solution.

In contrast to *Analogizer 1*, Vienna-born *Analogizer 2*, white-haired and somewhat frail and stooped, was intellectually energetic and engaging. He worked in the field of lubrication systems and analysis of surfaces. At one point he told me that in a project on the "cracking" operation (separating out the hydrocarbons) of crude oil, he had initially found a lot of leftover carbon. This was considered harmful because it would stop the cracking operation, but he had an idea for finding a way to make the carbon lubricating. Nickel-containing alloys, he decided, would produce carbon on the mechanical surfaces, and if there were continuous wear only thin layers of carbon would form close to the surface. These could be oriented in such a way that they would lubricate.

"I oriented this material," he said, "so that it would behave. I thought of a lubricant on the surface as being like an orderly bunch of soldiers standing up. With that analogy, it was in a straight line. Then, in order to make them slide, they would have to be laid down in one direction so that one could slide one soldier over the other. If they were in the opposite direction, then there would be difficulty moving."

Analogizer 2 used an analogy to the lineup of orderly, mobile soldiers as a means to induce lubricating qualities in surface carbon during oil-cracking operations. He applied their potential behavioral properties in space to the behavior of carbon as the lubricant, using properties required when soldiers are in a group to determine properties of the lubricant. He did not use a homo-spatial process by conceiving the carbon elements and the soldiers as occupying the same mental spatial location. He simply formulated two distinct images of carbon aligning like an analogous group of mobile soldiers. In other words, he compared the carbon and the line of soldiers. Superimpositions of the soldiers and carbon would instead have generated new properties and new identities as well as lineups. Analogies involve parallelism, similarity, and comparison rather than joining and construction. These may or may not lead to problem solution. They may enter into a part of a creative process, but they do not lead directly to creative results.

Connections

Another contrast between the engineers and the Nobel laureate group concerns the important factor of connections. Finding or making connections alone has been the proposed causative factor in creative thinking and creativity by both scholars and professionals.[8] As discussed in chapter 1, various ways of connecting have been proposed such as associating, combining, and blending. None of these formulations correspond with the creative process of sep-con articulation because the functionally separate factors connected are changed; they do not concretely or conceptually retain their identities. Connecting, combining, merging, or blending alone do not involve interaction among separate component factors, which leads to mutual modification, integration, and both newness and value.

Theorist/Connector was an engineering theorist, not a technician, and she therefore had devised no particular products or applied for patents. Both friendly and enthusiastic about her work, which was almost entirely computer based, she was dark haired, vigorous, and somewhat stately in a loose-fitting solid-color dress. As a woman in the engineering field, she told of having to overcome the obstacles of disparagement and suspicion by colleagues and students, even friends, regarding her motives and abilities. Her work, however, was considered outstanding. She described one connection, in her case a theoretical one she made during an engineers' conference, as follows:

> The magneto-hydrodynamic generator is a device for getting power out of an ionized [having a negative or positive charge as a result of gaining or losing electrons] gas. It's an advanced object with a conical shape, and it involves very hot gases. These gases radiate to the walls, and I had to predict how hot the walls would get to see if they would melt. I went to a conference and saw someone [Professor Tien] using equations regarding flow of gases which had nothing to do with radiation. I got the idea to use his coordinates [a magnitude serving to define a position] for a different set of equations, however, from what he was doing. I combined the techniques for one equation and brought it over into another field. That solved the problem.

Connector, who later left to become dean of the College of Engineering at another technological university, was spectacled, square jawed, and informally dressed with an open shirt and chino pants. He was working on the development of a different kind of coffee maker for a prominent coffee machine company and described a problem-solving connection he made. "The idea," he said, "was essentially to take all those parts and combine them into two parts. Then, I could mold both the couplings it needed into one plastic molding with hard silicone rubber pieces. These would go on the end and then one person could put it into the coffee maker instead of the two or three people who were required before."

Both *Connector* and *Theorist/Connector* connected components by combination—coffee maker parts for *Connector* and equation techniques for *Theorist/Connector*; in both cases, the product was different, a plastic molding for *Connector* and a different set of equations for *Theorist/Connector*. In neither case, however, was a creation produced comparable with the distinct newness and value of the products of the Nobel laureate group. In these as well as the instances of several other engineers who made connections, the separate identities of the components were lost or absorbed in the combinations, mergings, and the like. In no instance with any members of this group were functional separations preserved or continued with the connection. Concomitant functional separations and connections were in no case conceived or used. There were no applications of the sep-con articulation process and its resulting integrations and creations.

Emotional Factors, Collaboration, Development, and Aesthetics

None of the engineers indicated the kind or degree of passion in connection with their work or goals as the Nobel laureates did. They all were very interested in the problems they were working on, but there was little evidence of active or persistent motivations to create, deviations, risk taking, or courage. Independent problem finding was not apparent as almost all worked on problems contracted from industry or else needed for teaching or, sometimes, incidental interest. Competition with others in the field and, to some degree, with colleagues working on similar problems or in better academic positions, was present but much milder than the competition of the Nobel laureates. There was some interest in overturning previous ideas and procedures but little indication or application of aggressiveness or destructive feelings. Love of learning was, however, very strong throughout the group, and they applied that emotion to their problem-solving work as well as their teaching.

Collaboration was very common among the engineers, and many consulted with each other both on problems and teaching. Two, *Visualizer/ Collaborator* and *Theorist/Collaborator,* did their work consistently either with another engineer within the department or outside of it. These collaborators planned together and published together, and their individual procedures and thinking were intertwined. Overall, collaboration with other faculty was prized and encouraged. Family backgrounds and developmental histories of the engineers were very varied. There was no discernible pattern of parental occupations in this much smaller group similar to the Nobel laureates. Fathers of the men, for instance, ranged widely from poor working persons to surgeons and entrepreneurs.

As for aesthetics, only *Theorist/Connector* indicated that this feature played an important role in her work. Like Chandrasekhar and the other proponents of aesthetics in science cited earlier, she primarily employed mathematics in her theoretical tasks. "There is an aesthetic aspect to mathematical equations," she said. "Simplicity is one factor, another is symmetry. Symmetry is beautiful [See also Glashow regarding nonaesthetic higher mathematical symmetry, chapter 12]. I look for that all the time." She also gave significant emphasis to aesthetics in her work with the following statement: "I think all the equations that I come up with myself feel aesthetic to me. Otherwise, I wouldn't pursue them."

There was personal involvement with music without any creative connection to work. Five engineers (45%) indicated the same degree of musical interest as the Nobel laureates, including in some cases proficiency on a musical instrument. Two of the engineers said that they had thought of becoming professional musicians before they changed to engineering. Some worked in the field of acoustics where musical factors were measured but did not play a part such as structuralizing in their actual conceptualizing or problem solving.

Homospatial Process

Korean engineer *Creator* was the only comparison subject who described the use of the homospatial process in producing a creative discovery. A short, angular-faced, and solidly built man with a brisk, sharp-witted manner, he was somewhat unforthcoming and careful about industrial confidentiality regarding some of his work. Nevertheless, he did report the steps to one of his major creative achievements, the production of taffylike behavior in titanium alloys. The process has been contracted by the US Air Force at the value of billions of dollars for the wide production of jet engine parts, and it has had broad applicability to other types of metallic syntheses. Subsequent to completing this work, he planned to move back to South Korea and has now become a senior research engineer at an important research laboratory. Six patents in his name, in this case for aspects of the same unequivocally new and valuable procedure and product, are registered in the United States, and several more in Korea.

With regard to the development of the taffylike or plastic quality of certain titanium alloys, he explained that titanium had a high strength-to-density ratio, and the taffy effect was ultimately produced by a special three-dimensional procedure involving intense reciprocal heatings of the metal. He described the following process leading to his development of that procedure: "I thought of myself going inside the metal [molecule], conceiving in my own three dimensions how all this changing of atom positions takes place and at the same time how they affect the overall property. I was thinking of the crystal structure I might see from hexagonal atoms sitting at the corners of a hexagon and how they were changing into cubic structures and at the same time giving rise to this taffylike behavior." Nobel laureate Lederberg used a mental superimposition of himself, in his case upon a bacterium, to create, as I reported earlier (chapter 10). In a similar way, *Creator* conceived himself as superimposed and occupying the same space as the metal molecule. This produced a three-dimensional mental interaction leading to the production of a new, highly useful taffylike identity—a creative achievement.

The comparison control group subjects were all effective thinkers in the applied science field of engineering. In addition to the thought processes I have described, they used stepwise logic effectively, were skilled problem framers and solvers, and all at times expertly used analogic, deductive, and inductive conceptual modes.[9] The conclusion from the empirical findings is that the specific cognitive janusian, homospatial, and sep-con articulation processes were used and were operational only in the creative subjects—the Nobel laureates as well as the engineer *Creator*—and absent or not operative in the remainder of the less creative or noncreative comparison control group. The three cognitive processes serve to produce creative achievements.

the world and the beings that inhabit it. They have contributed to longevity, health, and beneficial products that have permeated every aspect of modern life. Recognized by science's highest honor, the awarding of the Nobel Prize, these achievements, although they build on past knowledge and accomplishments, either possess both newness and value or have been attained through creative thinking with those attributes and outcomes. The value aspect is quite prominent as the Nobel Prize is awarded primarily for scientific influence—the wide stimulation and applicability of a theory or discovery. Although scientists rely widely on cooperation and others' findings, the Nobel Prize singles out individual contributions and creative achievements. As I have tried to show earlier in this work, the creativity of individual scientists is comparable overall to individual creativity in literature and art and other fields.

The creative process in science, based on the findings in this investigation, begins with intense motivation. Very likely derived in part from a scientist's early development of mixed drives of competition and love, particularly with respect to a same-gendered parent, this motivation instigates the choice of a scientific field of investigation and ultimately involves a specific desire and intent to supersede and create. The competitive aspect also fuels later deviations from the mainstream and includes aggressiveness and a break from the past in creative achievement. The parental identification and loving aspect very likely fuels a passion for learning, the ability to collaborate, and the production of integration. Another factor for some is an identification with and learning from a parent's general inventiveness, game playing, and scientific interest as evidenced in the filial relationships of Fermi, Feynman, Arber, Glashow, Corey, and Köhler. For creativity in science, exceptionally high intelligence and the accumulation of knowledge also are necessary for the creative process to a more critical degree than in other fields of creative endeavor. On the other hand, the important possession of technical skills in scientific creativity is not of greater magnitude or intensity than comparable types of command over material in other fields such as literature, art, and music. Choice of a particular problem or area of scientific investigation is determined by cognitively determined value and importance, influence of mentors, personal emotional factors, chance, and occupational expedience.

The course of the creative process may be very long, taking place over a large number of years or, as in the case of some of the younger, successful Nobel winners, it may occur fairly rapidly and early in the course of an investigation. This was especially the case with Nobelists who did very successful work as graduate or postdoctoral students, such as Köhler and Lederberg. As a general characteristic, creative processes were applied in ongoing projects that involved extensive preparation. Employed early and late were many types of thinking and analysis, including inductive and deductive logic, experimental assessment both in thought and practice, and the consideration of analogies.

Analogical thinking may be useful in the course of creative work because analogies may provide the content for the choice of specific elements primarily in the second phase following motivation to create within the cognitive creative processes. These elements consist of specific opposites, oppositions, and contradictions for the janusian process; discrete spatial configurations and images for the homospatial process, and functionally separate entities for the sep-con articulation process as well as factors in the fourth phase construction of the theory or product. Errors that occur along the way, as both Delbrück's principle of limited sloppiness and my articulation of error formulation suggest, may also lead to functionally separate content and different directions of investigation. Like other content, whether autochthonous or deviational, these functional separations may be concomitantly connected with others through the sep-con articulation process. Following the element content phase, as reported by the subject group, both theory making and discovery involve sudden illuminations, leaps of thought, irregular or divergent sequences, and step-by-step constructions. These experiences, which lead directly to a creative result, are produced, together or in sequence, by one or all of the cognitive processes- janusian, homospatial, or sep-con articulation.

As with every type of cognitive process, these are accompanied by emotional factors related to their structure. All three, especially the sep-con articulation process, are accompanied by the feel or sense of creating. Some of the emotions may be the same as guiding and jointly operating ones, such as the loving orientation leading to predilection for connections, and aggressive emotions involving a disposition to cleaving or obversity. All three cognitive creative processes involve emotional and cognitive conflict among components; this generates and leads directly to breaks with the past as well as the development of value in creative achievement. The janusian process supersedes elements of paradox and contradiction but retains a conflicting linguistic and ideational structure; the homospatial process supersedes spatial reality and ordinary sensation to produce conflicting mental images; and the sep-con articulation process supersedes ordinary linkages and produces structures involving connections conflicting with their functionally separate components. For all three processes, the conflict induces mutual interactions. For the janusian process this leads subsequently to linguistic and conceptual creation, and for the homospatial process this leads subsequently to metaphors, models, spatial structures, and identities; the sep-con articulation process produces both conceptual and physical integration.

Following the formulations produced through the creative cognitive processes, there is a phase of elaboration, logical construction, comparison, and the application of a broad variety of thinking skills, leading to the stage in scientific work known as verification. In this stage the full theory or discovery is formulated and the results are tested and assessed by the creators and their peers.

In distinction to the various creative processes in the work of the Nobel laureates, the comparison group of engineers, with one exception, engaged primarily in problem-solving activities. Their activities often produced different and useful results but not something truly new in the sense of a break with the past or the appearance of a new exemplar.[2] Nor did they generate any products with the same degree of value and influence as the Nobel laureates' achievements. Their problem-solving approaches were generally effective and they usefully employed some productive cognitive procedures, particularly the use of analogy and induction, which is quite useful in solving technical types of problems. There was no evidence, except for *Creator's* use of the homospatial process, that they employed any of the cognitive creative processes. Their problem solving, although good, was not the same as creative thinking. It was lacking in both novelty and comparably sufficient value. The term *creative problem solving* involves much more than finding an answer or solution, even a complex one. With its distinctive creative attributes it may be considered another kind of designation for the achievements of the Nobel laureates described here. Based on the comparison with the engineer control group, the three cognitive processes are proven components of scientific creativity.

Integrations, the characteristic result of the cognitive creative processes, are created within natural phenomena, in theoretical descriptions of natural phenomena, in the components of an invention, and in all types of artistic products. In science, Einstein's general theory of relativity integrated his special theory of relativity with Newton's gravitation theories; Bohr's complementarity integrated the dual and interactive wave and particle qualities of light and electrons; Darwin's theory of natural selection interactively integrated favorable and unfavorable characteristics as well as the extinction and survival of species; Arber's restriction and modification theory integrated hereditary mutation in bacteria; Benacerraf's immune-responsive genes integrated genetically determined cell structure; Lehn's interacting cryptate and cryptands integrated supramolecular chemistry; and Nüsslein-Volhard's interacting genetic pairs integrated genetic control of early embryonic development. All the remaining discoveries and theoretical breakthroughs of the Nobel laureates documented here led in some way to the integration of an aspect or the entire composition and operation of a natural phenomenon. Concomitant separation and connection—present to some degree with all three cognitive creative processes—produces interaction leading to integration, in which the whole is greater than its parts.

Shifting to the major emotional factors in the creativity of the Nobel laureate group, the most striking of these was intense motivation. All of the scientists worked tirelessly and devotedly to solve the particular problems they chose and to develop and extend their findings and theories. Many of the group worked often through the night, or during holidays and vacations, and all described being preoccupied with the problem day and night as well as over more extended periods. Outstandingly, all were extraordinarily persistent. In the face of difficulties and the usually protracted time required to make the discovery or solve the problem, they all stuck with it for months and years, sometimes for the major portion of their lives. It is nevertheless hard to say whether their drive was completely exceptional, because as is well known, many highly competent scientists who do not manage the same level of achievement also have been very highly devoted and hard working.

In addition to instigation from the family background constellation I have described, other motivational factors in the desire to create are very likely derived from early experiences of gratification and success with deviating from standard and mainstream activities in childhood, adolescence, and young adulthood. These include frequent engagement in fantasy play acting and expressive play, success in school and games by going beyond ordinary procedures, rewarded interests outside of age-appropriate group and sports activities (although Herschbach's achievements in football seem to be an exception), and learning early to be self-reliant and resourceful in practical matters and play. Ivar Giaever described as the source of his creativity his experience making all his own things during the Nazi occupation of Norway during the Second World War. He had to save random objects because someday any of them could be useful.

Stimulation, knowledge, and the example of mentors were also important. In the documented autobiographies of all the Nobel laureate scientists used in the developmental study, all attested to the importance of at least one science mentor. In Zuckerman's 1972 sample of US Nobel laureates in science,[3] specifically 41% (48% internationally) had worked in the laboratories of previous laureates. Seventy percent of the group I interviewed had done the same.

Competitiveness within the investigative work, particularly with other scientists working on the same or similar problems, was discernible throughout the science laureate group. Although only a few of the subjects interviewed openly acknowledged this, many made references to the "race to a finding" or "the challenge of an alternate point of view." Several made irritated references to other scientists who were falsely given credit for one of the laureates' particular concepts or findings. Particular aspects of a collaborator's contribution were sometimes privately or even publicly denied, as were some achievements of other laureates sharing the subject's Nobel Prize. In rare but notable cases, public accusations of gross scientific misbehavior or usurpation of another's work have been made.[4] Members of this Nobel laureate group openly admitted unabashed competition for the best conditions and personnel in their laboratories and for enlistment of talented graduate students and potential collaborators. Seldom was there outright denigration of competing groups and laboratories, but elaborate personal courting of prospective students, including fine wining and dining, was universally practiced. In a related way, competition for funding, both from government and private grants—surely a necessary matter in all countries in modern times—was also universal and very intense.

As signified by such competition for funding, the field of science is necessarily highly competitive, and the pursuit of the most minimal type of success requires personal acquisitiveness and contention. It could be argued that both competitiveness and intense motivation are necessary factors in scientific creativity because without these attributes in the present day, scientists would neither be consciously creative nor able to achieve the greatest success. Because of the nature of the rewards and the need for priority, competition and motivation in all degrees are continually pervasive. Even when ultimately achieving lower levels of success, competition and strong motivation are diffusely present, and possibly are still required. As with high intellect, competition seems necessary in science and in scientific creativity, but it is not so strongly requisite in other fields or all types of creative endeavor. Collaboration and co-operation also are particularly important in science.

Both rebelliousness and courage, which are related to competitiveness, have been distinct factors in scientific creativity. In several cases I have cited, such as the work of Planck, Giaever, Arber, Delbrück, Luria, Gilbert, Seaborg, and Baltimore, the creative discoverer has chosen a field or taken an investigatory tack that the main body of scientists have neglected or actively opposed. They also challenged or even ignored accepted canons of knowledge or procedure. Such rebelliousness, while not invariably necessary for creative discoveries or theories, may serve to fuel the production of the exceptional and new. Sometimes, even after a new discovery is made or theory formulated, it is necessary for creators to take a seemingly rebellious stance and hold their ground. In such cases, courage to stand alone, to believe in one's approach, findings, or concepts, is critical.

Continual courage, based on the companion element of self-confidence, is in fact required for any and all types of creativity. Whether associated with rebelliousness or not, creations are, by definition, new entities. As I suggested earlier, it is more than a truism to recognize that newness, especially regarding beliefs and formulations about nature and reality, invariably is widely doubted and often rejected. This has occurred throughout history and still is characteristic in all countries and places. Although valuable new ideas and discoveries eventually are fully or partially accepted, they are initially discomforting, even unnerving, and are then disbelieved by all types of people, even sophisticated scientists. Cases among the Nobel laureates here of such initial disbelief were the rejection by a scientific journal of Kornberg's first article reporting the synthesis of DNA, and another journal's rejection of the initial report by Huber and associates on the first growth of crystals of the photosynthetic reaction center. Although there may have been other defects in these papers leading to the rejections, it is nevertheless notable that, in both cases, they were soon accepted by other journals. In ways both more detailed and general, all of the Nobel laureates I investigated showed courage in their willingness to conceive new formulations, work them out within several contexts over extended periods of time, and finally stand by them. Sometimes, of course, as with courage shown by warring enemies, this has merged into wrongheaded stubbornness. Even after having been wrong many times or on a wrong tack, however, each particular laureate returned to the worthwhile aspects of a problem or project, or an aspect of it, and stood up for often unusual but ultimately correct outcomes.

I have described a few of the personal emotional factors that entered into the thinking involved in attaining creative ideas. Because personal emotional factors do enter into all thinking and behavior, it is very likely that they influenced the choice of scientific field and problems investigated as well. Examples are Benacerraf's personal experience with childhood asthma and intestinal allergies determining his choice of immunology, Arber's following his inventive farmer father with a devotion to nature and biology, and historian's son Delbrück's choice of an historically oriented problem. To determine other similar as well as deeper personal connections with the problem studied would, as I indicated, require another type of methodology than the one I have employed, involving more extensive confidential interviewing over longer periods of time. The topic is beyond the scope of this investigation and deserves further research.

Although, as scientists such as Poincaré, Hadamard, Chandrasekhar, and Dirac have particularly stressed regarding their mathematical work, aesthetic interests may have some role in creative scientific discovery, such interests do not appear to have been applied generally in the investigative Nobel group. Only Nüsslein-Volhard actively and consciously used aesthetic decisions in her research work. Moreover, systematic questioning regarding general aesthetic interests and performance in the group elicited primarily or exclusively a preference for music not included in their conceptualizing work.

The comparison control group of engineers did not essentially differ in this respect from the Nobel laureates. A small number of engineer subjects were interested in music, but no other aesthetic interests were designated or used except in the case of a mathematical theorist. All were intelligent, motivated, and productive; a few were highly competitive, but they otherwise differed with the Nobel laureates in goals, background, and emotional predispositions. None could be considered in any way rebellious, nor did they need to be courageous regarding their work or problem solutions, even when it resulted in patents. Rather than manifesting creativity, the large number of patents produced in this group consisted of different, not new, constructions with mild to moderate utilitarian value. None of the engineers referred to important mentors. Their family backgrounds showed no distinct patterns or influences on their professional choice or work.

Emotional forces that I have documented, no matter how strong, function as enabling factors in the creative process; they do not lead directly to creative results. Those are instigated and ultimately derive from the janusian, homospatial, and sep-con articulation processes. These processes are responsible for the innovation, the break with the past, and critical aspects of the production of value. Each of these processes concerns different features of human thought and experience. Formulations within the janusian process are based on simultaneity of the elements, which are therefore out of temporal succession; time is both literally and psychologically broken, and newness and novelty is a result. As oppositions and antitheses are primarily verbal and conceptual, joining these produces conflict and interaction leading to verbal and conceptual creation. The operations of the homospatial process are based on space and spatial considerations and all modalities of sensory imagery—visual, auditory, gustatory, olfactory, tactile, kinesthetic—and joining of components of these produces conflict and interaction leading to new identities involving space and sensation. Sep-con articulation operates in rational thought, emotional constellations, language, physical constructions, and sensory or spatial experience. Because of the conflict induced by concomitant functional separation and connection, it produces interaction resulting in integration and wholeness. Production of integration, ranging from minimal to quite extensive, as in the theories and discoveries as well as the artworks I have described, is its primary function. Sep-con articulation is fed by the other cognitive creative processes and is also used in conjunction with them. All three processes, together or separately in sequence, are found to be responsible for creative results in science as well as other fields. As I have pointed out with regard to the Nobel laureates investigated here, the findings apply to individuals and are therefore comparable with the predominantly individual creativity in the arts, as well as with consensually determined creation in diverse types of fields. As I have emphasized, other factors also operate, such as the very high intellectual capacity and the understanding of complex scientific knowledge necessary for science. For writers, particular sensitivity and skill with words is required for literary creativity; for creativity in art, music, and dance, manual and conceptual skills with visual and auditory media and bodily movements are required. Moreover, in any field creativity requires both skill and knowledge regarding the particular content and operations of that field.

The cognitive creative processes consist of unusual and out-of-the-ordinary types of cognition, and they require a good deal of emotional flexibility as well as freedom from anxiety to employ. All three processes are mentally healthy and psychologically, physically, and culturally adaptive. Regardless of whether a creator using them is in some other way psychologically ill, courage and freedom from anxiety, both features of psychological health, are necessary. This means that full psychological health and lucidity would be optimal for all types of creativity. Even within the bounds of mental illness, anxiety disorders (previously designated as neuroses), personality disorders, and bipolar disorders along with moderate or severe cases of psychosis, the healthy elements are always preserved to some degree during creative activities, sometimes on a daily basis or over prolonged lengths of time.[5] Although I did not perform a formal psychiatric assessment of the subjects of my investigations, only one in the science Nobel laureate group showed overt signs of clinical depression, and one other clearly evidenced a compulsive personality disorder. Overt signs of mental illness were not present with any of the other laureates.

The background and development of the cognitive creative processes, both physical and environmental, are complex, just as the nature and operations of the processes themselves. Although very little is known about genetic production of particular capacities and modes of thought, except for the likelihood that various types of intelligence are inherited, it may be that some type of genetic expression due to individual genes or gene interactions is necessary for the production of these singular types of cognition. Other types of physical processes may contribute or be directly involved in their operation.

A further speculation is that homologs or biological parallels of the processes may operate in the brain within the synaptic junctions. Neurotransmitter chemicals responsible for transmission of brain functions including thought are emitted within the synapse by the presynaptic terminal on the transmitting neuron. Ordinarily, the transmissions of "messages" by neurotransmitter chemicals are asymmetrical—that is, they go in one direction from presynaptic to postsynaptic terminals. At times, however, the chemicals may be reabsorbed into the presynaptic terminal. During this reabsorption, some type of chemical and electrical interaction may occur that is specifically isomorphic with the interactions within the creative process.

Together with possible genetic endowments, developmental factors also play a role. Although some precursors of creativity appear in childhood, such as free and figurative-like expression developing later into true metaphor, novelty, and risk taking in adult creativity, the fully structured types of cognition required for production of the new and valuable do not begin to form and develop until adolescence. According to developmental research, abstract reasoning first develops during this period. This includes capacity for representational and true metaphorical thinking, all of which are necessary for creative cognitions.[6] Although there surely have been historical exceptions,[7] effective art, musical composition, scientific reasoning, and creative writing are not produced prior to adolescence. Starting soon after that point, however, poetry writing, and various types of attempts at poetry particularly, are done in earnest throughout adolescence and become a characteristic of the period. A very high percentage of persons of varying intellectual, economic, and social levels report that they have written some type of poetry during their adolescent years, even though they did not continue to do so into adulthood.[8] Among the arts, attempts at poetry seem to function not as a necessarily truly creative but a generally valued outlet for the manifold emotionality of the adolescent period.

Boys and girls who are motivated early toward creativity, because of the family background structure and possible genetic factors as well as parental inventiveness, acceptance of deviant thinking, and nurturance of individuality, very likely will develop the basic properties of the cognitive creative processes during adolescence. In this sometimes tumultuous period of life, they experience and use, in particular ways, the universal developmental tasks of the period of adolescence involving contending with and mastery of physical, psychological, and social changes. As identified through extensive psychological research, these tasks concern the development of identity and individuality, coping with body change and sexuality, and accomplishment of adaptive relationships with others.[9]

The cognitive and emotional structures of the janusian, homospatial, and sep-con articulation processes are coordinate with the essential structures of these developmental tasks; therefore they are very likely derived as creative operations from the shaping and adaptive fixation of modes of experiencing and dealing with them. Some of this shaping may for one thing involve early turbulence because, for all adolescents, there is a tendency to overshoot goals. Their feature of rebelliousness as part of attempts at independence from parents is sometimes painful both for adolescents and for their parents who are the objects of their defiance. The strong component of opposition in rebelliousness, including opposition at some point to social and parental dictates is, unlike the short and superficial opposition phases of 2- to 3-year-olds in early childhood, continued throughout adolescence until it is modified and worked through. This opposition and contention does eventually contribute to the development of adult independence as well as to stable psychological identity through maturation. For creatively motivated adolescents, opposition has both deviant and innovative effects, and these are incorporated into the conceptions and uses of cognitive opposite predilections in the janusian process. Related also to the opposition and rebelliousness is risk taking, a frequent feature of adolescence; risk taking to some degree may become serviceable for adult creativity, or it ultimately may become maladaptive.

Emotional ambivalence involving shifting between opposite emotions and perspectives may also fuel deviant thought and action and at the time be experienced as intellectually broadening. The ambivalent adolescent wish to "have one's cake and eat it too" is overcome in varying degrees by experience, but it leaves an emotional imprint for the cognitive structure of janusian process involving rational use of simultaneous opposites. Evidence for a creative predilection toward opposition at the end of this period is suggested by the findings of the earlier described word association experiment (chapter 9) showing that creatively oriented Yale students—young adults just past adolescence—had, along with the tested Nobel laureate group, a tendency to rapid opposite verbal response.

Adolescence is also marked by bodily changes for both girls and boys. Girls develop breasts and start to menstruate, whereas boys are primarily aware of increases in girth, agility, and height relative to other boys as well as girls. Both genders develop increased interest and capacity for sexuality. Learning to adjust to the increased range and variety of images and sensations and the changes in height, weight, and shape in relative bodily space is a developmental task that leads to outcomes in adulthood ranging from accommodation to gratification. There are characteristic interests in sexual intermingling and sensation, and accompanying increased awareness of the body in spatial placement and dimension. In addition to a focus on personal bodily change, a telltale ambivalent and counterreactive attraction to the bodily distortions of horror films and literature is habitual, as is the attention to variably sized (both proportioned and disproportioned) characters within futuristic and extraterrestrial space. In modern times also, the spatial focus has become increased through exaggerated sensations from a wide range of adolescent popular dance movement and music. Bodily sensations and preoccupations during this period, together with spatial alterations and manipulation, form a basis for flexible orientations to space and, in creatively oriented adolescents, the use of mental spatial superimpositions and interpositions of the homospatial process.

Achievement of individuation and identity, a major developmental task of adolescence, requires acquisition of enduring connections together with separations from other people. Adaptive relationships with others, whether they are peers, lovers, parents, other authorities, or acquaintances, requires clear-cut functional separation in the form of privacy, self-determination, individual choice, and values and, at the same time, connectedness involving cooperation, friendship, and productive association. Such individuation is critical for psychological health and is an adaptive basis for both emotional and cognitive functioning. All or part is necessary for both deviation and courage in all types of creative processes. Whether consciously recognized or not, the stable structure of concomitant connection and functional separation seems to be internalized by creative adolescents and begins to be used in the sep-con articulation process to produce integrations.

It is an aphorism among writers that, unless persons are writing poetry in their forties, they are not poets. Although commonly used primarily as an emotional outlet in adolescence, effective poetry and other creative writing may nevertheless begin in that period and extend throughout life. Other types of creativity that manifestly begin in adolescence are manifested in visual artistic pursuits, musical performance and composition, abstract and formal thinking endeavors, and technical activities and exploration. All types develop rapidly during this period. Successful creative writing focused on personal feelings, ideas, and experiences may serve to externalize a constantly changing and developing inner sense of self and identity. Formal features of effective poetry seem also to provide a framework for experiencing a sense of order and organization. Through the structuring and specifying required by writing and expression, in poetry as well as other literary forms, identity features become progressively clarified and constructed. Experiencing success in any type of creative activity[10] serves in adolescence both to consolidate identity and facilitate incorporation of precursor factors in the specific cognitive creative processes. Creative identity, the sense of oneself as a creative person, tends to start in adolescence and continue throughout life. This creative identity itself serves as a motivating factor for the acquisition of necessary skills and the pursuit of creative undertakings.

Derivatives of the developmental tasks of adolescence may become excessive, even destructive, rather than creative. Rebelliousness and risk taking can become a fixated part of personality and lead to maladaptive behavior and mental illness. Separation initially oriented toward independence may be exaggerated and result in patterns of withdrawal or antisocial activities. Rather than creative identity, self-preoccupation and manipulativeness may be incorporated and routine. At the current state of our knowledge, all of the environmental and genetic factors that produce healthy adaptation rather than disjunction and disorder cannot be ascertained. With respect to creativity, it is clear, however, that forcing children to be creative or to excel in school certainly is not effective.

I have repeatedly asserted that my focus in creativity research has been on consensually designated creative achievers where empirical criteria for creativity are distinct and well grounded. Of necessity therefore my findings, both in science and the arts, have applied to performance and capacity at undoubted high creativity levels. Do they also apply to other levels and types of creativity? I believe they should and that they do. In the Introduction to this book, I attempted to trace the creative use in the everyday sport of baseball of the sep-con articulation process by the hallowed Yankee centerfielder Joe DiMaggio. Many other applications to everyday and workday creativity can be formulated and employed.

Applications of all of the cognitive creative processes, in whole or in selective part, certainly must play a role in other types of everyday and workday creativity, such as in business and advertising, popular music, farming, photography, building and mechanical projects, politics, speechmaking, clothing design, cooking, skilled crafts, and interpersonal relationships.[11] A distinct application of the sep-con articulation process in the sphere of cooking may be the concomitant connection of two functionally separate flavors in the same preparation. A French restaurant known for its creative cuisine, for example, regularly offers a dish consisting of Saint Jacques scallops together with small leaves of spinach. The two flavors are joined, not merged, both separately present and connected in a delicious overall food creation. In creative actions in other fields, the three cognitive creative processes, or key selected aspects of them, may be used. Motivation to create and deviance, which are partially and popularly termed "thinking outside the box," are characteristics of the first phases of all three processes. Aspects of the janusian process may operate in the complete turn to the unexpected or unbelieved antithetical or opposite—not simply reversal of procedure—in humor, building, and problem solving. A businessperson, or even a politician, may devise an approach based on bringing together completely opposite procedures or factions. I have elsewhere shown that the homospatial process may be used in many different ways in advertising and clothing design.[12] New and interesting images and new styles of clothing are proposed for manufacture and display. The sep-con articulation process is always involved in creative speechmaking and athletics and it may be universally applied in everyday creative thinking and creative problem solving. The use of significant whole or partial features of the cognitive processes in a variety of activities, both everyday and special, may produce the necessary alterations and interactions required for creative results.

The emotional factors of intense motivation, risk taking and courage, and competition and aggressiveness that characterize high-level creativity, especially in science, are probably matters of degree. These types of emotions may not generally be necessary, or only necessary to some extent, in certain types of commercial creativity such as in advertising, business, and industry.

Content features of imagination, intuition, and flexibility of thought and action may, together with aspects of the cognitive creative processes, be used to produce innovation in work, entertainment, and modes of living. The results will often be quite useful and valuable true creations.

Overall, full application of the cognitive creative processes breaks through time and space and produces interaction between connected functional separations to produce a radical type of newness, integration, and value in science and other fields. This work has primarily concerned findings regarding the creative process and their applications to the continual flight from wonder in the scientific field. Many of the most adaptive, progressive, and gratifying features of modern life result, and will continue to result, from these features of creativity.

{ NOTES }

Preface

1. Researchers on creativity also cite the idea that creativity is considered mysterious. Some nevertheless proceed to state extensive explanations. See M. Boden, *The Creative Mind: Myths and Mechanisms* (New York: Basic Books, 1990); R. J. Sternberg and T. I. Lubart, *Defying the Crowd: Cultivating Creativity in a Culture of Conformity* (New York: The Free Press, 1995).

2. There is a long history of mythmaking about connections between creativity and mental illness. Trying to find correlations between mental illness and creativity has today become a frequent concern in psychological and psychiatric literature. I shall not repeat here the shortcomings and fallacies of these studies as I have presented these extensively elsewhere. See A. Rothenberg, *Creativity and Madness: New Findings and Old Stereotypes* (Baltimore: Johns Hopkins University Press, 1990); A. Rothenberg, "Creativity and Psychopathology," *Bulletin of Psychology and the Arts* 1 (2000), 54–58; A. Rothenberg, "Bipolar Illness, Creativity, and Treatment," *Psychiatric Quarterly* 72 (2001), 131–48; A. Rothenberg, "Creativity—The Healthy Muse," *Lancet* 368 (2006), 58–59. The creative processes found and described in this book are all healthy; therefore, when a creative person is mentally ill, he or she is both motivated and able to use these processes in lucid, anxiety-free periods.

3. It might be suggested that a more appropriate control group would be composed of scientists of various types and at various levels who had not had distinct creative achievements. Donald W. Mackinnon, however, in his collaborative Institute of Personality Research study of creative architects, used that type of approach to investigate architects at three rated levels of achievement. He found it necessary to conclude redundantly that their characteristics corresponded to Otto Rank's conception of three stages or types of personality and creative development. See D. W. Mackinnon, "Personality and the Realization of Creative Potential," *American Psychologist* 20 (1965), 273–81.

4. A. Rothenberg, "Word Association and Creativity," *Psychological Reports* 33 (1973), 3–12; A. Rothenberg, "Opposite Responding as a Measure of Creativity," *Psychological Reports* 33 (1973), 15–18; A. Rothenberg and R. S. Sobel, "Creation of Literary Metaphors as Stimulated by Superimposed versus Separated Visual Images," *Journal of Mental Imagery* 4 (1980), 77–91; R. S. Sobel and A. Rothenberg, "Artistic Creation as Stimulated by Superimposed versus Separated Visual Images," *Journal of Personality and Social Psychology* 39 (1980), 953–61; A. Rothenberg and R. S. Sobel, "Effects of Shortened Exposure Time on the Creation of Literary Metaphors as Stimulated by Superimposed versus Separated Visual Images," *Perceptual and Motor Skills* 53 (1981), 1007–1009; A. Rothenberg, "Artistic Creation as Stimulated by Superimposed versus Combined-Composite Visual Images," *Journal of Personality and Social Psychology* 50 (1986), 370–81; A. Rothenberg, "Creativity and the Homospatial Process: Experimental Studies," *Psychiatric Clinics of North America* 11 (1988), 443–59.

Introduction

1. Originally in Plato's *Phaedrus* (265e) as, "Cut up each hand according to its species along its natural joints." See discussion of the applicability to nature in J. K. Campbell, M. O'Rourke, and M. H. Slater, *Carving Nature at its Joints* (Cambridge, MA: MIT Press, 2011).

2. G. H. Lewes's definition of emergent novelty is the following: "Every resultant is either a sum or a difference of the co-operant forces; their sum, when their directions are the same—their difference, when their directions are contrary. Further, every resultant is clearly traceable in its components, because these are homogeneous and commensurable. It is otherwise with emergents, when, instead of adding measurable motion to measurable motion, or things of one kind to other individuals of their kind, there is a co-operation of things of unlike kinds. The emergent is unlike its components insofar as these are incommensurable, and it cannot be reduced to their sum or their difference." G. H. Lewes, *Problems of Life and Mind (First Series),* vol. 2 (London: Trubner, 1875) 412. See also J. Goldstein, "Emergence as a Construct: History and Issues," *Emergence: Complexity and Organization* 1 (1999), 49–72.

3. J. Dorso, *DiMaggio. The Last American Knight* (New York: Little, Brown,. 1995), 32.

4. S. Shaikh and J. Leonard-Amadeo, "The Deviating Eyes of Michelangelo's David," *Journal of the Royal Society of Medicine* 98, no. 2 (2005), 75–76.

Chapter 1

1. See C. R. Hausman, *A Discourse on Novelty and Creation* (Albany, NY: State University of New York Press, 1984). Hausman distinguishes between what he calls "novelty proper," in which a new type or an exemplar of a class is produced, and simple difference, which can be perceived as an instance of what existed previously. Also see J. Goldstein, "Emergence as a Construct: History and Issues," *Emergence: Complexity and Organization* 1 (1999), 49–72.

2. Goldstein, "Emergence as a Construct."

3. Although Turner and Fauconnier use the term *integration* in their theory of cognitive blending, their formulation is different from the meaning of the term as defined here. Their conceptions refer to combining and unification rather than integration as the resulting whole greater than the sum of its parts. Their applications to creativity do not coincide with meanings and results presented in this book. See M. Turner and G. Fauconnier, "A Mechanism of Creativity," *Poetics Today* 20, no. 3 (1999), 397–418.

4. J. Joyce, *Finnegan's Wake*, (New York: Viking Press, 1939), p. 8.

5. A. Rothenberg, *Creativity and Madness: New Findings and Old Stereotypes* (Baltimore: Johns Hopkins University Press, 1990), 64–65.

6. See John Pedro Schwartz, "Monument and Museum Discourse in *Finnegan's Wake*," *James Joyce Quarterly* 44 (2006), pp. 77–93. See also the many ways Joyce uses the word *Willingdone* in the passage where it is introduced in *Finnegan's Wake*.

7. J. Barth, *Giles Goat Boy* (New York: Doubleday, 1966); T. Pynchon, *Gravity's Rainbow* (New York: Viking Press, 1973); L. Carroll, "Jabberwocky," *Alice's Adventures in Wonderland and through the Looking Glass* (Cleveland: World Publishing, 1946), 174–76

8. Raphael Holinshed, *Holinsheds Chronicles of England, Scotland and Ireland* (London, 1577); *The True Chronicle History of King Leir and His Three Daughters, Gonorill, Ragan, and Cordella* (London, 1605).

9. See S. C. Pepper, "Organistic Criticism" in *A Modern Book of Aesthetics*, ed. M. Rader (New York: Holt, Rinehart & Winston, 1965), 466–80, esp. 469–70, 476–80.

Chapter 2

1. See A. Rothenberg and B. Greenberg, *The Index of Scientific Writings on Creativity: Creative Men and Women* (Hamden, CT: Archon Books, 1974); A. Rothenberg and B. Greenberg, *The Index of Scientific Writings on Creativity: General, 1566-1974* (Hamden, CT: Archon Books, 1976); A. Rothenberg and C. R. Hausman, *The Creativity Question* (Durham, NC: Duke University Press, 1976); R. J. Sternberg, *Handbook of Creativity* (New York: Cambridge University Press, 1999); M. A. Runco and S. R. Pritzer, *Encyclopedia of Creativity*, vols. 1 & 2 (San Diego, CA: Academic Press, 1999, rev. ed. 2011).

2. B. Eiduson, *Scientists: Their Psychological World* (New York: Basic Books, 1962).

3. A. Roe, "A Study of Imagery in Research Scientists," *Journal of Personality* 19 (1951), 459–70; A. Roe, *The Making of a Scientist* (New York: Dodd, Mead and Company, 1953).

4. Eiduson, *Scientists,* 262

5. G. F. Feist, "A Meta-analysis of Personality in Scientific and Artistic Creativity," *Personality and Social Science Review* 2 (1998), 296–97.

6. Ibid., 290–309.

7. K. Dunbar, "How Scientists Think," in *Conceptual Structures and Processes: Emergence, Discovery and Change,* ed. T. B. Ward, E. M. Smith, and J. Vaid (Washington, DC: American Psychological Association Press, 2008), 461–93. Several investigators and theorists cited hereafter also specify analogy in connection with creative thinking. By itself, however, analogy may be facilitative but it does not directly produce creative results.

8. D. K. Simonton, *Creativity in Science: Chance, Logic and Zeitgeist* (New York: Cambridge University Press, 2004); D. K. Simonton, "Creativity as a Constrained Stochastic Process," in *Creativity: From Potential to Realization,* ed. R. J. Sternberg, E. L. Gigorenko, and J. L. Singer (Washington, DC: American Psychological Association Press, 2004), 83–102.

Previously, Simonton had proposed a "chance-configuration" theory of scientific creativity proposing that discovery was an evolutionary process in which chance ideas and events were configured by talented researchers into achievements. See D. K. Simonton, *Scientific Genius: A Psychology of Science* (New York: Cambridge University Press, 1988).

9. H. Gruber, *Darwin on Man: A Psychological Study of Scientific Creativity* (Chicago: University of Chicago Press, 1981).

10. Ibid., 4.

11. H. E. Gruber, *Creative People at Work* (New York: Oxford University Press, 1989); S. K. Sagarin and H. E. Gruber, "Ensemble of Metaphor," in *Encyclopedia of Creativity*, ed. M. A. Runco and S. R. Pritzer, vol. 1 (San Diego, CA: Academic Press, 1999, rev. ed. 2011), pp. 677–81.

12. A. Miller, *Imagery in Science* (Boston: Birkhauser, 1984).

13. A. Miller, *Insights of Genius: Imagery and Creativity in Science and Art* (New York Springer-Verlag, 1996), 335.

14. M. Boden, *The Creative Mind: Myths and Mechanisms* (New York: Basic Books, 1990).

15. R. S. Root-Bernstein, *Discovering* (Cambridge, MA: Harvard University Press, 1989); R. S. Root-Bernstein and M. Root-Bernstein, "Artistic Scientists and Scientific

Artists: The Link between Polymathy and Creativity," in *Creativity: From Potential to Realization*, R. J. Sternberg, E. L. Gigorenko, and J. L. Singer, eds. (Washington, DC: American Psychological Association Press, 2004), 127–52.

16. Root-Bernstein, *Discovering*, 318–27.

17. Ibid., 313.

18. Ibid., 335.

19. H. Poincaré, *The Foundations of Science: Science and Hypothesis, The Value of Science, Science and Method*, trans. G. B. Halstead (1913; repr., Washington, DC: University Press of America, 1982).

20. J. Hadamard, *The Psychology of Invention in the Mathematical Field* (New York: Dover Publications, 1954).

21. P. A. M. Dirac, "The Evolution of the Physicist's Picture of Nature," *Scientific American*, May 1963, 45–53.

22. S. Chandrasekhar, *Truth and Beauty: Aesthetics and Motivations in Science* (Chicago: University of Chicago Press, 1987), 73.

23. G. Holton, *Thematic Origins of Scientific Thought. Kepler to Einstein* (Cambridge, MA: Harvard University Press, 1973).

24. G. Holton, *The Advancement of Science and Its Burdens: With a New Introduction* (Cambridge, MA: Harvard University Press, 1998), 229ff.

25. N. Nersessian, "Conceptual Change: Creativity, Cognition, and Culture," in *Models of Discovery and Creativity*, eds. J. Meheus and T. Nickles (New York: Springer, 2009), 127–66.

26. M. Black, *Models and Metaphors* (Ithaca, NY: Cornell University Press, 1962).

27. M. Csikszentmihalyi, *Creativity: The Psychology of Discovery and Invention* (New York: HarperCollins, 1996).

28. Ibid., 111–113.

29. J. W. Getzels and M. Csikszentmihalyi, *The Creative Vision: A Longitudinal Study of Problem Finding in Art* (New York: Wiley, 1976).

30. T. M. Amabile, *The Social Psychology of Creativity* (New York: Springer-Verlag, 1983), 91.

31. R. J. Sternberg and T. I. Lubart, *Defying the Crowd: Cultivating Creativity in a Culture of Conformity* (New York: The Free Press, 1995).

32. R. J. Sternberg, "Intelligence," in *Encyclopedia of Creativity*, eds. M. A. Runco and S. R. Pritzer, vol. 2 (San Diego, CA: Academic Press, 1999, rev. ed. 2011), 81–88.

33. A. Rothenberg, "The Mystique of the Unconscious in Creativity," in *Creativity and Madness: New Findings and Old Stereotypes*, ed. A. Rothenberg (Baltimore: Johns Hopkins University Press, 1990), 48–56.

34. E. Kris, *Psychoanalytic Explorations in Art* (New York: International Universities Press, 1952).

35. L. S. Kubie, *Neurotic Distortion of the Creative Process* (Lawrence: University of Kansas Press, 1958).

36. A. Koestler, *The Act of Creation* (New York: Macmillan, 1964).

37. S. A. Mednick, "The Associative Basis of the Creative Process," *Psychological Bulletin* 69 (1962), 220–27,

38. Boden, *The Creative Mind*, 124.

39. Ibid., 132.

40. M. Turner and G. Fauconnier, "A Mechanism of Creativity," *Poetics Today* 20, no. 3 (1999), 397–418.

41. M. Turner, "The Art of Compression," in *The Artful Mind: Cognitive Science and the Riddle of Human Creativity*, ed. M. Turner (New York: Oxford University Press, 2006).

42. H. Gardner, *Art, Mind, and Brain. A Cognitive Approach to Creativity* (New York: Basic Books, 1982).

43. H. Gardner, *Creating Minds* (New York: Basic Books, 1993), 363ff.

44. B. Solomon, K. Powell, and H. Gardner, "Multiple Intelligences," in *Encyclopedia of Creativity*, ed. M. A. Runco and S. R. Pritzer, vol. 2 (San Diego, CA: Academic Press, 1999, rev. ed. 2011), 273–83.

45. Gardner, *Art, Mind, and Brain*, 351.

46. N. R. F. Maier, "Problem Solving and Creativity," in *Individuals and Groups* (Belmont, CA: Brooks/Cole, 1970).

47. D. Klahr and H. A. Simon, "Studies of Scientific Discovery: Complementary Approaches and Convergent Findings," *Psychological Bulletin* 125 (1999), 524–43, 539.

48. P. Langley, "The Computational Support of Scientific Discovery," *International Journal of Human-Computer Studies* 53 (2000), 393–410.

49. J. P. Guilford, "Creativity," *American Psychologist* 5 (1950), 444–54.

50. M. A. Runco, *Divergent Thinking* (Norwood, NJ: Ablex, 1991).

51. E. P. Torrance, *Torrance Tests of Creative Thinking* (Bensenville, IL: Scholastic Testing Press, 1987).

52. M. A. Runco, "Implicit Theories and Ideational Creativity," in *Theories of Creativity*, ed. M. A. Runco and R. S. Albert (Newbury Park, CA: Sage Publications, 1990), 234–54.

53. F. Barron and G. S. Welsh, "Artistic Perception as a Possible Factor in Personality Style: Its Measurement by a Figure Preference Test," *Journal of Psychology* 33 (1952), 199–203.

54. E. deBono, *The Use of Lateral Thinking* (London: Jonathan Cape, 1957).

55. See Preface, note 2.

56. N. C. Andreasen, "Creativity and Mental Illness: Prevalence Rates in Writers and Their First Degree Relatives," *American Journal of Psychiatry* 144 (1987), 1288–92.

57. K. R. Jamison, "Mood Disorders and Patterns of Creativity in British Writers and Artists," *Psychiatry* 52 (1989), 125–34.

58. A. M. Ludwig, *The Price of Greatness. Resolving the Creativity and Madness Controversy* (New York: Guilford Press, 1996).

59. D. W. Mackinnon, "Personality and the Realization of Creative Potential," *American Psychologist* 20 (1965), 273–81; D. W. Mackinnon, "The Personality Correlates of Creativity: A Study of American Architects," in *Proceedings of the XIV International Congress of Applied Psychology, Vol. 2*, ed. G. S. Nielsen (Copenhagen, Denmark: Munksgaard, 1962), 11–39.

60. R. Helson and R. S. Crutchfield, "Creative Types in Mathematics," *Journal of Personality* 38 (1970), 177–97.

61. F. Barron, "The Psychology of Creativity," in *New Directions in Psychology II*, ed. T. M. Newman (New York: Rinehart and Winston, 1965), 1–134.

62. R. Helson, "In Search of the Creative Personality," *Creativity Research Journal* 9 (1996), 295–306.

63. F. Galton, *Hereditary Genius: An Inquiry into its Laws and Consequences* (London: Macmillan, 1869).

64. A. Rothenberg and G. Wyshak, "Family Background and Genius," *Canadian Journal of Psychiatry* 49 (2004), 185–91; A. Rothenberg, "Family Background and Genius II: Nobel Laureates in Science," *Canadian Journal of Psychiatry* 50 (2005), 918–25.

65. G. Wallas, *The Art of Thought* (New York: Harcourt, Brace, 1926).

66. J. E. Bogen and G. M. Bogen, "The Corpus Callosum and Creativity," *Bulletin of the Los Angeles Neurological Society* (1969), 191–220; J. E. Bogen and G. M. Bogen, "Split Brains: Interhemispheric Exchange in Creativity," in *Encyclopedia of Creativity*, eds. M. A. Runco and S. R. Pritzer, vol. 2 (San Diego, CA: Academic Press, 1999, rev. ed. 2011), 571–76.

67. Ö. de Manzano et al., "Thinking Outside a Less Intact Box: Thalamic Dopamine D2 Receptor Densities Are Negatively Related to Psychometric Creativity in Healthy Individuals," PLOS ONE 5, no. 5 (2010), e10670, doi:10.1371/journal.pone.0010670.

68. N. C. Andreasen, *The Creating Brain: The Neuroscience of Genius* (New York: Dana Press, 2005).

Chapter 3

1. A. Einstein, quoted by permission of Otto Nathan and Helen Dukas, Einstein Archives, Pierpont Morgan Library. Translation: G. Holton.

2. This formulation has been a basis for what is known as Einstein's principle of equivalence.

3. F. Darwin, ed., *Life and Letters of Charles Darwin* (London: John Murray, 1887), 82–84.

4. T. R. Malthus, "An Essay on the Principle of Population," *Oxford World Classics* (1798; repr., Oxford, England: Oxford University Press, 2008).

5. H. Gruber, *Darwin on Man: A Psychological Study of Scientific Creativity* (Chicago: University of Chicago Press, 1981).

6. Personal correspondence from Margarethe Bohr, 1980.

7. N. Bohr, Notes for Letter to the Editor titled, "The Philosophical Foundation of Quantum Theory," published in *Nature,* 1927. Quoted with permission of the American Institute of Physics Library, Philadelphia.

8. H. Bohr, "My Father," in *Niels Bohr. His Life and Work as Seen by His Friends and Colleagues,* ed. S. Rozental (New York: Wiley, 1967), 328.

9. B. Maddox, *Rosalind Franklin. The Dark Lady of DNA* (New York: HarperCollins, 2002). Some scientists have also challenged Watson's work. It has even been alleged that Watson and Crick stole Franklin's X-ray findings without her knowing it.

10. Even his collaborator, Francis Crick, who objected to many aspects of Watson's account, did not at all question the section cited here. See F. Crick, *What Mad Pursuit* (New York: Basic Books, 1990).

11. J. Watson, *The Double Helix* (New York: Norton, 1968), 114–15.

12. H. Yukawa, *Tabibito* [The Traveler], trans. L. Browne and R. Toshida (Singapore: World Scientific, 1982).

13. Ibid., 190.

14. Ibid., 202–3.

15. Simonton has referred to these as "domain specific skills" in science and other creative fields; D. K. Simonton, *Creativity in Science: Chance, Logic and Zeitgeist* (New York:

Cambridge University Press, 2004). All such skills are necessary for application and development of the creative cognitive processes described here.

Chapter 4

1. This study first revealed the operation of the janusian process, then called "oppositional thinking," in the play's creation: A. Rothenberg, "The Iceman Changeth: Toward an Empirical Approach to Creativity," *Journal of the American Psychoanalytic Association* 17 (April 1969), 549–607.

2. F. A. Wilczek, "Asymptotic Freedom: From Paradox to Paradigm" (Nobel lecture, Cornell University Library, December 8, 2004), http://arxiv.org/abs/hep-ph/0502113.

3. G. Holton, *Thematic Origins of Scientific Thought. Kepler to Einstein* (Cambridge, MA: Harvard University Press, 1973), 375–76

4. G. W. F. Hegel, *Phenomenology of Spirit*, trans. A.V. Miller (New York: Oxford University Press, 1977).

5. The janusian process, which involves conscious formulation of simultaneous opposites, is neither the same nor a result of the equivalence of opposites in the unconscious primary process posited by Sigmund Freud; see S. Freud, *The Interpretation of Dreams*, The Standard Edition of the Complete Psychological Works of Sigmund Freud 4–5, edited by J. Strachey, London: Hogarth Press, 1900–1901. In the janusian process, the opposites and antitheses are simultaneously operative and equally valid; they neither substitute for each other nor, as with the condensation mechanism in the primary process, do they become blended. Although it could possibly be postulated that the unconscious equivalence of opposites in some way influences the production of the conscious janusian process, such a postulate would need also to explain how a universal human dynamism such as the equivalence of opposites in everyone's primary process thinking could be responsible for the singular processes of creation, including relatively rare creative breakthroughs.

6. L. Pasteur, lecture, University of Lille, December 7, 1854.

Chapter 5

1. A. Rothenberg, "Rembrandt's Creation of the Pictorial Metaphor of Self," *Metaphor and Symbol* 23 (2008), 108–29.

2. P. Hindemith, *A Composer's World* (New York: Doubleday, 1961), 70–71.

3. H. Moore, "The Sculptor Speaks," *Listener* 18 (1937), 338.

4. G. Holton, "What Precisely Is Thinking? Einstein's Answer," *Einstein: A Centenary Volume*, ed. A. French (Cambridge, MA: Harvard University Press, 1979).

5. W. Isaacson, *Einstein: His Life and Universe* (New York: Simon and Shuster, 2007), 114, 122–27, 181.

6. F. Galton, "Statistics of Mental Imagery," *Mind* 5 (1880), 301–18.

7. A. Roe, "A Study of Imagery in Research Scientists," *Journal of Personality* 19 (1951), 459–70.

8. A. Miller, *Imagery in Science* (Boston: Birkhauser, 1984).

9. A. Rothenberg and R. S. Sobel, "Creation of Literary Metaphors as Stimulated by Superimposed versus Separated Visual Images," *Journal of Mental Imagery* 4 (1980), 77–91; R. S. Sobel and A. Rothenberg, "Artistic Creation as Stimulated by Superimposed versus Separated Visual Images," *Journal of Personality and Social Psychology* 39 (1980), 953–61; A. Rothenberg and

R. S. Sobel, "Effects of Shortened Exposure Time on the Creation of Literary Metaphors as Stimulated by Superimposed versus Separated Visual Images," *Perceptual and Motor Skills* 53 (1981), 1007–1009; A. Rothenberg, "Artistic Creation as Stimulated by Superimposed versus Combined-Composite Visual Images," *Journal of Personality and Social Psychology* 50 (1986), 370–81; A. Rothenberg, "Creativity and the Homospatial Process: Experimental Studies," *Psychiatric Clinics of North America* 11 (1988), 443–59.

10. H. Poincaré, *The Foundations of Science*, trans. G. B. Halsted (New York: The Science Press, 1929), 387; H. Poincaré, *Science et Methode* (Paris: E. Flammarion, 1908), 50–51. The word *structure* inserted here was from *combinaison* (English = association, combination, structure) in the original *Science et Methode,* to be consistent in meaning with the foregoing "pairs interlocked." Poincaré's Fuchsian functions integrated two separate fields in mathematics.

11. J. Hadamard, *The Psychology of Invention in the Mathematical Field* (New York: Dover Publications, 1954), 142–43.

12. G. Holton, "Metaphors in Science and Education," *The Advancement of Science, and its Burdens* (Cambridge, UK: Cambridge University Press, 1986), 229–52.

13. A. Rothenberg, "Creative and Cognitive Processes in Kekulé's Discovery of the Structure of the Benzene Molecule," *American Journal of Psychology* 103 (1995), 419–38.

14. H. N. Claman, "T Cell-B Cell Collaboration," in *The Immunologic Revolution: Facts and Witnesses,* ed. A. Szentivanyi and A. H. Friedman (New York: CRC Press, 1994), 81.

15. J. Wheeler, "Our Universe: The Known and the Unknown" (Address before the American Association for the Advancement of Science, December 29, 1967), *American Scholar* 37 (1968), 248–74.

16. The differentiation is between a so-called source—literal entities, attributes, and processes—and the more abstract target, which, in a metaphor, takes its attributes from the source.

17. The similarity relationship is one of the distinct differences between these preceding formulations and Koestler's association of habitually unrelated entities. See A. Koestler, *The Act of Creation* (New York: Macmillan, 1964).

18. Both Beethoven and Schumann wrote of using superimposed visual mental images in musical composition. L. van Beethoven, *Letters, Journals, and Conversations,* trans. and ed. M. Hamburger (New York: Pantheon, 1952), p. 194. Schumann is quoted in M. Agnew, "Auditory Images of Great Composers," *Psychological Monographs,* 31 (1922), 282.

Chapter 6

1. For example, in the writing of a novel I have recently published (A. Rothenberg, *Madness and Glory* [Cambridge, England: Vanguard Press, 2012]), I both felt and consciously experienced the developing personalities, emotions, and behaviors of both protagonists, the psychiatrist and the patient, interacting with my own personality, emotions, and behaviors at many junctures throughout. Such interactions influenced their characterization and actions as well as the content and structure of the storytelling.

2. From J. Merrill, "18 West 11th Street," *Collected Poems, 2001,* Knopf Doubleday, New York, NY.

In what at least
Seemed anger the Aquarians in the basement
Had been perfecting a device

For making sense to us
If only briefly and on pain
Of incommunication ever after....

... The swallow-flights
Go word by numbskull word
Rebellion ... Pentagon ... Black Studies - ...

The carpet - its days numbered -
Hatched another generation
Of strong-jawed, light-besotted saboteurs.

A mastermind
Kept track above the mantel. The cold caught,
One birthday in its shallows...

... Your breakfast *Mirror* put
Late to bed, a fever
Flashing through the veins of linotype: ...

Rigorously chosen from so many called. Our
Instant trance. The girl's
Appearance now among us, as foreseen

Naked, frail but fox-eyed, head to toe
(Having passed through the mirror)
Adorned with heavy shreds of ribbon...

Drunken backdrop of debris, airquake,
Flame in bloom - a pigeon's throat
Lifting, the puddle...

... Forty-odd years gone by.
Toy blocks. Church bell. Original vacancy.
O deepening spring.

3. Ibid.

4. See more extensive discussion of the writing of the poem in A. Rothenberg, "The Articulation Process in Psychotherapy," *The Creative Process of Psychotherapy* (New York: Norton, 1988), 127–49.

5. Quoted in S. Shaikh and J. Leonard-Amadeo, "The Deviating Eyes of Michelangelo's David," *Journal of the Royal Society of Medicine* 98, no. 2 (2005), 75–76.

6. J. Hersey, *Too Far to Walk* (New York: Alfred A. Knopf, 1966).

7. Quotations from manuscript in progress. Personal research communication from John Hersey.

8. On another level, the author's apparent struggle in these passages for understanding a personal underlying psychological dynamic is a factor in aesthetic effectiveness in literature.

See A. Rothenberg, "The Mirror Image Processes," *The Emerging Goddess: The Creative Process in Art, Science, and Other Fields* (Chicago: University of Chicago Press, 1979), 53–81.

9. Quoted and translated from P. Ehrlich, "Zur Kenntnis der Antitoxinwirkung," *Fortschritte der Medizin*, 1897, in E. Bäumler, *Paul Ehrlich: Scientist for Life* (New York: Holmes and Meier, 1984), 65.

10. M. Planck, *Scientific Autobiography and Other Papers* (London: Williams and Norgate, 1950), 37–41.

11. Planck applied a known type of curve-fitting mathematical operation for the formula, but as applied it constituted a new and valuable structure, a creative breakthrough.

12. Despite later proposals by mathematicians of alternate routes to Planck's discovery, his explicit accounting here in his autobiography of the steps in his creative discovery unequivocally indicate his motivation to create, his deviation, his conceptions, and his recognition of the specific creative achievement.

13. In a previous article (A. Rothenberg, "The Janusian Process in Scientific Creativity," *Creativity Research Journal* 9 [1996], 207–32), I had presented both the Planck and the Dirac examples as well as the Köhler one (see chapter 11) as instances of the janusian process because each contained strong oppositions: small and large energy for Planck, positive and negative particles for Dirac, antibody and cancer cell for Köhler. I was in that place in error because there was no evidence that the oppositions themselves were operative in the sequence of the creative conceptualization. The positing of functional separateness and concomitant connection of the key components was the necessary form of cognition. Initially looking for opposites of the known (e.g., electron and positron for Dirac, minimum and maximum for Planck, and cancer cell and healthy cell for Köhler) would not, as the full accounts show, have led to these creations; the concomitant separation and connection and the resulting complex interactions were responsible. Therefore, sep-con processes rather than janusian processes, which are otherwise structurally closely related with each other, were the responsible factors in each case. See Dirac's indications of connections within "holes" here and in chapter 7.

14. P. A. M. Dirac, "Recollections of an Exciting Era," *Varenna Physics School* 57 (1977), 109–46.

Chapter 7

1. Quoted in A. Pais, *Niels Bohr's Times, in Physics, Philosophy, and Polity* (Oxford, England: Clarendon Press, 1991), 275; for the original, see W. Heisenberg, *Der Teil und das Ganze* (Munich: Piper, 1969), 879.

2. P. Bartlett, *Poems in Process* (Oxford, England: Oxford University Press, 1951).

3. T. Kuhn, *The Structure of Scientific Revolutions* (Chicago: University of Chicago Press, 1970).

4. L. Pasteur, lecture, University of Lille, December 7, 1854.

5. A. Maurois, *The Life of Sir Alexander Fleming* (London: Jonathan Cape, 1959).

6. O. Glasser. *William Conrad Röentgen and the Early History of the Roentgen Rays* (London: John Bale, Sons and Damielsson, Ltd., 1933).

7. Leo Sternbach, interview with the author.

8. A. Rothenberg, "The Articulation of Error," *The Creative Process of Psychotherapy* (New York: Norton, 1988), 149–68.

9. Dunbar has also described the value of the aspect of unexpected findings in his study of scientific groups; K. Dunbar, "How Scientists Think," in *Conceptual Structures and Processes: Emergence, Discovery and Change,* ed. T. B. Ward, E. M. Smith, and J. Vaid (Washington, DC: American Psychological Association Press, 2008), 461–93.

10. J. W. Getzels and M. Csikszentmihalyi, *The Creative Vision: A Longitudinal Study of Problem Finding in Art* (New York: Wiley, 1976).

11. Stuart Firestein has emphasized the importance of ignorance in motivating scientific and other investigations. Although it is possible that potentially creative scientists are more motivated by ignorance than others, the factor of ignorance as this author describes it is ubiquitous in all scientific inquiry. S. Firestein, *Ignorance: How it Drives Science* (New York: Oxford University Press, 2012).

12. W. J. Sinclair, *Semmelweis: His Life and His Doctrine* (Manchester, England: University of Manchester Press, 1909), 48–50.

13. K. Cullen, *Biology: The People Behind the Science* (New York: Chelsea House, 2006).

14. In the late 19th century, Poincaré made a series of creative achievements in the areas of geometry, the theory of differential equations, electromagnetism, and topology, as well as contributing to relativity theory.

15. H. Poincaré, *The Foundations of Science: Science and Hypothesis, The Value of Science, Science and Method,* trans. G. B. Halstead (1913; repr., Washington, DC: University Press of America, 1982), 54.

16. Ibid., p. 129.

17. H. Yukawa, *Tababito* [The Traveler], trans. L. Browne and R. Toshida (Singapore: World Scientific, 1982), 201–202.

18. M. Planck, *Scientific Autobiography and Other Papers* (London: Williams and Norgate, 1950), 38.

19. See H. Bloom, *The Anxiety of Influence: A Theory of Poetry* (Oxford, England: Oxford University Press, 1973). Literary critic Bloom believes that poets are always creatively motivated to supersede the poetic works of previous successful poets.

20. J. Watson, *The Double Helix* (New York: Norton, 1968), 32.

21. Yukawa, *Tababito,* 200.

22. C. Darwin, *The Autobiography of Charles Darwin 1809–1882,* ed. N. Barlow (London: Collins, 1958), 120.

23. R. D. Cartwright, *The Twenty-Four Hour Mind: The Role of Sleep and Dreaming in Our Emotional Lives* (New York: Oxford University Press, 2010).

24. Quoted in H. Gruber, *Darwin on Man: A Psychological Study of Scientific Creativity* (Chicago: University of Chicago Press, 1981), 3. Reference is also made in the dream to Darwin's medical school instructor Dr. Monroe saying that a person could not recover from hanging because of the blood.

25. The relationships between dreams and conscious thinking are overdetermined. Elimination pertaining to unfavorable variations is also embedded in Darwin's initial natural selection conception.

26. P. A. M. Dirac, "The Development of Quantum Mechanics," in *Directions in Physics,* ed. H. Hora and J. R. Shepanski (New York, Wiley, 1978), 17.

27. B. Eiduson, *Scientists: Their Psychological World* (New York: Basic Books, 1962), 248–49.

28. See W. Empson, *Seven Types of Ambiguity: A Study of its Effect on English Verse* (London: Chatto and Windus, 1930).

29. Gruber, *Darwin on Man*, 1–15.

30. Yukawa, *Tababito*, 199.

31. S.Chandrasekhar as quoted by E. Segrè, *Enrico Fermi: Physicist* (Chicago: University of Chicago Press, 1970), 80.

32. L. Fermi, *Atoms in the Family* (Chicago: University of Chicago Press, 1954).

33. Yukawa writes of this "catch" conception of the force field in several places in the autobiography; Yukawa, *Tababito*, 195–96, 201.

34. C. P. Snow, *The Two Cultures* (London: Cambridge University Press, 1959). Snow's position has been controversial over succeeding years but the general lack of aesthetic interests (other than music in large measure) among science Nobel laureates is borne out by a survey of biographies at www.nobelprize.org.

35. P. A. M. Dirac, "Recollections of an Exciting Era," *Varenna Physics School* 57 (1977), 136.

36. Poincaré, *Science and Method*, in *Foundations of Science*, 60.

Chapter 8

1. The model for interviewing used in the excellent studies of thinking by P. Langley et al., *Scientific Discovery: Computational Explorations of the Creative Processes* (Cambridge, MA: MIT Press, 1987), in which subjects were asked to speak all their thoughts aloud while engaged in a problem-solving or scientific creativity analog task, was not appropriate here. That model had the advantage of delimiting the elements of the investigation. In such an exploratory study, however, the constructed analog is subject to the preconceived theoretical conceptions of the investigator. This construct would not, therefore, necessarily reproduce the very complex thinking and scientific context involved in a highly creative Nobel laureate's scientific discovery. Analogs, even those as skillfully constructed by the Simon group, run the risks of misrepresenting and trivializing both the problems and thought processes. In addition, scientific discoveries are often made through collaboration, and it is necessary to assess the full circumstances of the actual discovery to define the contribution and thought functions of a particular individual. Such information is not available or applicable in a simulated laboratory exploration.

2. Including the primary source material cited earlier for Nobel laureates Albert Einstein, Max Planck, Paul Ehrlich, Paul Dirac, Neils Bohr, Werner Heisenberg, James Watson, Hideki Yukawa, Enrico Fermi as well as Charles Darwin and Henri Poincoré, the total number of Nobel and other outstanding scientists investigated was 45.

Chapter 9

1. I. Lindgren, Nobel Prize presentation speech, from *Nobel Lectures Physics 1991–1995*, ed. G. Eksprong (Singapore: World Scientific Publishing, 1997).

2. F. H. Crick "The Origin of the Genetic Code," *Journal of Molecular Biology* 38 (1968), 367–79; L. E. Orgel, "Evolution of the Genetic Apparatus," *Journal of Molecular Biology* 38 (1968), 381–93; C. R. Woese, *The Genetic Code: The Molecular Basis for Genetic Expression* (New York: Harper & Row, 1967), 168.

3. S. R. Eddy, "Non-coding RNA Genes and the Modern RNA World," *Genetics* 2 (2001), 919–29.

4. L. E. Orgel, "Some Consequences of the RNA World Hypothesis," *Origins of Life and Evolution of the Biosphere* 33 (2003), 211–18; M. N. Pownes, B. Gerland, and J. D. Sutherland, "Synthesis of Activated Pyrimidine Ribonucleotides in Prebiotically Plausible Conditions," *Nature* 459 (2009), 239–42.

5. J.-M. Lehn, "Alchimères," *Remanances*, 1991.

6. J.-M. Lehn, *Supramolecular Chemistry: Concepts and Perspectives, A Personal Account (Lezioni Lincee)* (Rome: Academia Nazonale de Lincei, 1995).

7. G. H. Kent and A. V. Rosanoff, "A Study of Association in Insanity," *American Journal of Insanity* 67 (1910), 317–90; P. Cramer, *Word Association* (New York: Academic Press, 1968).

8. J. B. Carroll, P. M. Kjeldegaard, and A. S. Carton, "Opposites versus Primaries in Free Association," *Journal of Verbal Learning and Verbal Behavior* 1 (1962), 22–30.

9. A. Rothenberg, "Psychopathology and Creative Cognition," *Archives of General Psychiatry* 40 (1983), 937–42. Note also the difference in this experiment between the results for creative subjects and mentally ill ones, reflecting the distinction between creativity and psychopathology.

Chapter 10

1. These elements are still rare in occurrence. They are primarily found in China, where access for international commercial purposes has become a political issue.

2. A. Roe, *The Making of a Scientist* (New York: Dodd, Mead and Company, 1953). Roe did not publicly report the names of the participants in her studies.

3. J. Deisendorfer et al., "Structure of the Protein Subunits in the Photosynthetic Reaction Center of *Rhodopseudomonas viridas at* 3Å Resolution," *Nature* 318, no. 6047 (1985), 618–24. In his Nobel Prize autobiography, Hartmut Michel reported that Robert Huber showed him how the diffraction pattern of a promising derivative should look; H. Michel, "Hartmut Michel—Biographical," Nobelprize.org, 1988, accessed May 1, 2014, http://www.nobelprize.org/nobel_prizes/chemistry/laureates/1988/michel-bio.html.

Chapter 11

1. According to newspaper accounts at the time of his death, Köhler perished in an accidental laboratory fire. His former colleague Klaus Eichmann, however, gives a detailed, purportedly authentic, but unsubstantiated account of Köhler's death following his rejection of any treatment for severe heart disease in K. Eichmann, *Köhler's Invention* (Basel, Switzerland: Birkhauser, 2005).

2. This reaction disproved a phenomenon known as "allelic exclusion" (alleles are different types of chains), the suppression of one chain by the other.

3. In a written response to my transcribed and exactly documented report of Georges Köhler's account, his wife, Claudia Köhler, vouched for its complete accuracy. Personal communication, 2011.

4. Hans Wigzell, "The Nobel Prize in Physiology or Medicine, 1984, Award Ceremony Speech," trans. from the Swedish, Nobelprize.org, 1984, http://www.nobelprize.org/nobel_prizes/medicine/laureates/1984/presentation-speech.html. Köhler and Milstein called the initial product a "hybridoma" because of its double features, and this imprecise

and incorrect term has continued to be used. The "hybrid" portion refers to the two components, but does not correctly indicate the factors of interaction and organic integration in the multinuclear monoclonal antibody. To correct the misapplication, I have avoided using the term in the exposition and edited it out of the above quotation.

5. E. Schrödinger, *What Is Life? The Physical Aspect of the Living Cell* (Cambridge, England: Cambridge University Press, 1914).

6. Rothenberg, "The Articulation of Error," *The Creative Process of Psychotherapy* (New York: Norton, 1988), 149–68.

7. P. Reichard, "The Nobel Prize in Physiology or Medicine, 1978, Award Ceremony Speech," trans. from the Swedish, Nobelprize.org, 1978, http://www.nobelprize.org/nobel_prizes/medicine/laureates/1978/presentation-speech.html.

8. The idea of a fourth or charmed quark had been a radical one. Glashow's associate, Bjorken, was "extremely skeptical of the whole idea; so skeptical," Glashow emphasized to me, "that he used his Norwegian surname with an accent line through the "O" (ø) in order to disguise the paper so that it wouldn't be included in his bibliography." Glashow himself, however, was very confident. "There was no doubt in my mind," he continued, "that the charmed quark was going to be found and I would give lectures all around the world saying that you guys are incompetent, go out and find this particle. At one conference, I bet them, I said I would eat my hat if the particle were not discovered by the next meeting of that group in two years. One year later, the particle was discovered and the next year, when the group met again, the organizer distributed little (foul tasting) candy hats for the audience to eat."

9. S. L. Glashow, L. Iliopoulos, and L. Maiani, "Weak Interactions with Lepton-Hadron Symmetry," *Physical Review* 2 (1970), 1285–92.

10. J. Bardeen, L. N. Cooper, and J. R. Schreiffer, "Theory of Superconductivity," *Physical Review* 108 (1957), 1175–1205.

11. S. Lundqvist, "The Nobel Prize in Physics, 1973, Award Ceremony Speech," trans. from the Swedish, Nobelprize.org, 1973, http://www.nobelprize.org/nobel_prizes/physics/laureates/1973/presentation-speech.html.

Chapter 12

1. H. Zuckerman, *Nobel Laureates in the United States* (New York: The Free Press, 1977).

2. See also L. Alvarez, "Our Computer Programs Produced X-ray Like Photographs Which Would Show a Chamber in the Same Way an Abdominal X-ray Would Show a Gas Bubble in the Intestines," in *Discovery Alvarez: Selected Works of Luis W. Alvarez with Commentary,* ed. W. P. Trower (Chicago: University of Chicago Press, 1987), 180.

3. Note the similarity between Nusslein-Volhard's aesthetic analysis and the creative outcome of integration as discussed in chapter 1.

4. Ambivalence especially, with its focus on opposites, probably routinely plays a role in the constructions of the janusian process. See Rothenberg, *The Emerging Goddess.*

Chapter 13

1. One of the challenges was by physicist Oreste Piccioni, who claimed that the Segrè group had stolen his ideas in the discovery of the antiproton. This led to legal action eventually submitted 18 years later to the U.S. Supreme Court. The action was, however, rejected because the case had exceeded the statute of limitations.

2. P. W. Mattisch and B. R. Monsey, *Collaboration: What Makes It Work. A Review of Research Literature on Factors Influencing Successful Collaboration.* (St. Paul, MN: Amherst H. Wilder Foundation, 1992).

3. The members of the engineer comparison group were also university-level professors, and ultimately did not appear as distinctive in communication and teaching overall as the Nobel group.

Chapter 14

1. D. K. Simonton, "Biographical Determinants of Achieved Eminence," *Journal of Personality and Social Psychology* 33 (1976), 218–26; J. M. Cattell, "A Statistical Study of Eminent Men," *Popular Science Monthly* 42 (1903), 359–77.

2. H. Gardner, *Frames of Mind: The Theory of Multiple Intelligences.* (New York: Basic Books, 1983).

3. R. J. Sternberg and T. I. Lubart, *Defying the Crowd: Cultivating Creativity in a Culture of Conformity* (New York: The Free Press, 1995).

4. US Bureau of the Census, "Lifetime Occupational Mobility of Adult Males, March, 1962," *Current Population Reports, Series P-23,* No.11 (May 12) (Washington, DC: US Government Printing Office, 1964).

5. V. Goertzel and M. G. Goertzel, *Cradles of Eminence* (Boston: Little, Brown & Co., 1962); V. Goertzel and M. G. Goertzel, *Three Hundred Eminent Personalities* (San Francisco: Jossey-Bass, 1978).

6. L. Terman, "Mental and Physical Traits of a Thousand Gifted Children," *Genetic Studies of Genius,* vol. 1 (Stanford, CA: Stanford University Press, 1925).

7. Biographers usually cannot procure reliable information about personal parental matters including information about parental wishes, expressed or implied.

8. J. Gleick, *Genius: The Life and Science of Richard Feynman* (New York: Pantheon Books, 1992).

9. A. Rothenberg and G. Wyshak, "Family Background and Genius," *Canadian Journal of Psychiatry* 49 (2004), 185–91.

10. Goertzel and Goertzel, *Cradles of Eminence;* Goertzel and Goertzel, *Three Hundred Eminent Personalities.*

11. Terman, "Mental and Physical Traits."

Chapter 15

1. It might be argued that the panel (anonymous because of the necessarily negative judgments) employed a too-demanding criterion for creativity, as many levels of value or usefulness may be culturally and socially designated for creative actions, events, and results. Scientifically, however, it is necessary to apply clear-cut, consensually agreed-upon value criteria (social, scientific, and instrumental), and those have been widely and consistently applied to the creative achievements of Nobel laureates. The findings therefore apply distinctly to creativity. As I stated in the Preface and chapter 1, other varied or related types of determinations of creative activities and achievements are certainly feasible and, if rigorously applied, may be employed for a wide variety of social and physical areas: for example, business, cooking, and the like. To develop an appropriate comparison

group for study, however, significant factors must be controlled. In this case, it was the level of value and degree of newness produced by the engineers; with one exception, these were not comparable with the distinct creative achievements of the Nobel laureates.

2. Although "creative" problem solving is a meaningful designation and valid factor for consideration and study. I shall not here conflate creativity and problem solving, in order to be clear about the separate cognitive factors in each.

3. N. R. F. Maier, "Problem Solving and Creativity," in *Individuals and Groups* (Belmont, CA: Brooks/Cole, 1970).

4. E. deBono, *The Use of Lateral Thinking* (London: Jonathan Cape, 1957).

5. A. Miller, *Imagery in Science* (Boston: Birkhauser, 1984); A. Roe, "A Study of Imagery in Research Scientists," *Journal of Personality* 19 (1951), 459–70; N. LeBoutillier and D. Marks, "Mental Imagery and Creativity; A Meta-analytic Review Study," *British Journal of Psychology* 94 (2003), 29–44.

6. The use of visual imagery in problem solving by *Visualizer 2* was similar to *Visualizer 1* and the other control subjects and no specific account therefore is presented here.

7. A. Rothenberg and C. R. Hausman, "Metaphor and Creativity," *The Creativity Research Handbook,* vol. 3 (New York: Hampton Press, 2012), 133–61. See its extensive discussion of differences between analogies and metaphors.

8. This is sometimes construed as the making of *new* connections—see S. Arieti, *Creativity: The Magic Synthesis* (New York: Basic Books, 1976)—but this actually moves the issue more to obscurity because explaining *new* is a part of finding the basis of creativity.

9. Deduction and induction, though not specifically mentioned for the Nobel scientist group earlier, are standard conceptual modes and skills for all scientists.

Chapter 16

1. Alvarez was awarded the Nobel Prize for the discovery of resonance particles and the hydrogen chamber, but the data presented in this book have pertained to his creative thinking in a field outside of physics, the construction of the theory of dinosaur extinction.

2. C. R. Hausman, *A Discourse on Novelty and Creation* (Albany, NY: State University of New York Press, 1984).

3. H. Zuckerman, *Nobel Laureates in the United States* (New York: The Free Press, 1977), 99–100.

4. Nobel laureates have been accused of such malfeasance as purposely disrupting or even stealing a colleague's data.

5. Although some references to the issue of creativity and mental illness have been made earlier in the book, this work is not at all focused on that issue. See A. Rothenberg, *Creativity and Madness: New Findings and Old Stereotypes* (Baltimore: Johns Hopkins University Press, 1990). Pertinent evidence exists, however, that that poet Robert Lowell, and artists Jackson Pollock and Edvard Munch, are notable creators who suffered from bipolar disorder, but all did some of their best creative work during periods of remission from the disease. See A. Rothenberg, "Bipolar Illness, Creativity, and Treatment," *Psychiatric Quarterly* 72 (2001), 131–48.

6. D. Yurgelin-Todd, "Emotional and Cognitive Changes during Adolescence," *Current Opinion in Neurobiology* 17 (2007), 251–57; J. S. Eccles, A. Wigfield, and J. Byrnes, "Cognitive Development in Adolescence," *Developmental Psychology,* Vol. 6 of *Handbook of Psychology,* ed. I. B. Weiner (Hoboken, NJ: Wiley, 2003), 325–50; H. E. Gruber and J. J. Vonèche, *The Essential Piaget* (New York: Basic Books, 1977). L. S. Vygotsky," Imagination and Creativity in Childhood," *Journal of Russian and East European Psychology,* 42 (2004), 7–97.

7. Wolfgang Amadeus Mozart, Felix Mendelssohn, and Srinivasa Ramanujan, among others, have often been cited as childhood creative prodigies.

8. I carried out a survey of 300 adult men and women from both urban and rural populations at varied socioeconomic levels regarding lifetime writing of poetry. Depending on the socioeconomic group included, percentages of persons who had written poetry during their adolescence ranged from 47% to 100%, the upper ranges consisting, as might be expected, of college-educated groups; A. Rothenberg, "Poetry Writing in Adolescence" (unpublished manuscript, 1995).

9. Studies of the developmental tasks of adolescence have been carried out, most prominently by E. H. Erikson, *Identity: Youth and Crisis* (New York: W. W. Norton, 1968), and R. J. Havighurst, *Developmental Tasks and Education* (New York: McKay, 1972). The tasks designated here include the essentials of their designations. Also see: A. Mazor, Adi Alfa, and Y. Gampel, "On the Thin Line between Connection and Separation: The Individuation Process, from Cognitive and Object-Relations Perspectives, in Kibbutz Adolescents," *Journal of Youth and Adolescence,* 22 (1993), 641–69.

10. Creative work in scientific pursuits is included here. The Intel Science Talent Search identifies creative scientific achievements in middle and late adolescence.

11. Creativity in the social sciences, touched on in the studies of A. Roe, "A Study of Imagery in Research Scientists," *Journal of Personality* 19 (1951), 459–70, and M. Csikszentmihalyi, *Creativity: The Psychology of Discovery and Invention* (New York: HarperCollins, 1996), and through studies of Nobel laureates in economics, but otherwise often overlooked in discussions of scientific creativity, may also be fueled in whole or part by the processes described in this book.

12. See A. Rothenberg and R. S. Sobel, "A Creative Process in the Art of Costume Design," *Clothing and Textiles Research Journal* 9 (1990), 27–36.

Note: Page numbers followed by "*t*" indicate a table; "n" indicates a note.